THE HUMANIST

AS CITIZEN

THE HUMANIST
AS CITIZEN

EDITED BY JOHN AGRESTO

AND PETER RIESENBERG

NATIONAL HUMANITIES CENTER

Copyright © 1981 National Humanities Center

All rights reserved

Manufactured in the United States of America

Distributed by The University of North Carolina Press

Library of Congress Cataloging in Publication Data

Main entry under title:

The Humanist as citizen.

 Published as a memorial to Charles Frankel.
 Bibliography: p.
 Contents: Why the humanities? / Charles Frankel
—The true political man / Samuel Scolnicov—
Isaac Newton and humanistic values in science /
B. J. T. Dobbs—[etc.]
 1. Humanities—Addresses, essays, lectures.
2. Frankel, Charles, 1917–79—Addresses, essays,
lectures. I. Agresto, John. II. Riesenberg,
Peter N., 1925–   . III. Frankel, Charles,
1917–79.
AZ103.H84   001.3   81-4021
ISBN 0-8078-1450-4   AACR2

❦ CONTENTS

❦ INTRODUCTION

FROM SEPTEMBER to May 1978–79, a small group of scholars in history, philosophy, literature, art, and education gathered together at the newly established National Humanities Center in North Carolina. Charles Frankel, whose career spanned the full range of liberal scholarship, was the Center's president and director. In May of 1979, toward the very end of the year's activity, Charles Frankel was murdered in his home in Bedford Hills, New York. This volume was conceived upon his death by those Fellows at the Center as a memorial to the man. It was also conceived as a tribute to the vision by which he guided his life, a vision of the civilizing integration of humane learning and citizenship.

"The humanities," Charles Frankel said in a speech reprinted here, "are a curious combination of involvement and detachment." Yet, between involvement and detachment, no ready calculus exists to help us put the humanities in their proper place. Too great an involvement in the present and the public soon converts the humanities into ideology and partisanship. Too high an expectation of the immediate uses of the humanities—or of humanist scholars—leads quickly to disappointment. Yet this book is written with the conviction that the humanities are vital for life and that the imposition of too great a detachment reduces the humanities to a mere frill on the borders of human affairs, to pleasant ornamentation and irrelevance. Thus, to attempt to address, as this volume does, the "uses of the humanities" will surely seem both awkward and, at the same time, fully necessary.

Though the belief that ideas affect life, that ideas have meaning in history, is true to the point of platitude, the question of the appropriate role of the man of ideas in history is hardly settled. That question is the single thread that weaves together the otherwise diverse strands in this book.

Thus, beyond the broad theme suggested by the title, no constraints were placed upon the group of Fellows who contributed to this volume, no collective answer to the question of the proper role of ideas in history was envisioned. If these essays, taken as a whole, seem diverse, even disparate, it is because we agreed only on the validity of the question, not on any one solution.

This, then, is not a *Festschrift* in the usual sense, a collection of essays written by the students and peers of a great scholar in his field. It is, rather, a volume whose raison d'être derives from the quality of the man whose inexplicable death it commemorates and whose scope bears witness to his range. If this book can contribute to a better understanding of the proper uses of the humanities, if it illuminates for scholarship both the importance and the limits of its involvement in human affairs, it will begin to be a fitting tribute to the memory of Charles Frankel.

John Agresto
Peter Riesenberg

PART ONE

THE HUMANIST AND

THE PUBLIC LIFE

CHARLES FRANKEL

❧ WHY THE HUMANITIES?

WE HAVE MET to discuss a subject of great practical and professional interest to almost all of us here—the proper role of government in relation to the humanities and the proper requirements humanistic endeavors should meet if they are to be supported by government. In addressing myself to this subject I am unhappily aware of a double disqualification. The first is that I have agreed to be the keynoter. Anyone who has accepted an assignment to discuss the relationship between government and the humanities had clearly placed his own good judgment under justified suspicion.

My second disqualification is one I share with most of the people in this audience. In the main, we are professional scholars or educational administrators or officers of government. Our experience and knowledge have their gaps, but we are probably ahead of most of our fellow citizens, nonetheless, in the ability to conduct— if we choose—a knowledgeable discussion of government and the humanities. Society has assigned us special responsibilities with regard to the nurturing of the humanities and the maintenance of a fruitful partnership between government and the humanistic community. Yet it is for just these reasons that we may also suffer from a disability.

It is an impediment that goes with our special acquaintance with the issues and special responsibilities toward them. It is what the French call a "professional deformation." Being who we are, we are likely to think that the problem of government and the humani-

This is an address delivered by Charles Frankel at a symposium on government and the humanities, the Lyndon Baines Johnson Library, the University of Texas at Austin, 4 December 1978.

ties is peculiarly *our* problem. But if we do, we shall be picking the problem up at the wrong end and seeing it in the wrong proportions. That, at any rate, is the position I should like to consider as a point of departure.

For what is at stake in a review of the history of government support for the humanities or in an examination of possible future policies is not the convenience and contentment of congressional committees or Endowment officials. It is not even—if my academic colleagues can forgive me—the contentment of humanistic scholars or their cozy feeling when they go to work that their government loves them. What is at stake is the quality of the environment in which Americans live, that environment in its most important aspect—not its physical aspect, though that, too, is involved, but its imaginative, its moral, its aesthetic, its intellectual aspect.

What will our country offer its members as a diet for their minds and souls? They are the citizens of a free society. They must make their own decisions about the good, the true, and the beautiful, as well as about the genuine article and the fake, the useful and the useless, the profitable and the unprofitable. But their individual minds, their individual schemes of value and structures of belief within which they make their choices, are largely formed by the social and cultural atmosphere, with all its educational and mis-educational effects. And they can choose only from among the alternatives that our institutions, public and private, make available to them. Further, they must do their choosing within a pricing system that inevitably affects their choices and that is influenced not only by market forces but by public policy and the movement of public revenues.

No institution within our society, certainly not government, has the capacity to control this cultural and moral environment. We can be thankful this is so. Nevertheless, any citizen—and certainly anyone with public responsibilities or anyone who is a trustee for a tradition of civilized achievement—must ask what part he or she can play in shaping the environment in which we Americans must live and find our being.

What images of human possibility will American society put

before its members? What standards will it suggest to them as befitting the dignity of the human spirit? What decent balance among human employments will it exhibit? Will it speak to them only of success and celebrity and the quick fix that makes them happy, or will it find a place for grace, elegance, nobility, and a sense of connection with the human adventure? What cues will be given to our citizens, those who are living and those still to be born, that will indicate to them the values authoritative institutions of our nation, such as our governments, national, state, and local, and our halls of learning, regard as of transcendent importance? These are the questions that I believe are really at issue when we consider the place of the humanities on the national scene and the role that government should play in their care and feeding. And they are important enough questions to suggest why it may be worthwhile to continue to live and struggle with the paradox and challenge of government programs in the humanities.

For it should not be possible any longer to deceive ourselves. The troubles that have been experienced in making these programs work are inherent in them. They are not caused by foolish administrative errors or philistine pressures or disagreements that grow out of clashes between personalities or political parties. Such things aggravate tensions that are already unavoidably present and that are as intrinsic to the game, and as much a part of its fun, as tackling is to football. The paradox and the challenge of government programs in support of the humanities reside in the attempt, on the government side, to spend public money in an accountable manner without managing or directing or intruding on free intellectual enterprises. The paradox and the challenge lie in the hope of the humanistic community that it can receive government assistance in solving its problems and yet persist in its established habits and attitudes that probably are the most highly individualistic of all the departments of intellectual activity. A government doing business with humanists? Humanists meeting in committee with congressmen or budget makers or presidential appointees? This is to set before ourselves the task of maintaining a modus vivendi between politicians and poets, accountants and admirers of Kandinsky, bureaucrats and followers of Thoreau. It is as though we were to take two radical extremes of the American character—the capacity to plan and to pull together and to be members of a team, and the disposition to lawlessness and to anarchic individualism—and demand that they make peace and learn to profit each from the other.

Still, it can be done; it has been done. And if it can be done, the achievement is so considerable that we have some reason to look to the future with confidence and to believe the effort worth continuing. Yet, given the known troubles, the abrasions, and the misunderstandings that inevitably surround that effort, it is also natural to ask, Why bother? There are other reasons to ask that question as well—the growing conviction that government has been seeking to do too much, the apparently declining confidence, felt by humanists themselves, in liberal education, and, not least, the disillusionments over two decades with professors and their doings, whether they give their advice to presidents in the Oval Office or from picket lines across the street. In the present national mood it is not only inevitable but it is necessary and imperative to ask, Why seek to maintain so odd a relationship as one between government and the humanities? Why should government give specific support to the humanities? Why should the humanities claim such support, and do they accept any reciprocal responsibilities when they do?

Although I would like to try, I shall not seek to offer a general definition of that elusive phrase "the humanities." But I should like to focus on some curious features of the humanities, noticed by most people who look at them closely. I believe this may help in understanding some of the functions of the humanities. The humanities are a curious combination of involvement and detachment; of the search for scientific objectivity and irrepressible personal idiosyncrasy; of piety toward the past and the critique of the past; of private passion and public commitment. Some humanistic disciplines display one or another of these tensions more conspicuously than others, but I would hazard the opinion that they are characteristic, by and large, of all the humanistic enterprises.

Let me begin with the mixture of involvement and detachment that characterizes the humanities. The humanistic disciplines can be described, maliciously, as parasitical disciplines. They are, that is, second-order disciplines; they feed on other people's work. They would not exist if human beings did not, quite independently of these disciplines, engage in certain distinctive kinds of activity. Human beings worship; they talk, dance, sing, paint, praise the beauties of their beloved; they tell stories, maintain legends, build monuments, try to discover facts, live by rules, make choices between better and worse, complain about injustice; they puzzle over the mysterious ways of God and man. And to all these activities human beings bring passion. They engage in them from motives of fear or awe or love or practical advantage and sometimes out of sheer physical excitement or emotional exaltation. They do not engage in them coldly or because it has been proved to them, by some abstract intellectual formula, that they should do so. They are learned activities, yet it is as though they were done by instinct.

Yet in all these activities there is a tendency in sophisticated civilizations toward a certain turning inward, a certain process of feeding on what has gone before. The arts, like religion, law, war, or politics, develop a professional tradition. In the arts, for example, the playwright, painter, or novelist, employs old myths and symbols; in using them he presents his own ideas and images on one level and on another, he offers an implicit commentary on what his predecessors have done with those same myths and symbols. He addresses a living audience, but he is also speaking to and with a company of men and women with whom he feels bound across the ages, people who have worked the same territory and used the same pathmarks for their own purposes. In speaking to a living audience he is counting on their having minds and eyes and tropisms and aversions that have in part been shaped by this company that stretches across the centuries and by the myths, images, and symbols he is now reshaping. The artist's or writer's spontaneity and originality are products of a dialectical process in which he plays with and against a received heritage. The sharpness and depth of the effects that Sophocles achieved in retelling the story of Oedipus, that Renaissance painters achieved in painting Christ with muscles and in flesh tones, that Joyce achieved in transplanting Ulysses to Dublin and turning him into a wandering Jew, are due to this dialectic, this consistent double entendre, that emerges when an inherited system of symbols is exploited and remade.

And the humanities? The humanities are not, except incidentally, the repositories of an art's or a profession's techniques for doing things successfully; nor is it their business directly to write poems or fight battles or legislate for society. They do their work at another level. They are the disciplines that comment on and appraise such activities, that reflect on their meaning and seek to clarify the standards by which they should be judged. Humanist scholars detach themselves, as it were, from that in which their fellows engage with passionate commitment. Yet their detachment is not an act of rejection, nor is it a useless frill. It grows, usually, from affection, from a desire to understand more deeply and appreciate more intensely what has aroused a sense of beauty or awe. And it contributes to that atmosphere of informed expectation, to the forming of that audience whose sympathies are broad but whose standards are severe, that is the element in which every first-rate talent in every field flourishes best. The humanities are parasitical, but they also enrich that on which they feed.

Nevertheless, humanistic scholars are often resented and seen as killjoys or troublemakers. They are lovers of man's works but strange lovers—ironical, resistant, and seeming to prefer talk and talk about talk to the straightforward embrace of that which they love. They are like the Unitarian minister of whom it was said that there was one thing he preferred to heaven and that was a lecture on heaven. Thus Nietzsche's condemnation of Socrates. Socrates was a critic, a philosopher, a mere parasitical, second-order mind. He fed on other people's vitality; he took the passionate and turned it cold. He made the unconscious conscious and therefore separated the Greek genius from its Dionysian inspiration.

If, however, we turn Nietzsche's judgment of Socrates, which is perverse, into an observation about the character of humanistic scholarship, it takes on a certain truth. It grossly overstates that truth, yet the story is incomplete if it gives no account of an inherent danger in the humanistic disciplines to which humanistic scholars do succumb from time to time. In my own discipline, philosophy, it is possible for philosophers to detach themselves so completely from primary materials that they no longer offer commentaries on science or law or education but instead merely give us commentaries on the commentaries on the commentaries. Philosophy then becomes an exchange among members of a closed club who live by taking in one another's laundry and have forgotten the original business—human inquiry, human practice, human choices and hope—that once aroused their common attention. In every humanistic discipline there is a necessary and desirable concentration on refining the ideas and tools that the discipline has developed over the centuries and that it needs in order to do its work. But no one who has ever contributed greatly to a humanistic discipline has not brought to that discipline a passion from outside it, an aesthetic or moral or religious passion or an intellectual curiosity that was not idle but painful and urgent.

Most people find it painful to have their activities analyzed and their joys dissected; humanists, too, engage in these exercises with divided feelings. They put on trial their capacity to do something difficult and testing—to maintain involvement and detachment in equilibrium; and it is the larger society's capacity to tolerate and appreciate such a state of precarious balance that gives the measure of its level of civilization. For this strange exercise in involvement and detachment rests on a certain faith: the faith that as human beings grow more conscious of themselves and what they are doing, more self-aware and self-critical, they do not reduce their enjoyment of life, but intensify it; the faith that discrimination and taste do not weary the emotions but make them fresh. We ask, What use are the humanities? What good do they do? The answer does not seem easy to find because we look for a chain of causes and effects; we look down the line for a distant result. But the result is immediate: it is in the difference in people's experience if they know the background of what is happening to them, if they can place what they are doing in a deeper and broader context, if they have the metaphors and symbols that can give their experience a shape. Think of what the lore and legend, the analyses and arguments, that surround baseball contribute to our enjoyment of that game. They *make* the game, as anyone can discover by sitting next to someone who is uninitiated. Would anyone say, What is the use of all that talk, all those stories, let us just get on with throwing and hitting the ball?

These observations take me to a second of the polarities that seem to me to characterize the humanists. It is their mixture of concern for an impersonal or scientific objectivity and their irrepressible elements of personal idiosyncrasy. Take historians whose works are monuments in the discipline of history—Thucydides, Gibbon, Lord Acton—as three examples. Their effort to make sure of their sources, to evaluate alternative explanations, to connect the stories they tell with principles that do not apply only to these stories but to broad ranges of human experience—all this qualifies them as scientific minds. They were impelled by an ideal of impersonal truth, they sought explanations from which wishful thinking, prevailing prejudices, individual quirks had been removed. Yet the work they produced bears their own unmistakable individual mark, as clearly as a work of Dickens or a poem of Yeats bears the mark of its creator. We cannot confuse any one of them with anyone else. There is an ultimate pathos in most great works of history. The authors' horizons will be broad; they will see farther than the conventions of their time; they will offer a vision that will allow them to speak and to be understood by people who live in vastly different periods. Yet such historians never escape themselves or their time. Reading their work we learn not only independent facts. Although the great historians may transcend their age, they also speak for it, expressing its outlook in its clearest, most coherent, most spacious form. Thus, we learn about the set of mind of an age. We learn about a period in mankind's wanderings, an episode in our race's effort to come to terms with its doings, to appraise their meaning. And we read not only a history, we meet a man: we enter the temple of his private faith.

I would not for a moment suggest that the humanistic disciplines are not disciplines; I do not mean to imply that they are entirely expressive or lyric in their functions. But they partake of the lyric. At their most vivid, they are like the arts as well as the sciences. The humanities are that form of knowledge in which the knower is revealed. All knowledge becomes humanistic when this effect takes place, when we are asked to contemplate not only a proposition but the proposer, when we hear the human voice behind what is being said. The humanities sink into pedantry when they lose this quality. They no longer give us knowledge with commitment. Whitehead speaks somewhere of the difference between significant knowledge and knowledge that is merely inert—knowledge that gives us no sense of its bearing on our lives or that throws no light on the image we entertain of human nature and destiny. One function of the humanities is to bring knowledge alive, to put it to moral and philosophical use; and one way they serve this function is to maintain the ironic tension between the personal and the impersonal.

But let me turn now to a more obviously public and civic function of the humanities. For almost two hundred years, during the period when modern humanistic studies took their distinctive shape, there occurred in France and England an intense debate among scholars and men of letters known as "The Quarrel of the Ancients and the Moderns." The Greek and Roman writers had been revived. Were their works to be presented to the European mind as models of achievement and wisdom which artists, writers, and critics could do no better than to imitate? Were these ancient personages, the creators of an extraordinary tradition, to be viewed as authority figures? Or could it be supposed, as the "moderns" argued, that the life of a civilization was like the life of an individual and the maturer years were those years that came later?

It was living men and women, the "moderns" argued, who were the true Ancients. They stood on the shoulders of their predecessors, benefited from the accumulated experience of the ages, and could see farther than their predecessors who had come at the dawn of civilization. Accordingly, it was incumbent on teachers, scholars, and critics of literature, history, the arts, or philosophy not to bow down before the authority of the past. Matthew Arnold described a modern age as one that is characterized by a general tendency to criticize received dispensations. In this sense, the Greek enlightenment was a modern age, and the self-conscious modernity of our own civilization took shape in the sixteenth and seventeenth centuries. The Quarrel of the Ancients and Moderns played a crucial part in the process.

I offer this example as one among many that might be presented. The humanistic disciplines are caught curiously between the poles of continuity and change, piety and rebellion. Few of these disciplines can be understood except as parts of a continuing historical tradition. They are rooted in problems, symbols, judgments, values that came to us from the past; they are among our principal means for maintaining continuity with that past. And if we do not retain such continuity, we are without bearings for the future. But in no dynamic and rapidly changing society is it possible to maintain continuity with the past merely by acts of veneration. The past has to be brought to life—and that means it has to be interpreted and reinterpreted. This is a major function of the humanities.

We cannot underestimate its significance. The modern world, almost by definition, is a world in which new knowledge and techniques produce rapidly changing social conditions that in turn produce vertiginous changes in human beliefs and values. The coherence that people have thought they have seen in things is regularly broken; their sense of connectedness with what has gone before and of an intelligible direction in where they are going is disrupted. Humanistic scholars are more knowledgeable, perhaps, yet they are only occasionally wiser than their fellows. They may be as lost as their unscholarly neighbors. But surely the effort to find coherence, to restore a sense of continuity and direction, cannot be left only to impulse and unguided inspiration, to visionaries or sloganeers, or to newspapermen or leaders of political parties. If people with knowledge of philosophy, literature, and history do not take part, if people who have time specifically set aside to permit them to think do not take part, the results are likely to be thin and fragile. Humanistic scholars have been conspicuous participants in such an effort in the past—Matthew Arnold and John Stuart Mill, to take two examples from Victorian England, George Santayana, Oliver Wendell Holmes, John Dewey, Perry Miller, Richard Hofstadter, to take a few disparate examples from twentieth-century American intellectual history.

Nor need we be discontented if we are not given great synoptic visions. When a wrenching event like that in Guyana takes place, we can unnecessarily lose our intellectual moorings. We ask, even without the help of the Russians—every pundit and headline-writer in the United States, it seems, encourages us to ask—What has happened to the country? What unsolved social problems, what rooted social ailments explain this horror? In the early sixteenth century in Münster in Westphalia there was established a community based on a combination of theocracy and communism that saw itself as the destined center for the reconquest of the world for righteousness; and when the surrounding world descended on it, its inhabitants in frightening numbers accepted the mandate that they must die. There are many other analogies—in the Middle Ages, in ancient Rome, in the cultures of disparate peoples who have never known technology or capitalism or the historically parochial explanations of surprised sociologists. This, too, is a function of the humanities. If they keep us in touch with the past, they keep us in touch not only with the changes in the human scene but with the recurrences. It may not be comforting to be reminded that our progressive age is subject to old-fashioned forms of madness, but it is enlightening. It saves us from that special version of the sin of pride that holds that we twentieth-century Americans, no matter what we do, whether it is good or evil, are always bigger and better and more original.

Much more could be said about the uses of the humanities; much could be said about the many abuses to which they are prone. I have discussed them at their best. But we may ask, Why the Senate and House of Representatives? Why the oil industry? Why water and wine and men and women? What are the functions of all these? We cannot mean, in asking such questions, to consider these things at their worst but at their best, or at least their average. At their best, and quite often at their average, the humanities are the activities that ask us to lead double lives, to note what we are doing, to reflect on why we care. To say that our nation does not need the humanities is to say that it does not need irony, a sense of humor about itself, a set of purposes for itself that honest and reflective men and women can credit.

But it is one thing to recognize the uses of the humanities; it is another to ask whether government is needed, or can be useful, in helping these disciplines. That it is needed there can be little doubt. The pressures of the present student culture, of the educational marketplace, of the current economic situation, are all adverse to the healthy evolution of humanistic studies. In many ways, the existing structure of universities is also adverse. At the moment, the financial crisis in higher education puts us in grave danger of losing a generation of talent that will be forced into other occupations.

The federal government, of course, cannot support the humanities by itself. Even in recent years its financial contributions have been marginal as compared to the contributions of state and municipal governments and of private colleges and universities, libraries, museums, foundations, and individual philanthropists. Nor should we imagine that the financial aspect of the problem is grave from the point of view of the federal budget. I happen to be among those who believe in fiscal caution at this moment; nor would I wish to argue that that part of the federal budget devoted to support of the humanities is the only part that should not be inspected stringently. But on a comparative basis, the amounts spent by the federal government for the humanities are not large; and it is not here that the battle of the budget will be won or lost.

Yet what the federal government does will be critical. We are probably not in a period of growth. But the humanities will be diminished if they do not receive the extra support from government that they are unlikely to receive from any other source. And they will be diminished not only in size, not merely in the material aspects of their needs, but in what is most important—their own sense of themselves and their potential role in the world. Nothing has happened of greater importance in the history of American humanistic scholarship than the invitation of the government to scholars to think in a more public fashion and to think and teach with the presence of their fellow citizens in mind. It would be tragic if that invitation were now made less urgent or if it were withdrawn.

For humanistic scholarship grows—in the end, it develops confidence, freshness, original ideas—when it is fed not by its own professional concerns alone but by the doings of human beings outside the study. Those doings are the humanities' primary material. And when humanistic scholars have been persuaded that they really are part of the larger community they have also made the largest contributions to their own disciplines. Plato, Machiavelli, Erasmus, John Locke, Diderot, James Madison, Ralph Waldo Emerson are not remembered for being intellectual recluses. Not even Spinoza, who was forced into physical retreat, took this as an excuse for intellectual retreat. He sought a measure of dispassion, a perspective from which he might see the issues of his time *sub specie aeternitatis*. But he addressed himself to these issues.

Government support can stimulate humanist scholars to turn their minds and eyes outward. It can symbolize a nation's decision that it respects and needs what they are doing. It can help give them what they do not always seek but surely is a prescription for their health and vigor—a larger, better informed, more sophisticated, and demanding audience—an audience that expects them to write well, and to think in large terms, and to think with it. Humanistic scholars do not always seek such an audience, but there are few things that have done more for their health and vigor.

But to say that a government can do such things for humanists is to say that it can, through its support, lay down a challenge to them. It can put their capacities for vision, lucidity, and dispassionate civic commitment to the test. But it is for humanist scholars themselves to recognize that challenge and pass that test.

SAMUEL SCOLNICOV

❧ THE TRUE POLITICAL MAN:

SOCRATES ON KNOWLEDGE

AND POLITICS

QUITE SURPRISINGLY, at *Gorgias* 521 D, Plato makes Socrates affirm that, among his contemporaries, perhaps he alone truly practices the political art. No doubt, such is not the picture of Socrates we are accustomed to in this and other dialogues. More typical are the passages in Plato's *Apology* where Socrates maintains that he would rather converse with individuals than try to influence the multitude. "He who really intends to fight for what is right," says Socrates in one such passage, "if he expects to hold on even for a short time, must do it in private and not in public" (*Apology* 32A cf. 32E). Xenophon ascribes to Socrates a similar sentiment: "In which way could I play a more important role in politics: by engaging in it single-handed, or by making it my business to turn out as many good statesmen as possible?" (*Memorabilia* 1.6.15).

Socrates' avoidance of political activity has been sometimes interpreted as a recognition on his part of the incompatibility of politics and morals. He would thus have seen politics as the art of the possible and detected among the presuppositions of political activity at least some readiness to compromise, to aim at what one can reasonably expect to reach. "Socrates implies here [*Apology* 32A]," writes a recent author, "that it is impossible for a politician to remain honest and just. Either he gives in sooner or later to the

16

reckless and foolish demands of the many, and thus achieves success at the expense of his peace of mind, or he antagonizes the many by seeking justice at the expense of his life."[1] One can indeed recognize in our several Socratic portraits the root of what later became a main Cynic trait—the shifting of interest from the body politic to the private individual, even to the exclusion of all political activity. But there was between Socrates and the Cynics the more important difference that Socrates' ethical ideal was not the imperturbability that the Cynics believed to be possible only by the dissociation of oneself from, among other things, all political struggle and ambition. For Socrates—or at least for Plato's Socrates—what was at stake was not his "peace of mind," but the very possibility of success in the fight for what is right. Given Socrates' conceptions about what is right, he must rule out as unfeasible any public action, not because it conflicts with the private aims of the individual but because it is ineffectual in achieving the real aims of the political art.

Possibly, the main contribution of Socrates to moral philosophy was the discovery of the personality as the unifying element of thought and action. He seems to have been the first to forge the concept of *psyche*, "soul," as that in us by which we are good or bad, knowing or ignorant, and which becomes better when just, worse when unjust; in short, what we should call today "I" or "self."[2] It is the integration of one's opinions and one's actions, at least to some extent, into a consistent, if not a coherent, pattern. To be a person is to display in one's actions and opinions a recognizable degree of unity and coherence. The lack of such coherence, in extreme cases, is considered pathological, as Plato points out in the *Gorgias*.

The idea of a unified personality to account for the acts of the individual was, in the fifth century B.C., an innovation. In archaic thought there was no such unity. Each of man's actions was explained separately. In the Homeric world, a god was involved, more often than not, in the origin of important acts, although concomitant personal responsibility was not thereby necessarily excluded.[3] It was only with Heraclitus, toward the end of the sixth century, that a notion of personal responsibility based on the unity of the moral agent was reached. "A man's character is his daimon," he said (fr. 119). One's fate is determined by the whole of one's habits and ways of acting, not by any outside agent. But for Socrates it is the whole of one's activity *and* one's cognition that becomes the focus of the moral inquiry. The stress on the intellectual element within the unified personality picks up the conscious deliberation as the morally relevant aspect of the action. The moral agent is now not only a unity of habits and ways of acting but chiefly a unity of thought and of action following upon thought.

Greek tragedy had already emphasized the intellectual element in human action, pitching conflicting points of view against one another on the stage. But apparently it was Socrates who strictly made the rightness of one's action dependent upon deliberation based on knowledge.[4]

Socrates seems to have been interested not so much in right action per se as in the impact of thought upon action. The rightness of the action was for him in the element of thought, in the deliberation, not in a certain feature of the act itself, to which the deliberation was merely accessory or heuristic. True, deliberation is for the sake of right action, but the rightness of the action is not independent of deliberation and knowledge. This is part of the meaning of the Socratic dictum that virtue is knowledge.

The determining factor in action is thus knowledge, not the unreflective will that chooses between aims whose intrinsic values are incommensurable with each other. Indeed, the Socratic concept of deliberation implies that knowledge itself is sufficient to decide between conflicting aims and hence also to initiate action. *Akrasia*, the weakness of the will, is impossible, but must in fact be, on Socrates' account, ignorance.

Of necessity, then, the arousal of knowledge is of central moral and political import, and conversely, the principal way of rightly influencing moral and political action is to arouse knowledge and reflection. Thus, for Socrates in the *Apology* (18 A5), as for Plato in the *Phaedrus* (261ff.), the excellence of the orator is to speak the truth. But truth is not a matter easily taken care of. It requires a "longer way," which is impracticable in court or in parliament.

To the rhetoric of Protagoras and Gorgias, Socrates opposes his dialectical method as the only adequate tool of politics. He is very careful to mark off the differences between these two ways of persuasion. Rhetoric brings the listener to a state of having been persuaded, dialectic to a state of having learned.[5] Dialectic proceeds step by step, by question and answer, and at each step the questioner has to secure the respondent's assent. Whereas rhetoric appeals to the judgment of the majority, or of the influential people ("the leaders of the public opinion"), dialectic aims at convincing the individual alone. In this sense dialectic is both antidemocratic and antiaristocratic: the results of the inquiry—and consequently also the course of action to be taken, for the Socratic inquiry is always into a practical question—should not be influenced by show of hands, neither should they take into account status, wealth, power, or authority (*Gorgias* 471 Eff.).

The main difference between Socrates and the ancient orators (and their modern heirs) is in his appraisal of the role of truth and knowledge in the process of deliberation. Socrates firmly believed that by freely examining the alternatives presented to him at each juncture of the dialogue, the respondent—other things being equal —must decide for the right alternative. No one errs willingly, but always because he is disturbed by irrelevant opinions, interests, or habits, which it is the function of the elenchus to eradicate. But Socrates was well aware how difficult it is to purify the mind of these impediments and how dubious, at best, are the prospects for success.

For the educated Athenian, influenced by Gorgias and others, the art of politics consisted in the efficient manipulation of the psychological conditions of persuasion and of moving the masses through that persuasion.[6] The objective of the political orator is to influence decisions, to "make things happen." Political oratory is thus concerned with inducing conviction about right and wrong. Socrates, however, stressed that decisions about right and wrong cannot be dissociated from the knowledge of what is the case.

Those who have knowledge on the matter to be decided upon decide on the strength of their knowledge. It is only when knowledge is lacking or insufficient that psychological motives can carry the day (cf. *Gorgias* 459E–459B).

For Socrates, then, politics was essentially the art of education. And yet, education as he understood it could never be the education of the masses. It would always be an individual affair. As in Greek tragedy, it was an *agon* between two characters, to which the chorus was merely accessory. And as in tragedy, the future of the protagonist, for better or for worse, hinged on his recognition of himself and of his moral predicament.

Yet, Socrates denied educating, as Gorgias, Prodicus, and Hippas claimed to do (*Apology* 19E; Protagoras is not mentioned because he was already dead by the time of Socrates' trial). Socrates knows he cannot "hand down virtue" like Euthydemus, nor can he promise to make those who associate with him "better from day to day," like Protagoras. The results of a Socratic dialogue can never be predicted, for dialogue always means interaction between two personalities. And, indeed, most of the early Platonic dialogues depict Socrates' failures rather than Socrates' successes. The commitment to truth requires that the course of the conversation be jointly determined by the inquirer and the respondent. Socrates saw the dialogue as essential to the emergence of knowledge in the individual, and where there was no true dialogue he could find no true conviction.[7]

That conviction sought by Socrates does flow from an inner source: it is in one's psychic recesses that the final discrimination between true and false is made. When presented with a question (in its simplest form, a yes-or-no question), the respondent must consider it himself and answer "as it seems to him." The answer to each question in the dialogue is always somewhat unpredictable to the questioner—or it must be if it is not given only to please the questioner or to save the respondent's face.

On the other hand, that conviction can receive its legitimation only in interpersonal examination. Subjective certainty is not sufficient for Socrates: he requires that one's opinions be open to public scrutiny and to the most exhaustive inquiry, conducted according to the fixed rules of the elenchus. Even then, the most that can be conferred on opinions is a prima facie validity, ever open to reexamination. One's inner resources provide merely the raw material from which knowledge and true conviction have to be hammered out in open conversation.

Socrates' morality was, then, not founded on the privacy of conscience but rather on the communality of discussions. Thomas More, for example, could base his opposition to his King on "his conscience and his soul."[8] But Socrates could not dissociate the validity he ascribed to his innermost opinions from the interpersonal process of their verification. For the Christian statesman, conviction is ultimately a matter of faith: the religious dogma provides a certainty that, although subjectively immediate, is not open to verification or challenge. Hence, when brought to court, More stood obstinately for the inviolability of his private beliefs. Greek religion, however, was not a religion of belief, but a state cult, in which citizens were required to partake not as a matter of conscience but of civic duty to the common good.[9] That subjective certainty of faith, which is central to Christianity and which was the historical ground of the concept of private conscience as we know it and as More used it, a private conscience which does not need, and in fact may be opposed to, public expression—that sort of inner conviction is lacking in Greek religion.

It is then understandable that for Socrates truth was possible only if publicly shared and publicly arrived at. Correspondingly, Socrates saw the central concept of action in *boulesis*: volition that includes deliberation. This deliberation is always open to social scrutiny because it turns on objective considerations susceptible of examination through dialogue. But, the requirements of the situation in which reasons can be given and evaluated cannot possibly be met in the political sphere. Restrictions of time and the necessity of speaking to many listeners at once, the one-sidedness of the set speech, and the almost complete impossibility of dialogue with the audience convinced Socrates that the usual ways of politics would force him to forego any serious attempt to influence action by the arousal of knowledge. What was left was at best the manipulation of the psychological conditions of persuasion or the expeditious use of the conflicting interests of the multitude. What Socrates objected to was the very concept of deliberation current in politics: deliberation that is not necessarily based on rational discussion and on clarity of thinking.

Socrates thus restricted himself to private conversations. He shunned public activity in the accepted sense of "public" because he thought it was at best ineffective and at worst misguided. Yet his activities were in an important sense public too. Socrates was a well-known figure in Athens; about his fortieth year he had been the subject of two comedies.[10] Socrates' acts and omissions could not fail to have had repercussions in the city. When, for example, the Thirty Tyrants tried to implicate him in their unlawful deeds by sending him along with others to arrest Leon of Salamis, he quietly went home. For Socrates, however, going home was a public act just as his conversations in the gymnasium were public acts. He points out that much in the *Apology*: "and about this many of you can testify" (32E). His further comment on the affair, to the effect that "it is possible that I would have died for it, if the Government had not quickly been put down," is a piece of understatement that takes a Socrates to make and a Plato to appreciate.

Nevertheless, it would be perverse to see in Socrates primarily a political figure. He was that, too, no doubt, and some of his contemporaries did understand him so, as well as some modern interpreters, although in a rather straightforward and simplistic way.[11] This, however, seems to have been only part of Socrates' complex personality. He seems to have been interested primarily in the nature of virtue—for a practical purpose. The aim of his inquiry was always right action, never theoretical knowledge for its own sake. As the Stoics were to learn from him, knowing is for the sake of acting; but acting rightly requires knowing.

Socrates saw the only remedy for Athens's political plight in a new morality, whose prerequisites were clarity of thinking and a new concept of the coherence of the personality and its moral worth. These, however, can be attained only by the individual himself, and there can be no short cuts to virtue. Political reform can come only through the differential education of individuals, not through the leading of the masses toward a predetermined goal. Socratic dialectic is, in an important sense, elitist. Oddly enough, it was Plato who saw the problems inherent in a political-educational view that does not provide for the masses. Hence the political significance Plato concedes to right opinion, although he retains the supremacy of knowledge and a hierarchy of capabilities.

For Socrates there is only one road to salvation. This is not because his care or his love for his fellow citizens is limited or conditional.[12] Socrates loved Athens, but he did not weep for her, as he did not weep for himself, because he was convinced that salvation lies in self-knowledge alone, not in compassion. He who cannot save himself cannot be saved by another.

NOTES

1. Anton-Hermann Chroust, *Socrates, Man and Myth* (London: Routledge & Kegan Paul, 1957), p. 166.

2. *Crito* 47f., *Protagoras* 312f. See John Burnet, "The Socratic Doctrine of the Soul," *Essays and Addresses* (London: Chatto and Windus, 1929), pp. 126–62.

3. See Arthur William Hope Adkins, *Merit and Responsibility* (Oxford: Clarendon Press, 1960), pp. 50–55, with Gregory Vlastos's strictures in *Plato's Universe* (Seattle: University of Washington Press, 1975), pp. 13–17.

4. See further Bruno Snell, *The Discovery of the Mind*, trans. T. G. Rosenmeyer (New York: Harper Torchbooks, 1960), ch. 8.

5. Cf. the distinction at *Gorgias* 454 c7ff. between *memathēkenai* and *pepisteukenai*. Cf. also *Meno* 87 c7, D1.

6. For a modern parallel, cf. *Gorgias* 45 2 E with Arnold Sherwood Tannenbaum's definition of leadership as "making things happen through others," in *International Encyclopedia of the Social Sciences* (New York: Macmillan Free Press, 1968), 9:101.

7. Cf. my "Three Aspects of Plato's Philosophy of Learning and Instruction," *Paideia* 5 (1976): 50–62.

8. On Socrates and Thomas More, see Eva Brann, "The Offense of Socrates," *Interpretation* 7 (1977–78): 1–21.

9. The political or civic import of the charge of *asebeia* (irreligiosity) against Socrates and its relation to the charge of corruption of the youth has been pointed out already by Adolph Menzel, "Untersuchungen zum Sokratesprozess," *Hellenika: Gesammelte kleine Schriften* (Baden bei Wien: Rudolf M. Rohrer [1938]), pp. 21–26.

10. Aristophanes' *Clouds* and Ameipsias' *Connus*, both produced in 423. Socrates is also mentioned by Callias, Eupolis, and Telecleides.

11. As in the interpretation revived by Chroust, which still has its adepts. A very recent version of it, from an unexpected quarter, is I. F. Stone's article on the trial of Socrates in *The New York Times Magazine*, 8 April 1979.

12. As Gregory Vlastos has it, "The Paradox of Socrates," *The Philosophy of Socrates*, ed. G. Vlastos (Garden City, N.Y.: Doubleday, 1971), p. 16.

B. J. T. DOBBS

℞ ISAAC NEWTON AND HUMANIST

VALUES IN SCIENCE

IT IS COMMONLY held today that the universe described by modern science has a cold, chancy inexorability about it that makes the existence of man an unexplained accident on a minor planet of a third-rate star. Gone forever is the comfortable geocentric and anthropocentric cosmos where the stars wheeled majestically around us and we were the summit of creation, the reason for the existence of it all. Gone also is the comfortable, albeit terrifying, cosmic drama of man's salvation, when heaven and hell waited to see what we would do.

With our displacement from the center of affairs, there have grown up persistent doubts about the reality of meaning and values on the cosmological scale. The "objective" universe seems to have no place for them; they are appropriate only in the small world of human life and are sometimes hard pressed to survive even there. One concomitant of this ontological decline in the human meaning of cosmic processes is a rising sense that the scientist, if he wants to do good "objective" science, had best divorce his search for meaning and values from his scientific work. He may legitimately look for personal meaning and values in his work, in his peer relationships, or in the benefits to accrue to mankind from his discoveries. But he may not look for cosmic meaning and values. "Science" has demonstrated that they do not exist, and the scientist must match nature herself in "objectivity" or else fall into error.

I would like to challenge that general point of view by the

introduction of some historical material. Whether or not the reader is convinced by my material, he can hardly deny to the principal subject of my discourse the right to be counted among the scientists. For my subject is Isaac Newton, whose *Philosophiae naturalis principia mathematica* (1687) marked the culmination of the scientific revolution and whose *Opticks* (1702) was only slightly less influential. Newton perhaps made more significant scientific discoveries than any other human being who has ever lived, and, I shall argue, he did it all through a passionate search for God.

Born in 1642 into a deeply religious age, Newton grew into manhood as a sincere though hardly orthodox religious thinker. We had long lost sight of this dimension of Newton's character, partly because of historical processes that had recast him in more "suitable" heroic molds for every successive age. But partly we had lost sight of the seventeenth-century Newton because so much of his thought was never published. Masses of his private papers, especially those on theology and alchemy, remained in manuscript and in private hands until this century. Dispersed at auction in 1936, most of these papers have in the last forty years been acquired by major university, college, or public libraries and so have become available for scholarly study. In the last twenty years or so a veritable "Newton industry" has grown up, as historians of science struggle to piece together the scattered fragments of the historical Newton. The result has been a startlingly different portrait of the man, one far removed from the austere, "objective" fountainhead of modern science so often presented in the science textbook tradition.

Newton was not alone in the seventeenth century in giving a religious meaning to the pursuit of science, or, to use terminology more appropriate to the seventeenth century, to the study of natural philosophy. The primary motivation for many of the founders of modern science was religious in character. Francis Bacon in the *New Atlantis*, for example, called his research foundation the "College of the Six Days' Works," meaning that it was to study the work done by God in the six days of creation. Johannes Kepler called himself a "priest of God to the Book of Nature." The Book of

Nature was coming to have equal standing with the Book of the Word. One could learn of God by studying either one, for the latter was divinely inspired while the former was God's handiwork and reflected His nature. So Newton was not alone, but he may have been more conscious of the religious meaning of his natural philosophy than most and more insistent in his dedication to it. "When I wrote my Treatise about our System," Newton said in 1692 (referring to the *Principia*), "I had an Eye upon such Principles as might work with considering Men for the Belief of a Deity and nothing can rejoice me more than to find it useful for that Purpose."[1]

We may take Isaac Newton then as the prime example of a man who thought the pursuit of knowledge about nature to have profound humanistic meaning—meaning for the individual seeker and for mankind. In doing this, we must perforce look not only at his work in mathematics and natural philosophy but also at part of his less well-known work such as that in alchemy and history. For there was a consistency in the total shape of Newton's intellectual life that, once we have grasped it, will enable us to see the meaning of natural philosophy to him.

Let us first examine the assumptions with which Newton operated. Primary and fundamental was his belief that the purpose and duty of human life is to seek knowledge of God and to worship Him. The more man knows about God, the more his faith is strengthened and the better able is he to discharge the duty of worship.

A second assumption of Newton's was that of the unity of truth. In its ultimate, its purest form, that assumption implied the identification of truth with God, and from thence it followed that all paths of knowledge would lead to God. It mattered little where one started. If one pursued wisdom diligently and humbly, one would learn something more of God's nature. Truth was one, and for Newton that included the true, pure knowledge of God and of nature that mankind had held before the fall from grace. Before man corrupted himself, as Newton would have put it, he had truth directly from God. But after the fall, truth had been lost, or mangled by the passage of time, or it had been deliberately hidden in mythic language to keep it out of the hands of evil men who might misuse it. Implicit also in his doctrine of the unity of truth was Newton's belief that God's attributes were reflected in the nature of nature. Natural philosophy thus took on immediate theological meaning to him. It served to reveal those characteristics of God that were not to be so readily found in the written Word, for nature was the work of God's hands. Thus by whatever route one approached truth, the goal was the same. Experimental discovery and revelation, the productions of reason, speculation, or mathematics, the cryptic, coded messages of the ancients (if correctly interpreted), all found their reconciliation in the infinite unity and majesty of the Deity.

With these assumptions, Newton set out on his voyage "through strange seas of Thought, alone," as Wordsworth put it in *The Prelude*. His first venture probably led him through Scripture, and large numbers of his surviving papers attest his thorough familiarity with all parts of the Bible. Scripture was divinely inspired, and it contained truth, though of course he thought one must interpret it carefully, wisely, and rationally. He was never a literalist in his interpretations, but neither did he ever abandon his belief in the inspiration of the Word.

In his mature years, Newton's great mind absorbed and digested almost every branch of knowledge available to him. He read not only Scripture but also the early fathers of the church. He read theology and philosophy, natural philosophy and natural history. He read mathematics and mythology; he read history and alchemy. He experimented with the materials of the physical world and equally he sought a technique for the interpretation of prophecy. All would lead ultimately to truth.

We can see obvious links between some of these studies, but to comprehend the linkages among them as they existed for Newton, we must divest ourselves of many modern notions and burrow into matters with which the seventeenth-century intellectual concerned himself. We see that a biblical scholar would want to read theology. We can understand that a thorough grasp of metaphysics would enhance the study of theology. We know, at least in an abstract way, that in the seventeenth century philosophy proper shaded readily over into natural philosophy and that natural philosophy shaded into natural history.

We would have no argument at all with the proposition that mathematics is closely related to the natural philosophy, though interestingly enough that was a rather unorthodox view in Newton's time. He had John Dee and Kepler and Galileo and a few others to guide him, but many seventeenth-century thinkers held that mathematics was ungodly, being the province of astrologers and cabbalists, or, if not actually wicked, probably useless. Dee and Kepler, however, had seen God as the Great Mathematician, creating the world according to Platonic mathematical forms, and Galileo had agreed that the world had mathematic bones at the center of it.

Again, we see experimentation as naturally related to both natural philosophy and to mathematics. Indeed, we would see those three subjects as the ones Newton wove together to create his *Principia* and *Opticks*, the two books that may reasonably be said to have launched modern science. But that is a post-Newtonian point of view, and we come here to one of the less obvious linkages in Newton's mind between these various paths to truth. Experiment was important to him because of his voluntaristic theology. If one emphasizes the rational side of God's nature (that is, if one is a theological rationalist), one may be tempted to employ—or over-employ—his own rationality in deducing God's mode of operation in the universe. But if one assumes that God's will is primary (that is, if one is a voluntarist in theology), then man's puny rationality is immediately seen as inadequate. One may still deduce how God might have acted in a rational manner, yet man's mind is not the measure. It is seen that God has the power to act in any way He wills; therefore it is necessary to look at the world as it exists to find out what God actually did in creating it. So Newton looked.

A very similar line of reasoning led to Newton's interest in history. History, Newton thought, was the story of God's action in the world, and as such it was a key for the interpretation of prophecy.

Prophetic writings in the Bible were divinely inspired, but man could understand prophecy only after it had been fulfilled, for it was written in "mystical" language. Newton spent untold hours on the prophecies of Daniel and the Apocalypse of St. John, involved in an intricate attempt to match historical events with the various prophetic passages. In a very real sense there was a direct link between history and experiment in Newton's mind, because history provided the experimental—or at least experiential—verification of the correct method for the interpretation of prophecy. And as in experiment, man's mind was not the measure. Man was not to presume to interpret prophecy in a way that allowed for the prediction of future events. Only after the events had occurred could one see that they had been the fulfillment of prophecy: then God's action in the world was demonstrated. God gave prophecies, Newton said, "not to gratify men's curiosities by enabling them to foreknow things, but that after they were fulfilled they might be interpreted by the event, and his own Providence, not the Interpreters, be then manifested thereby to the world. For the event of things predicted many ages before, will then be a convincing argument that the world is governed by providence."[2]

There was likewise a religious dimension to Newton's study of alchemy. For theological reasons Newton rejected the purely mechanical universe of the Cartesians, arguing with Henry More and the other Cambridge Platonists that God had to be present in an active way in the universe. It was unacceptable to postulate a closed mechanical system that could run on indefinitely by itself once God had set it in motion. God needed to be in constant contact with His creation in order to maintain His providential governance of it. In any case there were some obvious processes in the natural world that could not be explained mechanically. By "mechanical," these seventeenth-century philosophers meant that physical events were all caused by matter and motion, by bodies impacting with other bodies. Processes that gave the mechanical philosophers grave difficulties were electricity, magnetism, gravity, sympathetic vibration, and what Newton called "vegetation" (life and growth). These processes required "active principles," not

mechanical ones, for their explanation, and the alchemical literature dealt with just such an active principle at work in the "vegetation" of metals. It was a spiritual principle, sometimes described
almost as a Neoplatonic "soul of the world," but in any event it
was God's agent. It was the agent by which He had given the
power of life and "vegetation" to all three kingdoms in the beginning (animal, vegetable, and mineral), and it was the agent by
which He continued to support life and growth with providential
care. A demonstration of the truth of alchemy by a successful
experiment in the "vegetation" of metals would be equally a demonstration of God's active participation in the natural world, and
Newton—we now know on the basis of the manuscripts he left
behind—studied, wrote, and experimented in alchemy for thirty-
five years.

Alchemy in its turn was closely related to the interpretation of
prophecy. Alchemy, like prophecy, was written in obscure symbolism. Techniques developed for deciphering prophecy might be
applied to the decoding of alchemy as well.

Then there was the possibility that the alchemical texts might
contain some of the pure wisdom of the ancients, wisdom that had
been divinely inspired in the beginning. That was especially likely
with the Hermetic texts, for Hermes (Newton thought) was himself
one of the ancients. If so, the wisdom had clearly been encoded to
keep it from "the vulgar," but one might get clues from other rem-
nants of ancient learning, such as myths. Newton was quite sure
that many important secrets were hidden in classical mythology.

Myths held secrets not only about alchemy, but also about history. The gods and goddesses in the myths, Newton thought, were
divinized kings and queens who had once actually lived and who
had been falsely given divine status in the process of mythopoeia
because of great deeds or great benefactions to humanity. He
attempted to sort out all of their various relationships in order
better to understand the "chronology" of ancient kingdoms. So we
see his study of mythology feeding complex strands into both his
study of alchemy and his study of history.

From the treasure trove of his private papers, Newton drew out only a relatively few items for publication or even for limited circulation in manuscript: some on mathematics; those incorporated into the *Opticks* and the *Principia*; one on the nature of acids; one on degrees of heat and some on light and color sent to the Royal Society; those that finally went into the *Chronology of Ancient Kingdoms, amended*. His *Observations upon the Prophecies of Daniel and the Apocalypse of St. John* was found in manuscript and published after his death. In many of these works, one finds threads from Newton's many lines of investigation interwoven in a manner that at first baffles the modern reader. What, for example, is God doing in the *Principia*? Why has Newton calculated the exact floor plan of the Temple at Jerusalem and inserted it in the *Chronology*? Why are there glimmerings of alchemy in the *Opticks*, in the *Principia*, and in the paper on acids? How could he possibly have thought that he could combine celestial mechanics (the precession of the equinoxes) with interpretations of myth to reassess the chronology of ancient kingdoms? What conceivable relationship is there between Germanic tribes and the ten horns of the fourth beast of Daniel? Many of our difficulties with the superficial anomalies in Newton's published works can now be resolved, thanks to the fresh insights into his thought that the recent study of his unpublished manuscripts has given us. We can now see, as I have argued above, that to Newton it was all related. To Newton, though not to us, it did not seem in any way strange to weave all those strands of investigation together, because they were all ways to truth and to a fuller knowledge of God.

It was Newton's fondest hope, as we have already seen, that his discoveries "might work with considering Men for the Belief of a Deity." Atheism was not widespread in the seventeenth century by any modern standard, yet it was there and it threatened to spread. Hence the acute fear expressed by the Cambridge Platonists that Descartes's mechanical system of the world would lead to more of it. Hence Newton's pleasure in finding that his system could be used for the confutation of atheism. Let us now turn to two of those elements of the Newtonian system of the world that he thought made it "useful for that Purpose": the nonmechanical nature of gravity and the evidence for ordered design in nature.

One of the basic tenets of the Cartesian philosophy was that gravity, like every other event in nature, took place through bodies impacting upon each other. To explain gravity, Descartes had postulated the existence of invisible vortices of very fine matter. A solar vortex, for example, whirled the planets around the sun. An earthly vortex supplied the impacts needed to force objects downward to the surface of the earth in a manner consonant with the recognized laws of terrestrial gravitation. Newton himself had imbibed much of this system through the reading of his student years, but his subsequent experimental and mathematical investigations had revealed the fallacies of the Cartesian gravitational hypothesis to him, and a good part of the *Principia* is devoted to an exposé of Descartes's errors in the matter of vortices. There was no adequate mechanical explanation of gravity that Newton could find, only his famous mathematical law for it. That means that most of space is empty once one removes the hypothesized vortices of fine, invisible particles, and the implication is that the cause of gravity is nonmechanical in nature, that is, not caused by the impact of bodies. If the cause of gravity is not corporeal, then it must be incorporeal and spiritual and must be God Himself. In the end, Newton believed that his work on gravity had demonstrated the literal omnipresence of God in the universe. In 1705 he talked the matter over with David Gregory, and Gregory entered the following note in his journal.

> *What the space that is empty of body is filled with.* The plain truth is, that he [Newton] believes God to be omnipresent in the literal sense; And that as we are sensible of Objects when their Images are brought home within the brain, so God must be sensible of every thing, being intimately present with every thing: for he supposes that as God is present in space where there is no body, he is present in space where a body is also present. But if this way of proposing this his notion be too

bold, he thinks of doing it thus. *What Cause did the Ancients assign of Gravity.* He believes that they reckoned God the Cause of it, nothing else, that is no body being the cause; since every body is heavy.[3]

The thoughts that Newton expressed that day to Gregory eventually found their way in modified forms into later editions of both the *Principia* and the *Opticks.*

Then there was the matter of design in nature. Once he had found that the solar system was kept in order by a single mathematical law, Newton immediately looked past the law to the One who had established the order in the first place.

[B]ut though these bodies may, indeed, continue in their orbits by the mere laws of gravity, yet they could by no means have at first derived the regular position of the orbits themselves from those laws. . . .

[I]t is not to be conceived that mere mechanical causes could give birth to so many regular motions. . . . This most beautiful system of the sun, planets, and comets, could only proceed from the counsel and dominion of an intelligent and powerful Being.[4]

And finally, after a long passage on the attributes of this Being who is omnipresent, who constitutes duration and space by His very existence, who set the stars in their courses and keeps man under His providential care, Newton concludes triumphantly, "And thus much concerning God; to discourse of whom from the appearances of things, does certainly belong to Natural Philosophy."[5]

One may of course argue that Newton was mistaken in what he took to be the thrust of his achievements, that the religious dimension of his natural philosophy comprised a nonessential scaffolding for his "real" science, a scaffolding subsequent generations have quite correctly dismantled. That may be, and it is not my intention here to debate that point. On the contrary, my intention has been to bring forward historical material that bears on a matter of some importance in our own culture. It is clear, I think, that the case of Isaac Newton adequately demonstrates that a search for cosmic meaning and values need not preclude the doing of good "objective" science. Whether those values and that meaning may yet be found in the physical universe is another question.

NOTES

1. Isaac Newton, *The Correspondence of Isaac Newton*, ed. by H. W. Turnbull, J. P. Scott, A. R. Hall, and Laura Tilling, 7 vols. (Cambridge: Published for the Royal Society at the University Press, 1959–78), 3:233 (Newton to Richard Bentley, 10 December 1692), quoted from the version in *Isaac Newton's Papers & Letters On Natural Philosophy and related documents. Containing Newton's contributions to the Philosophical Transactions of the Royal Society, his letter to Boyle about the aether. "De Natura Acidorum." Newton's letters to Bentley and the "Boyle Lectures" related to them. the first published biography of Newton. Halley's publications about Newton's "Principia," &c.*, ed., with a general introduction by I. Bernard Cohen, assisted by Robert E. Schofield, with explanatory prefaces by Marie Boas, Charles Coulston Gillispie, Thomas S. Kuhn, and Perry Miller, 2d ed. (Cambridge, Mass., and London, 1978), p. 280.

2. Isaac Newton, *Observations upon the Prophecies of Daniel and the Apocalypse of St. John. In Two Parts* (London: Printed by J. Darby and T. Browne in *Bartholomew-Close*. And Sold by J. Roberts in *Warwick-lane*, J. Tonson in the *Strand*, W. Innys and R. Manby at the West End of St. *Paul*'s *Church-Yard*, J. Osborn and T. Longman in *Pater-Noster-Row*, J. Noon near *Mercers Chapel* in *Cheapside*, T. Hatchett at the *Royal Exchange*, S. Harding in *St. Martin*'s *lane*, J. Stagg in *Westminster-Hall*, J. Parker in *Pall-mall*, and J. Brindley in *New Bond-street*, 1733), pp. 251–52.

3. *David Gregory, Isaac Newton and Their Circle. Extracts from David*

Gregory's Memoranda, 1677–1708, ed. W. G. Hiscock (Oxford: Printed for the Editor, 1937), p. 30.

4. Isaac Newton, *Sir Isaac Newton's Mathematical Principles of Natural Philosophy and His System of the World. Translated into English by Andrew Motte in 1729. The translations revised, and supplied with an historical and explanatory appendix, by Florian Cajori*, 2 vols. (Berkeley, Los Angeles, London: University of California Press, 1934), 2:543–44.

5. Ibid., 2:546.

LEWIS LEARY

❦ JOEL BARLOW: THE MAN

OF LETTERS AS CITIZEN

THERE HAS NOT been unanimity of opinion on whether the man of letters can or should be in any ordinary sense a good citizen. The function of the poet, Emerson once said, is not to settle, but to unsettle, to surprise, even disturb, by quick revelation, to examine, as Thoreau did, things as they are and invite resistance to them. Poets have been most effective in a public sense in time of revolution, as Milton was when he turned to admonitory prose. But neither the American nor the French revolution produced a distinguished man of letters, any more than did the incipient revolution of the early 1860s in the United States. Each was heralded and sustained by a chorus of voices, few rising in solo above the rest. For revolution most often breeds repetition of ideas or ideals already spoken and restless for approval.

The man of letters in proper guise confronts his age, to mend or amend, providing shocks of recognition that what is should not or need not be. In periods of stress, he may become a translator, an echo voice effectively reciting programmatic measures. His words then may so reflect his time that they resist timelessness. As citizen, he serves; as artist, he provides skillful popular instruction. Instead of confronting his age, he embraces it. If a Milton, the stress removed, he returns to his art. If a lesser person, he may become crippled by good intentions. The revolution in seventeenth-century England did not produce Milton. It might almost be said, though quietly, that revolutions do not produce, but seduce, the man of letters.

37

The Enlightenment of the late eighteenth century was particularly seductive. It counseled benevolence and cooperative goodwill. It called for sacrifice of individual rights for the good of society at the same time that it insisted that all men are endowed with equal rights, thus posing the democratic dilemma that would later beguile Emerson, of to what extent a person can remain single and separate, a law unto himself, and to what extent he must put self aside to become a cooperative and contributing member of a group. The Enlightenment called for a reformation of society on rational principles: the past must be examined anew, catacombs of superstition emptied, and the inherited power of any person or class over the lives or destinies of other people stripped away. America's Declaration of Independence was the first public harbinger of an aspiring view that would keep the Western world in precarious balance for generations, like an equestrian, Emerson would say, with one foot on one horse, the other on another.

Moving through a period when human rights were enforced by riot and bloodshed, Joel Barlow of Connecticut, perhaps more than any of his countrymen, can profitably be examined as a person who, fumbling through inherited ideas, produced a pattern that has not yet effectively been used to provide a protective cloak for what he called the poor, troubled race of humankind, an infant still, struggling toward maturity.

His was not a talent fitted to the task he undertook. His visions were larger than his ability to make them clear. Tied to tradition as a poet, he seemed often so intent on smoothing his verse to requirements established by the beguiling but stultifying example of Alexander Pope that sense often gives way to sound, with the result that it is sometimes difficult to determine his meaning. His prose is more direct, but as much the product of enthusiasm as of logic. He therefore defies precise explication. He must be taken unaware, grasped at in those instances when he escapes from traditions of form or substance to say or suggest something perhaps quite beyond his knowing that he was saying it. For he thought more freely, though no less clearly, than he wrote. Through all his life, he was a religious person, and his religion was that of universal love. Because the religious is more difficult to explain than other attitudes, taking on the coloration of the explainer, Barlow was misread by many of his generation and perhaps has been by ours.

As the first activist offspring of the Enlightenment, the American Revolution was more than political. It has been said to have been, besides that, moral and philosophical,[1] which of course it was, but it was religious also. It contributed toward a revision of the way people thought about deity and of the degree to which deity might be expected to respond to the ways of people. As the struggle for freedom drew to a close, the Reverend Charles Chauncy, long a leader among the clergy of New England, and his younger colleague, the Reverend John Clark, startled but did not surprise Boston by striking at the roots of New England Calvinism by declaring salvation available to all persons. Even some of their more liberal colleagues thought they had spoken precipitously, perhaps too strongly. "They had let the cat out of the bag" too soon, said the Reverend John Eliot, for people, "even the most rational part of the town," were not ready for it. But the people heard, some disturbed, some pleased, others relieved.

For "the doctrine of universal restitution," explained the Reverend Jeremy Belknap, "has long been a secret among learned men." Though most sensible people shrugged aside the militant deism of Ethan Allen's *Reason the Only Oracle of Man* as the rantings of an inadequately educated wild man, the unbagged cat showed alarmingly sharp claws. People flocked to listen to the Reverend John Murray, an Englishman who preached Universalism, or were attracted to the blunt pronouncements of the Reverend William Hazlitt, from Ireland, who doggedly attempted to convert the new world to Unitarianism. Neither of these was to the New England manner bred, and that bothered clergymen who with less forensic display must keep their pews filled. But created equal, people would decide for themselves what they would believe. Swedenborgianism was making a stir in Philadelphia. And Freemasonry, what of that?—a secret conspiracy certainly, meant to pervert the world.

"A belief in God's universal love for all his creatures, and that he will finally restore all . . . to happiness," advised Dr. Benjamin Rush from Philadelphia, "is a *polar* truth. . . . It establishes the equality of all mankind." All persons created equal—John Murray's wife, Judith Sargent Murray, of good New England ancestry, argued that women also deserved equality—"the book of Nature and the book of Scripture," explained Belknap, "are open to the inspection of all." The people had democratic license to examine them for themselves.

This Joel Barlow would do. Though educated under the tutelage of the Reverend Timothy Dwight, who was described in 1783 by John Eliot as "a compleat bigot, . . . a mean-spirited divine,"[2] and who five years later would spew anathema on Ethan Allen, Charles Chauncy, and all others—Voltaire more than most—who contributed to what he called *The Triumph of Infidelity*, Barlow remained his own man. Unorthodox to the extent that it required the influence of friends and some quick evasionary tactics on his part to become certified as a chaplain during the Revolution, he preached patriotism rather than piety. Encouraged by Dwight, he wrote poems. He spent years, as Dwight did also, on what has been called an epic attempt. Dwight's would be published in 1785, a militant poem on *The Conquest of Canäan* that explained how Joshua had led his chosen people to a promised land, by which many people thought him to have intended an analogue to Washington's leading his people toward freedom. Barlow's, published two years later, told of *The Vision of Columbus*, a forecasting of what the New World might become. Barlow protested that it was not an epic, but it almost was.

Nine years before, on graduating from Yale, he had read a conventionally pious poem on "The Prospect of Peace," in which he forecast the beginning of a "golden age," a millennium where "Love shall rule, and Tyrants be no more." Three years later, on receiving a second degree, he read another poem, inserting into it "several passages from a longer work" yet unfinished. Dedicated now to verse-making, he hoped that he might attract "some liberal benefactor," some modern Maecenas, to support him while he completed his *Vision*. For the new nation, rising toward independence, needed "peace inspiring song" to explain its "progressive plan/Which draws for mutual succour, man to man." The poet's voice was the necessary voice, to sing, not the clash of arms, but peace, with "nations . . . leagued" by common interests ensured by a mutually profitable commerce among them.

Underlying Barlow's vision was an optimistic certainty that men could improve themselves and that self-improvement was basic to concord among people.[3] Emerson, half a century later, would have used the terms in a different sense, but might have nodded approval as Barlow in an address to the Society of Cincinnati on 4 July 1787 counseled listening to the *"still small voice,"* the voice of rational reflection. "The Revolution," he warned, "is but half completed": we must now conquer ourselves. Government was "the child of reason" and "America the empire of reason," where neither pageantry nor superstition need cloud the mind. Reason required the "noblest effort of human nature" in *"the conquest of self,"* the "sacrificing of private . . . advantages for the good of the majority." Within the self are "passions and prejudices more powerful than armies and more dangerous to our peace." But self-interest was at root common interest. "Unite," he advised; "put your commerce on a respectable footing"; then "your arts and manufactures, your population, your wealth and glory will increase." Our "strongest duty," he concluded, "is to enlighten and harmonize the minds of our fellow citizens, and point them to a knowledge of their interests," thus bringing "peace . . . to future ages, and through the extended world."

These were more than catchwords of his time. They outlined a vision that Barlow would state and restate over many years. It informs the melange of rationalism and native pride in *The Vision of Columbus*. Dwight's long poem of *Conquest* is accompanied by the thunder of great battles and the thunder of great storms that foreboded or accompanied them. Barlow's is a poem of peace universally triumphant. Columbus, instructed by a seraphic guide, is allowed a vision of amity among nations. Dwight's retells a tooth and claw Old Testament story. Barlow's, so far as it has biblical analogy, looks to the New Testament. In the great chain of being, culminating in the "harmony of the human frame," there "God's first works and nature's are the same." Beneath this, however, is a subliminal vision of nature's god, the life-giving sun as emblem of the New World.

Though encouraging Barlow as through the years he struggled to complete his poem, Dwight could not have read all of the manuscript with approving care, especially not the long footnote added to its second book "but a few days previous to the Poem being put to press," or the fifteen pages in prose, "A Dissertation on the Genius and Institutions of Manco Capac," that followed it, the one admitting indebtedness to, the other admiration of, Dwight's bête noire, Voltaire. There Manco Capac, the Incan chieftain, is celebrated as having had established "a most benevolent and pacific" religion, based on worship of a god of nature, the sun. Such a religion "tended to humanize the world and make his people happy." Capac's conception of deity was "so perfect as to bear comparison with the enlightened doctrines of Socrates and Plato."

Moses had not done so well. He had indeed brought to power an uncivilized people, servile and savage and superstitious, by presenting himself "as an interpretor of divine will." By enforcing "religious observations of certain rites, he formed his people to habitual obedience." But he withheld from them the mysteries of their religion as not a proper subject for "profane and vulgar investigation." More than that, he "prohibited any intercourse with foreigners" so that enmity rose among and against them. Lycurgus at Sparta had done much the same, inspiring his people with "a contempt for others." Neither provided for the "future progress of society." Each would mire his nation "forever in a state of ignorance, superstition, and barbarism." Nor had Mohammed done better. Knowing the natural propensities of people, he had lured his followers with promises of pleasure in a sensual paradise. His people remained in ignorance. Their monarch was sacred and supreme. The "most important end of government, that of social happiness, was deplorably lost."

Like Moses and Mohammed, Manco Capac had presented himself to his people as a monarch from heaven. But Capac's God bestowed "blessings of light, and warmth, and vegetation." He was "the God of order and regularity," controlling the seasons, enriching products of the earth, and bringing "Blessings of health to his people." Most Christians, Barlow interjected, "ascribe their afflictions to the hand of Heaven, and prosperity to their own merit." They do not discover deity "in the usual course of nature, in the sunshine and shower, the productions of the earth and the blessing of society." Capac's was "the most surprizing exertion of human genius to be found in the history of mankind, . . . rendering religion and government subservient to the general happiness." Dwight must have sputtered in indignation. Religion subservient to happiness indeed!

Returning to verse, Barlow continued to proclaim "the bounties of our sire the Sun." Rocha, son and heir to Capac, speaks, but the words are the young poet's as he celebrates a visioned land where

> No furious God disturbs the peaceful skies,
> Nor yields our hands the bloody sacrifice.
> But life and joy the Power delights to give,
> And bids his children but rejoice and live.

In the heavens, "the all-delighting Sun" on "golden throne" reigns as

> our only God: in him we trace
> The friend, the father of our happy race.

But, though beguiled by Incan legend, Barlow did not look back to a time of pastoral bliss. He knew, and in his prose confirmed, that Capac's kingdom was finally destroyed by war and internal dissension, but in verse allowed a triumphant leader to assure his people that their God, the god of nature, "commands to stay the rage of war."

And how will this pacific end be accomplished? His guiding spirit informs Columbus that "United nations" will finally move toward amity. Columbus is pleased. He hopes that, avarice put aside, people of his new found world will finally "learn the various blessings that extend/Where civil rights and social virtues blend," and "arts and laws in one great system bind,/By leagues of peace, the labours of mankind." Commerce will flourish, science reveal new secrets, and art inspire a "new creation," where

> Though different faiths their various orders show,
> That seem discordant to the train below;
> Yet one blest cause, one universal flame,
> Wakes all their joys and centers every aim.

To the "darkling race of poor distrest mankind," the voice of God proclaims,

> I reign the Lord of life; I fill the round,
> Where stars and skies and angels know their bound;
> Before all years, beyond all thought I live,
> Light, form and motion, time and space I give.

"Thro' nature's range, progressive paths design'd" one simple scheme in which "beauty, wisdom, power" are bound in "one harmonious system" in which "moral beauties bid the world attend" and to "distant lands their social ties extend." Discarding "pride of name, the prejudice of schools," people might yet discover "laws in every breast,/Where ethics, faith and politics may rest," first through sense, that "great source of knowledge," then through reason that restrains "wild fancy" and "calms the impassion'd soul,/Illumes the judgment and refines the whole." As he brings his *Vision* to an end, Barlow speaks, not in terms of conventional belief, but of "nature's God, . . . one simple universal cause, . . . the eternal mind" from which radiates one great "mystic scheme." Sense policed by reason discovers "the attracting force of universal love" that, centered in God, spreads to all his creatures.[4]

The lumbering of his verse may sometimes dim Barlow's meaning. Written over many years, his *Vision* had grown as he grew. It contains vestiges of older conventional thought on which new convictions are grafted. It is a hunchbacked poem, distorted, or enlivened, by discovery of the god of nature in the legend of Manco Capac. He never started over again to write it to unity, only patched it in revision, but the tension between the lure of Capac's myth and Barlow's increasing conviction that myth is incompatible with a life of reason livens much that Barlow would later write. Now he seems to be saying that America need not look abroad or to some pagan past for a controlling legend. It was there in the deification of nature in the New World. He observes now of religions that, however diverse their creeds, one "finds in all, what nature might approve," and that is a "God of justice reconciled by love." This was enough for a young man who, like Manco Capac, would strive

> In bands of mutual peace all tribes to bind,
> And live the friend and guardian of mankind.

Almost exactly a year after *The Vision of Columbus* appeared, in late May 1788, Barlow sailed for France as an agent of the Scioto land company that would recruit immigrants to settle the western territories. In Paris, he enjoyed the company and confidence of Jefferson and Lafayette and their infectious enthusiasm for ideas quite contrary to those of many of his friends in New England. He was a fascinated and undoubtedly sometimes frightened bystander during the Revolution of 1789, but its principles, he thought, were his principles. The land company failing, he crossed to England where he associated with such liberals as Horne Tooke, Mary Wollstonecraft, William Godwin, and Thomas Paine, bad company indeed as measured against home-grown standards. After the publication late in 1790 of Edmund Burke's caustic *Reflections on the French Revolution*, he joined Paine in spirited reply. Sandwiched between the first and second parts of *The Rights of Man* was the first part of Barlow's *Advice to the Privileged Orders*, which made him friends, but enemies also.

The revolution in France seemed to promise fair new policies derived from "principles approved by reason." Undertaken "for the benefit of the people, it originated in the people and was conducted by the people." The example of the United States had demonstrated that political change resulted, not from pontifications of such people as Burke, but on decisions of "a much more important class, . . . the class that cannot read. It is to be determined by men who reason better without books, than do all the books in the world," for "little instruction is needed to teach a man his rights." Barlow's commitment to democracy was complete. The past must be thrust aside. Aristotle must be corrected, just as Ptolemy had been. Traditions that upheld entailment and primogeniture must be done away with and freedom of the press ensured. Each person would speak in his own voice, and each would speak for all.

As for religion, all people were, of course, religious, but a creed sustained by "mysteries and invisibilities" did not reflect the true "light of religion." None "had right to interfere with the religion of another." The *"existence of any kind of liberty is incompatible with the existence of any kind of church* . . . declared to be national, or declared to have any preference in the eye of the law." Like Druids and Augurs of the past, priests "pretend supernatural powers, and invest themselves in the cloak of infallibility." Away with them. Christian polytheism is certainly as evil as that of Greece or Rome: "But it is not the *church* that is corrupted by men, it is *men* who are corrupted by the church." Like a canny debater, Barlow avows that "he will not mention," but then goes on to speak of the corruption of morals resulting from "the ardent passions of restrained celibacy" that tempt men of the cloth to doing what comes naturally. He is proud that in his country no such restraints are necessary. Without quite saying that all people are by nature good, he wonders "how many of our vices are chargeable on the permanent qualities of man, and how many result from the mutable energies of state."

Still using familiar catchwords, he attacked in turn the feudal system, the national church, the military, and the administration of justice as these prevailed throughout Europe. He planned then a second volume that would review public expenditure and revenue, the means of subsistence available to people, the place in their lives of literature, science, and the arts, and of war and peace. But circumstances intervened, so that he completed discussion only of the first subject, speaking of national debt, national credit, and funding. Unable to find a publisher in England because of "violent attacks on the liberty of the press" there, he had it published two years later in Paris, where as a man of letters and citizen he then labored to sustain the civic millennium that the new Republic seemed to promise.

Before leaving London in the spring of 1792, Barlow published *The Conspiracy of Kings* as a versified companion to *Advice to the Privileged Orders*, blasting that "strange man," Burke, as a "degenerate slave" in whose chaotic utterances "darkness frowns" as "Truth, Error, Falsehood, Rhetoric," joined with "Pomp and Meanness, . . . Strain to an endless clang." But they strain in vain, for "Freedom at last, with Reason in her train,/Extends o'er earth her everlasting reign," as "Truth's blest banners . . . shake tyrants from their thrones." In October, he addressed *A Letter to the National Convention* of the new French Republic, urging it to adopt principles similar to those set forth in the Constitution of the United States. Thomas Paine, who sat as a member of that body, formally presented the letter to the National Convention, which thereupon made its author an honorary citizen of France.

What Barlow said was not original, only strongly spoken. But the publication of the *Letter* established him as a useful person. Late in November, he was chosen to address the National Convention, bringing it assurance that members of the London Constitutional Society, to which he was proud to have been elected, approved and encouraged its republican principles. Hardly a week later, he was off to the south, to Savoy, with a delegation charged with instructing that area on measures to be taken in electing delegates to the French National Convention. He liked the Savoyards. They were rigorous and hardy, "just born to liberty," and he was given some reason to suspect that he might himself be elected as one of their delegates.

He was not, but while among them, he wrote *A Letter Addressed to the People of the Piedmont*, advising them on the advantages of adapting the principles of the French Revolution. French and Italian versions were printed in Nice and Grenoble and distributed widely on both sides of the border. "You are my fellow citizens," Barlow wrote, and "as such I love you." He reminded them that "their Gospel of Jesus Christ preaches . . . in the strongest language the great doctrine of equality, that all men are equal in the sight of God." The principles of the revolution in France, which he invited them to join, "are those of universal peace."

While in Savoy, attracted to the quiet of the countryside of rocks and hills and of fertile valleys snuggled between mountains, Barlow was reminded of his New England home, and he wrote a homesick poem that has often been considered lightly and brightly his best. "The Hasty Pudding," singing praise of bowls of hot, golden cornmeal, milk-cooled with exact precision to please the palate, mocks "the excessive sentimentality associated with popular pastoralism," at the same time, Robert D. Arner has suggested, that it affirms a "native American's unique and personal relationship to the land that sustains him." Arner calls attention to the "abundance of religious terminology in the poem" and to its "affirming faith . . . in the undying life of the natural world" to which the sun is central: "It grows the corn, which in its color reflects the hue of the sun . . . and the pudding, golden like the sun, is heated over a fire that is not only sun-colored, but also possesses some of the sun's light and warmth."[5]

Again Barlow turns to the myth that had struggled for precedence in *The Vision of Columbus*. America is not only the rising sun among nations that will dispel fogs of corruption that smother the Old World; the new nation finds within its own past, in native Indian lore existing long before Columbus sighted its shores, its own foothold in legend. As Pocahontas was to be seen as a "mythical nature symbol" by Hart Crane, who would also attempt an epic of the New World, so Barlow now, repelled by the stagnation of Europe ("Paris, that corrupted town, . . . Where shameless Bacchus" reigns, and London, "lost in smoke and steep'd in tea"), where fear of the sun's bright rays allows the Old World no growing of golden corn, discovers an Indian girl to be a "tawny Ceres," goddess of fertility, whose "complexion reflects the hues of the sun." The New World was nourished by a god of nature. Not through Manco Capac's

> rich Peruvian fields alone
> The fame of Sol's sweet daughter will be known,
> But o'er the world's wide clime shall live secure,
> Far as his rays extend, as long as they endure.

But then almost ten years passed before Barlow again turned seriously to literature. They were years of strenuous service to himself and to his country, in building a fortune through shipping and adroit investment and in drawn-out negotiations as an agent of the United States in obtaining freedom for American seamen prisoned in Algiers and, that done, in writing letters to people in power at home in an attempt to ward off war with France, letters that were intercepted and circulated to prove him a traitorous Jacobite. He did putter over materials for a history of the French Revolution and for a history of the United States that Jefferson encouraged him to write, but little came of either.

Robert Fulton, bursting with ideas, lived with the Barlows in Paris. He had published in London *A Treatise on the Improvement of Canal Navigation*. With Barlow's encouragement and assistance, he worked on a submarine, a torpedo-boat, he called it, that might rid the English Channel of marauding British vessels. It did well, but not well enough, and they abandoned it to work on a boat propelled by steam. Though Napoleon had come to power, to shatter their republican vision of a free world, there were still things to do for the melioration of people. Both believed that free commerce among nations, large and small, even those landbound, was essential to the well-being of all people, so they projected "The Canal: A Poem on the Application of Physical Science to Political Economy." There were to be four books, Fulton supplying the ideas, Barlow the verse. The first book begins:

> Yes, my dear Fulton, let us seize the lyre,
> And give to science all the muses fire.

Poetry as handmaiden to science! Two worlds joined? Barlow thought they might be, but the muses' fire seems not to have ignited Fulton, who had steamboats on his mind. Barlow, however, lingered over the poem for some time, reading in Erasmus Darwin, Lucretius, Ovid, and other poets who had written of the usefulness of nature. And he worked on a revision of *The Vision of Columbus*, to make it reasonable. Of "The Canal," its first book "about half completed" by January 1802, he wrote, "Should I not live to complete the poem, which is probable, I desire that it be printed as a fragment."[6] It has not been, and perhaps never should be, except as an example of what can happen to rhyme when measured by reason.

Soon another enterprise beckoned. Some years before, Jefferson had begun but as president thought it inappropriate to continue a translation of Constantin Volney's popular but controversial *Les ruines*. Barlow took over the task and, with some assistance from the author who was a neighbor and friend, completed late in 1802 *A New Translation of Volney's Ruins; or Meditations on the Revolution of Empires*, a subject, he said in preface, "perhaps the most universally interesting to the human race that has been presented." Instructed, as Columbus had been, by a supernal spirit, the narrator of the meditations is informed that people, rather than ascribing their misfortunes "to *obscure and imaginary agents*," must learn to look instead to *"natural laws"* as the *"common source of good and evil."* Religions of all the world are examined. All are rejected. Finally, a "General Assembly of Nations" examines God in his many guises, discovering him to be, however variously described, "the *hidden power*, which *animates the universe*." To live in harmony and peace, people must put aside "the world of fantastical beings" for "the world of reality."

In Volney, Barlow found reinforcement for his own less well formulated ideas. Christianity, he was there told, was "an allegorical worship of the sun, under the cabalistic names of Chris-en or Christ, or Yes-us or Jesus." Cabal had no place in religion, nor had ritual. Free yourself from fetters, Volney urged. Discover "the religion of evidence and proof." Admit to nothing that reason cannot explain. The rest is mystery, delusive and not worth the time it takes to worry about it. In his cumbersome way, Barlow was entering what Emerson would later call the post-Christian era, when spirit would be recognized as spirit, not bound to creed. But no more than Emerson did he renounce Christianity. Born a Christian, he was to say, he remained a Christian, just as if born a Mohammedan, he would have remained a Mohammedan. But reason would be his guide.

Three years later, Barlow returned to the United States, after seventeen years of absence, his head filled with reasonable plans. Among them was the establishment of a national university, of which he offered himself as chancellor. In it, he would have professors engaged in research, but not too busy to meet classes. Laboratories would seek out secrets of the earth and heavens; the science of politics would be "founded on principles analogous to the nature of man"; studies in literature, to which too little attention had been paid among English-speaking people, would be encouraged. Libraries would be provided, botanical gardens and agricultural experimental stations, and a university press to publish results of investigation. No longer would Americans have to go abroad for proper education. Barlow's blueprint for what would have been much like a university as organized today was, however, to remain a blueprint. Jefferson had the plan submitted to the Congress, but that body, perhaps suspicious of his motives, allowed it to die in committee.

Few Americans of his generation were more widely read than Barlow in books that in the late eighteenth century tempted toward a fresh look at people and politics, and few more good-heartedly would share what he had learned in kindly instruction. But, like Herman Melville almost half a century after him, Barlow came to his reading late, so that it became a disturbing overlay on earlier teachings that it seemed to challenge, if not contradict. Melville found in whale and wall images through which his vision could be made, if not clear, in essence transmittable. Barlow's vision became straight-out homily. As Leon Howard has said, he "had lost the impulse of the poet and become a scholar."[7] When in 1807, at the age of fifty-two, encouraged by Fulton, who supplied the plates to illustrate it, he published *The Columbiad* as a revision and extension of *The Vision of Columbus*. It was a book complete with the apparatus of scholarship: a dedicatory acknowledgment of Fulton's aid, a preface of sixteen pages, thirty-two pages of notes, and an index of just over five pages.

In revision, Barlow smudged many passages of youthful vision. Lines that twenty years before had reached toward poetry became rhymed instruction. In the earlier version, the morning star, as "type and promise of the sun," had heralded the appearance of "blest religion" that leads the "raptured mind/Thro' brighter fields." In *The Columbiad*, the morning star, again "type and promise of the sun," is herald of "Physic science" that in turn prepares the way for "Moral science" that "leads the lively mind/Thro' broader fields." The raptured mind becomes a lively mind; religion becomes science. Small wonder that Barlow's friends in New England clucked their tongues in disapproval. Not a cat unbagged, but a wild cat was loose among them.

He dimmed his bright vision of the sun and of the benign monarchy of Manco Capac. Monarchies of any kind, he explained, "fail to embrace the extensive scope of human nature which is necessary in forming republican institutions." Capac then must be put aside, as Aristotle must, and Homer also, whose martial verse has "caused more mischief to mankind than any other." It is not the fine arts, Barlow now said, "which tend the most to the general improvement of society"; it is the "sciences of Geography, Navigation, and Commerce, especially the last," that "open an amicable intercourse between all countries, . . . to soften the horrors of war, to enlarge the field of science, and to assimilate the manners, feelings and languages of all nations."

All this is set forth reasonably in prose commentary. In verse, Homer is not set aside: his "monumental songs" are admired as having more durably built "his splendid throne/Than all the Pharaohs with their hills of stone." And in verse, the sun is not eclipsed, though sun worship is no longer "the purest plan,/That e'er adorn'd the unguided mind of man," but is now an "ungov-ern'd flame, . . . That dazzled erst, and still deludes." But as it had twenty years before, the sun shines occasionally through, pro-claimed a god in bounty and power supreme, the "parent Sun," a "great Godhead" and "our only God" in whom we "trace/The friend and father of a happy race." It reflects "the great soul of na-ture, man's immortal Sire." For Barlow was not careful enough, perhaps not enough convinced, entirely to submit the life-sustain-ing sun to measurement by reason. Nor, as he fumbled through sureties that rational thoughts required, did he turn his back on God. In both versions, he proclaims, in the first a "sovereign," in the second a "prime" power that has "produced all humankind;/ Some Sire supreme, whose ever ruling soul/Creates, preserves and regulates the whole."

Barlow took great pains in explaining and expanding what as a younger man he had visioned of the New World. The vision re-mained, of a free people united by commerce in peace. He posited, but did not effectively use, a new tradition-free American language and told why in a long prose postscript. He has been said to have been "the only poet (or would be poet) before Whitman who had enough conviction and ability to run the risk involved in striving to use traditional means and forms to break away from tradition it-self."[8] But he positioned himself outside the poem, so that the ardent voice of the younger man is muted. *The Columbiad*, as a statement of stolid assurance, becomes more polemic than poem: "My work," Barlow said, "is only a transcript of my mind." His purpose, he said, was moral and political: "I wish to encourage, in the rising generation, a sense of the importance of republican in-stitutions as the great foundation of public and private happiness."

He never learned, as Thoreau did, that truth is a wary, wild thing that will not be approached directly, but must be come upon by indirection, unaware. Reasonable definition will distort it be-cause words get in the way. What remains viable in Barlow's verse is not what he laboriously said. Breaking occasionally through his rejection of what will not submit to mind is a young poet's voice rising in rapturous response to a god of nature, the life-giving promise of the sun, which is also the promise of the Western world. He can be thought of as reaching toward but unable properly to phrase what Thoreau explained in the last sentences of *Walden*: "There is more day to dawn. The sun is but a morning star."

To say that the man of letters cannot be a good citizen is to speak unreasonably. Older men of any persuasion are not likely to listen carefully to what a younger man has said. Arteries harden, fancies fail, fact overrides fiction. Barlow remained a useful person. He served just before the War of 1812 as minister to France, and he died in Poland on a diplomatic mission to Bonaparte. Only a month before his death, he wrote another poem, livened with passion. Reason is put aside as in "Advice to a Raven in Russia" he lashes out in bitter scorn at Napoleon whose depredations had shattered the poet's vision of a world united. "If the same passionate outcry had informed *The Vision of Columbus* or *The Columbiad*," suggests James Woodress, "Barlow would have been a major poet."[9]

But would have been is not was. Barlow perhaps had too little talent to qualify as an expert witness to whether a man of letters can or should be effectively a good citizen. He stands beside the best of his time in reasoned prose, but his verse is seldom allowed to fly on unclipped wings. To say that he soiled his vision by too much handling or by submitting it to polemics is, however, to dismiss him too casually. His mind was a melange of rational certainties that seldom submitted precisely to order. His recognition of a god of nature as an inexplicable great force and of the sun as symbol of a rising young republic run as undercurrents beneath strong tides of obsessive rationality.

Subliminal, but hauntingly present, is his legend of the parent sun, the rising sun of the West, the sun as protector and provider, the god of order and regularity, controlling the rotation of the seasons, the productions of the earth, and the blessings of health. Barlow knew that "the muse but poorly shines/In cones, and cubes, and geometric lines." He said so in "The Hasty Pudding." He knew in *The Conspiracy of Kings* that "the bliss that Freedom sheds" depends on "rights of nature, and the gift of God," and he discovered with Volney that God was a *"hidden power,"* illusive and undefinable.

He never developed this completely, in prose or verse. The inner voice to which as a young man he counseled listening seems seldom to have been heard amid the clatter of public demands. As citizen, Joel Barlow gave his day what in his judgment his day most needed. Much of what he said is now submerged beneath waves of other writings by other people who said much the same. He sang in chorus, with seldom a solo part. But, like Whitman, he was confident that the New World could produce an unsoiled new Adam. Like Emerson, he knew that all people had access to the still small voice of truth, and like Poe, considered this truth submissive to reasoned explanation. But Barlow is not a person to return to. He was there, and he helped measure some areas of what John Dos Passos has called the ground we stand on.[10] If seduced, Barlow was gladly submissive, and he may still remind a generation immersed in certainties of its own that "Man is an infant still," with a long way to go before he can enjoy security and peace, or comprehend the magnificence within the mystery of nature's God.

NOTES

1. Merrill D. Peterson, "Thomas Jefferson's *Notes on Virginia,"* *Studies in Eighteenth-Century Culture* 9 (1975): 49.
2. This and the colloquy on religion in Boston are from "The Belknap Papers," *Collections of the Massachusetts Historical Society*, 5th ser., 2 (1877): 171, 324–25; 3 (1877): 236–37; 6th ser., 4 (1891): 324–25.
3. See Leon Howard, *The Vision of Joel Barlow* (Los Angeles: The Grey Bow Press, 1937), pp. 11–12, who explains that belief in the perfectibility of all people is central to Barlow's vision.
4. For a more complete discussion, see John D. Richardson, Jr.,

"The Enlightenment Myth and Joel Barlow's *The Vision of Columbus,*" *Early American Literature* 13 (Spring 1978): 34–44.

5. "The Smooth and Emblematic Song: Joel Barlow's *The Hasty Pudding,*" *Early American Literature* 7 (Spring 1972): 76–91.

6. Two manuscript copies of "The Canal" are in the Pequot Library in Southport, Connecticut.

7. *The Connecticut Wits* (Chicago: University of Chicago Press, 1943), p. 308.

8. Roy Harvey Pearce, *The Continuity of American Poetry* (Princeton: Princeton University Press, 1961), p. 69.

9. *A Yankee's Odyssey: The Life of Joel Barlow* (Philadelphia: J. B. Lippincott, 1958), p. 304.

10. "Citizen Barlow of the Republic of the World," *The Ground We Stand On: Some Examples from the History of a Political Creed* (New York: Harcourt, Brace, 1941), pp. 256–80.

JOHN AGRESTO

LINCOLN, STATESMANSHIP, AND THE HUMANITIES

It is something of an embarrassment—it may almost be scandalous—for educators in the humanities to write about the education of Abraham Lincoln. Lincoln—lawyer, inventor, philosopher, writer, and statesman—had, by his own calculation, less than a year of formal schooling all totaled. He went to school, as he said, "by littles." He never set foot in a classroom after he was fifteen, and never, it would seem, did he speak of his former teachers. When elected to the House of Representatives in 1848 he had to fill in a standard government form and in the blank after "education" he wrote "defective." So it is not without its humbling irony for American educators to reflect on the training and career of Abraham Lincoln.

Yet, perhaps, we are safe. For even if Lincoln was not "taught" he was, by any measure, "educated." To those who have a historical interest in the humanities, both Lincoln and his boisterous Illinois audiences can indicate the degree to which even the ranks of the formally unschooled were molded by exposure to those areas we now broadly call the "humanities." In Lincoln we can catch a still picture of the scope and breadth of humane learning in the motion-filled life of mid-nineteenth-century America.

But, although interesting, this historic aspect of the humanities in America is only part of the story. In searching for the role of the humanities in America we need to see more than their history. We need to know what good the humanities did and can do. Here again, we can return to Lincoln, not for an insight into what was current in his day but for an indication of the strength, the vision, and the human greatness possible in a mind and a person civilized, that is, humanely educated. If Lincoln shames us by never having been taught, he raises up our profession by being himself a teacher.

Of Lincoln's literary self-education everybody knows a little. We all know that he read the Bible and Shakespeare, although, contrary to our casual expectations, he scanned the Bible for poetic images and studied Shakespeare for the lasting truths of human life. Like others of his generation, he read *Pilgrim's Progress*, *Robinson Crusoe*, Byron, Poe, and Robert Burns. Once, when asked for an account of his early life, he gave his audience not private history but a public literary picture: he quoted to them from memory some words from Gray's *Elegy*. In there, he said, was *his* life, "and that's all you or anyone else can make of it." Unlike his college-trained contemporaries, he knew no Greek and read no Latin classics. At best all he had of the literature of antiquity was a volume of Aesop's Fables. But what he did read, he read deeply, slowly, and purposefully.

Shortly before Lincoln was born, another president-statesman, John Adams, issued a rather fatuous critique of literature and poetry by noting that, amid the bowers of knowledge, philosophers searched for the fruits, the truth, while poets saw only the flowers. Lincoln flatly rejected such hollow caricature. Although Shakespeare and the poets both embellished and strengthened Lincoln's future powers as a writer, his first notion of literature was that it could enlighten and inform, not merely prettify. For Lincoln there was, in literature, the potential to find both truth and flowers. And he attached himself to literature, especially to poetry, because he knew that it was "relevant"—relevant not in any narrow, practical sense, as means toward ends preset by prejudice, calculation, or predisposition, but relevant in the sense that he wanted from literature, as Lord Charnwood, his greatest biographer, said of him, to find in it patterns of what a man's life should be like. He spent no time with all the scholarly crossword puzzles we academicians construct for ourselves in our literary pursuits—influence tracing, historicist reductionism, symbolic reconstructions, or superficial psychological rationalizations. Unlike some of his more educated contemporaries, he studied literature not to learn about it but from it.

Perhaps if we insist on tracing literary "influences" on Lincoln's life and thought we can begin and end with Shakespeare. In the deepest senses of the word, that poet informed him. Especially through the study of the more "political" plays, his mind was given shape and content. We know he read *Lear, Hamlet, Richard the Third, Henry the Eighth*, and *Macbeth*. He sometimes repeated speeches from *Richard the Second*. And upon hearing the news of Lee's surrender at Appomattox, Lincoln gathered his friends around him and read to them from *Macbeth*. His biographers say that he paused at one point and read the following lines twice:

> Treason has done his worst: Nor steel, nor poison
> Malice domestic, foreign levy, nothing
> Can touch him further.

If a Te Deum would be sung for the defeat of Lee and of rebellion it would be in the words of a tragedy of treasonous but still great men brought down.

Literature not only clarified Lincoln's ideas but strengthened his own capacities as a writer. One of the best examples of the power and the clarity of Lincoln's own speech is what he said from the back of his train as it started to leave Springfield, Illinois, for his first inauguration. This is the entire speech:

> My friends, no one not in my situation can appreciate my feeling of sadness at this parting. To this place, and the kindness of these people, I owe everything. Here I have lived a quarter of a century, and have passed from a young to an old man. Here my children have been born, and one is buried. I now leave, not knowing when, or whether ever, I may return; with a task before me greater than that which rested upon Washington. Without the assistance of that Divine Being, who ever attended him, I cannot succeed. With that assistance I cannot fail. Trusting in him, who can go with me and remain

with you and be everywhere for good, let us confidently hope
that all will yet be well. To his care commending you, as I
hope in your prayers you will commend me, I bid you an
affectionate farewell.

That little speech is a jewel of majesty, imagery, and depth. It also
was, to the best of our knowledge, impromptu.

One last word on the role of literature in Lincoln's life and
Lincoln's age. On 8 November 1863, two speeches were given at
Gettysburg, and their comparison is shocking. Edward Everett,
classics scholar, Harvard graduate and professor, editor, congressman, ambassador, and governor, preceded Lincoln and spoke for
two hours. His speech was in the classical style, with literary allu-
sions, mythological figures, and long, elegant, and ornate phrases.
Lincoln's speech was only fifteen lines. Like Everett's, it was laden
with symbolism, the symbolism (in the midst of a graveyard still
covered with unburied dead) of birth and life and childhood. In the
midst of death it was a poem about a nation once newborn, "conceived in liberty," and dedicated, baptized, in the name of an idea:
that all men were created equal. And it was a speech about the
resurrection of that country and those people ransomed by the
blood of innocent and brave men, a resurrection into "a new birth
of freedom." It was symbolic for the sake of insight, and poetic,
too, for Lincoln meant to move men. Perhaps the most startling
part of the address is the ironic sentence in the center: "The world
will little note, nor long remember what we say here." Lincoln
knew its irony, as do we; for he knew that the strength of the
immaterial word, "the word fitly spoken," is often the most powerful of all our human forces. He had learned from poetry; and now,
through it, he sought to teach.

If Lincoln should strike us as an anomaly in literature, he seems
a manifest enigma in philosophy. Within the corpus of Lincoln's
extant works there is not one reference to Aristotle or Hobbes or
Kant or even Locke. He never studied them. Yet there was not, up
to that time, nor has there been since, an American mind more

morally clear or philosophically compelling. In political philosophy he studied Jefferson in place of Locke and found himself convinced by what he read. In place of Aristotle or Aquinas he studied the Bible. And, after long reflections, he rejected much of it. His self-education in the humanities gave him a mind that taught him to distinguish and accept, criticize and reject; not a mind that sponge-like absorbed learning and catalogued quotes into holding bins for future use. Philosophy made Lincoln not pedantic but wiser. That, again, was the relevance of the humanities.

To help him in analysis and logic he studied Euclid. He started and mastered the first six books of Euclid when he was forty, in 1848, during his first year as a United States congressman. His crystalline speech would now be clearer, his powers to persuade himself and others even sharper.

Almost alone among his contemporaries, Lincoln cut into the very core of the arguments for slavery. There was no bombast, no spurious pomposity. And although there was pity, there was little sentimentality. "If A can prove," he wrote in 1854, "that he may, of right, enslave B, why may not B snatch the same argument, and prove equally, that he may enslave A?" By the end of Lincoln's analysis, slavery is left intellectually speechless. He could, more-over, recast the most abstract concepts and give them graspable, public life. "This," he said, "is the sentiment embodied in the Declaration of Independence"—"that the weights should be lifted from the shoulders of all men and that *all* should have an equal chance." As Jacques Barzun said of Lincoln, his speeches glow with both depth of thought and transparency of medium.

Lincoln knew, also, something easily forgotten in a world of rapid technological change and massive economic and military force: the power, the regal domination, of ideas. The idea of slav-ery's evil, for example, or, conversely, the idea of its positive good, would, in the end, rule history. No people who thought slavery wicked could long defend it, justify it, or forever preserve it in their lives; no people who thought it either good or indifferent could long restrict its spread. For Lincoln, the debates were not spoken or the war first waged to eliminate slavery as much as to eliminate the idea of human slavery. The extinction of slavery could wait, but the extinction of the principle of slavery could not.

To change the course of human events involves, then, the ability to change the course of ideas, to change men's minds. In a democratic government "public sentiment," as Lincoln called it, "is everything. With public sentiment nothing can fail; without it nothing can succeed." A nation whose people know their true aims has little need for enlightened statesmen. In the daily meshing and compromising of public and private interest, politicians, not statesmen, are sufficient. And as a politician Lincoln was hardly a success. Before he was elected president he had spent only two years in any elected national office. He was defeated for the United States Senate twice, he was never governor, he served one term in the House, only to have his party fail to nominate him for another. Lincoln succeeded, not as a politician, but as a statesman-president in a nation puzzled about its purpose and unsure of its true principles. It was here, in a nation torn and confused, where the public powers of the humanities, in the person of Lincoln, began their greatest work.

By an inseparable mixture of accident and inexorable destiny, Lincoln became president. The man who had taught himself Shakespeare and Euclid now ruled. It was, in one sense, a philosophic rule. His insights gave us back the reasons for existence. Through him we saw why this nation was "that last, best hope of earth," that last chance, as he said, for "all people of all colors everywhere" to have the burdens lifted from their shoulders. Through his mind we learned why the question was not, Can free democracies be established? but, rather, Can they endure?

But knowing the truth was not enough. We had to act on it. Public opinion, the final sovereign of a democratic people, is sometimes swayed by argument, but it is more often swayed by speech. The mutability of opinion through rhetoric is, on one hand, surely an ever-present danger in democratic life—Caesar's ambition with Antony's tongue can be more destructive than all the arms of foreign powers. But it also means that the ability to move men's hearts through rhetoric, through speech, must not be absent from the man who would be statesman. Great-souled public men must love rhetoric and speech; such powers should never be relegated only into the hands of demagogues or tyrants. And because what is said can infuse public opinion and give it form, in America what statesmen say is often as important as what they do. For that simple reason the Gettysburg Address, the Speech at Independence Hall, and the Second Inaugural are not only profound understandings of the essence of our nation, they are purposefully superb poetry as well.

In this essay, I have tried to touch on only one small portion of a very large field—how the "humanities" informed and nurtured one historic life. That life, if nothing else, might indicate the power of our disciplines, for they shaped not only the mind of one great man, but the destiny of a great nation. From that life we may get a sense of both the private and the public uses of the humanities, a sense not only of their power, but something of their value for each man and for all men and for all future time.

PART TWO

THE HUMANITIES AND

HUMANE LIFE

GERALD F. ELSE

❦ FRIENDS AND FRIENDSHIP,

GREEK STYLE

IT IS WELL KNOWN that the Greeks and Romans set great store by friendship. Cicero's treatise on the subject (*De Amicitia*) is not only a classic but one that can still move the ordinary reader. Why did the classical culture assign so high a place to friendship that even if we are touched by it we may find it difficult to understand?

Cicero's essay summarizes the Roman experience and his own; it also stands on the shoulders of a series of Greek discussions going back to Aristotle and beyond: see Books 8 and 9 of his *Nikomacheian Ethics*. (Aristotle rather than Plato is Cicero's model here; Plato talks about love, Eros, not friendship.)

My concern here is not so much the concept of friendship in Greek thought as the meaning of friendship and its emotional overtones in Greek life. (The former was derived from the latter.)

The Greek word for friend is φίλος, *philos*; friendship is φιλία, *philia*. We do not know the etymology of φίλος, but we do know its ambience and its emotional charge. Its original application was not to friends but to that primeval locus of all emotionally charged attachments, the family. Thus one's φίλοι, in the original sense, are the members of one's family, especially the closer ones, and the emotional burden of the word is "near *and dear.*" One's children are φίλα τέκνα, "dear children." Chryseïs is the dear child, παῖδα φίλην, of the old priest Chryses (*Iliad* 1.20), and he is her dear father (ibid., 441). Agamemnon addresses Menelaos as φίλε κασίγνητε, "dear brother," at 4.155; cf. φίλος ὦ Μενέλαε, "dear Menelaos"

67

(ibid., 189). These examples delimit the original scope of φίλος (-οι): it refers to close blood kin. But its connotation is not the closeness of the kinship as such but the closeness of the affection that binds one to the person or persons in question. Thus, although according to one primitive idea a mother is not blood kin to her child (who belongs wholly to the father), in practice mothers are recognized as φίλοι along with fathers: cf. *Odyssey* 6.287. In *Odyssey* 2.333 one of the suitors of Penelope mentions that Odysseus is τῆλε φίλων, "far from (his) φίλοι," where the φίλοι certainly do not include the speaker himself; the persons meant are Laertes, Telemachos, and Penelope. The connection of the thought is implicit in the formulaic phrase for the wedded state, εὐνῇ (-ῆς) καὶ φιλότητι (-τητος), "with (from) bed and love," where φιλότης denotes the tenderness that—normally—comes over a man who sleeps with a normally loving woman. So in *Iliad* 3.138 Aphrodite informs Helen that Menelaos and Paris are going to fight over her; τῷ δέ κε νικήσαντι φίλη κεκλήσῃ ἄκοιτις, "and to the winner you shall be called dear wife" (literally, bedmate).

As this example shows, wives were included among one's φίλοι at least as early as the Homeric poems (those poems, especially the *Odyssey*, give evidence of an unusually, perhaps abnormally, high estimate of wedded love).

At what point did the term φίλος come to mean "friend"? For evidence on this point we cannot do better than look at the prime specimen of friendship in Homer, that between Achilleus and Patroklos. At no point are they called simply φίλοι, "friends," outright. Certainly Patroklos—in his colloquy with Nestor in *Iliad* 11, for example—does not refer to Achilleus as "my φίλος," "my friend"; he uses much more polite and honorific terms. At 11.611–14 Achilleus instructs Patroklos to go and ask Nestor who the wounded hero is who is being carried off the field; πάτροκλος δὲ φίλῳ ἐπεπείθεθ᾽ ἑταίρῳ, "and Patroklos did the bidding of his dear companion." In Book 18.80, after the first prostration of grief over Patroklos's death has passed, Achilleus says to his mother, "Yes, Zeus granted my wish [that the Achaians be humiliated to pay him back for the dishonor they had done him], but what joy have I

from that, since φίλος ὤλεθ᾽ ἑταῖρος, my dear companion is gone?"
Here the terminological situation is clear. Patroklos's status was
that of ἑταῖρος, companion, but he was something special, a dear, a
beloved companion. In other words, the specific meaning of φίλος
is not yet simply "friend"; it means "beloved."

But we must not subjectivize this state of affairs unduly. Φίλος
may mean "beloved," but it also denotes an objectively perceived
and accepted situation—as φίλη κεκλή-ση ἄκοιτις, "you shall *be
called* his dear bedmate," in Aphrodite's words to Helen implied an
emotionally charged status that at the same time is officially recognized and accepted by the surrounding society. This combination
—objective status, but emotionally colored—is characteristic of
early Greek language and culture in general, and especially of
Homer. So φίλος, on its way to meaning "friend," is accompanied
throughout by the emotional overtone "beloved"; it never has the
cool, neutral connotation of our modern word "friend" (as when a
movie star, asked about her relationship with a certain man, says,
"Oh, we're just friends").

This peculiar (from our point of view) state of affairs can be
documented from another side as well. Homer does not make the
familiar distinction between body and soul, or body and mind.
Homeric man's mind or spirit is perceived in very concrete, physical terms; conversely, the parts of the body are never perceived
as merely physical—they are alive with spirit, feeling, emotional
force. Thus a hero's arms and legs are not simply bodily members;
they are his φίλα γυῖα (*Iliad* 13.85), his dear limbs. So heart, spirit
(breath), breast, hands (arms), knees, throat, eyes (lids) are dear
(ibid., 1.491; 3.31; 4.313; 5.155; 7.271; 19.209; *Odyssey* 5.493).

I have had ominous experience of a parallel between dear ones
and dear limbs. I have lost three dear ones: a father, a wife, and a
son, and each time, especially at the death of my wife, I felt as if I
had lost an arm or a leg. Not only was the amputation painful; a
part of me, an essential part of me, was gone. (Ultimately, of
course, the pain diminished; that is a natural part of living, and
I am sure the body, too, eventually accepts and overlooks its
impairment.)

We distort the Greek record when we speak of φίλος being "on its way to meaning 'friend'." It would be more accurate and to the point to say that the Greek word was extended to cover persons who were not near and dear in the sense of blood kin but linked with oneself by other ties, such as the companionship among fighting men. The φίλος ἑταῖρος becomes the φίλος tout court. Community of interests and feelings was the basis: κοινὰ τὰ φίλων, "(in) common (are) the things of φίλοι," said the proverb. Carried to an extreme—and the Greeks were extremists, notwithstanding their constant adjurations to sobriety and restraint—this arrives at the thought of the φίλος as an ἄλλος ἐγώ (Latin alter ego), "another I." The Greeks were devotees of φιλία precisely because they, earlier and more thoroughly than most peoples, relaxed the grip of the family on the individual and so made it possible for him to form near and dear relationships with other individuals who were not his kin. In other words, friendship was an extension of family ties for a people as devoted to individualism as the Greeks were—or as we are—and its proper name was "love." But the Greeks had a great advantage over us in possessing two distinct sets of words for love: ἔρως, ἐράω (verb), for sexually inspired love, desire, and φίλος, φιλέω, φιλία, for nonsexual love and its objects, whether within the family or outside. Thus the line was drawn in an entirely different place than it is for us. By the fatality of our language, "friend" lies outside the orbit of the family and of love, so that when we speak of loving a friend we are conscious of pressing the word a little. The Greeks, on the other hand, could speak of φίλος (-οι) or φιλία without infringing on the dangerous realm of ἔρως, or of ἔρως without implying that it ever necessarily leads to φιλία, real affection.

This is the way in which I saw my friendship with Charles Frankel. Many of us in the "class of '79" did not know him well, but we felt the *potentiality* of φιλία with him: a possibility of indefinite extension of the friendliness he manifested toward us. His luminous look spoke to us of goodwill, courage, generosity, capacity, and willingness to share our best and our worst: all the good qualities we like to ascribe to ourselves. The relationship was potential rather than actual, at least in my case, but I was confident that it could be realized in depth if circumstances ever permitted such a development. That is why I felt the old pang of organic loss at Charles's death, and why I make bold to say that he was my φίλος.

CARL NORDENFALK

🦅 THE MORAL ISSUE

IN SEBASTIAN BRANT'S

THE SHIP OF FOOLS

IT IS MOST UNUSUAL for an author to make clear to his readers that he does not care to have his book sold. Yet this is what Sebastian Brant does at the end of his *Narren-Schyff*:

> My fool's book, does it anger you?
> I beg of you to pass it by
> I ask no one to come and buy![1]

As a matter of fact, when the book first appear in Basel, on All Fools' Day 1494, it sold out almost immediately, and in less than a year the same thing happened to a second edition.[2] Even prior to the second edition, a number of pirated reprints had appeared elsewhere in Germany. Within a few years a Latin edition was published; the book was translated twice into French; and this was followed by two English and one Dutch paraphrases. In the history of the printed book no contemporary piece of writing had reaped a similar spontaneous success. It was the first known "best seller."

There has been some speculation as to why the book appealed to people so much and so quickly.[3] Some of the answers are fairly obvious. First, it was a typographically attractive volume, and its appearance established Brant's fellow student, Johann Bergmann von Olpe, a well-to-do Swiss cleric and a printer by avocation, as a leading representative in Basel of the flourishing craft of fine print-ing.[4] It pleased the eye not only with clear and well-balanced type-setting, framed on both sides by rinceaux borders, but also with a wealth of illustrations, the majority of them by a rising star on the artistic firmament of Germany, the young Albrecht Dürer.[5] Its more than a hundred woodcuts made *The Ship of Fools* as much a picture book as a piece of literature, and for that reason it appealed even to those bibliophiles—ridiculed by the author at the begin-ning of his poem—who collect books without caring to read them.[6]

In addition to that, the work was cleverly written in rhymed couplets, pleasing both by their easy-flowing rhythm and witty slogans. "The style," says Edwin H. Zeydel, who has made an excellent modern translation of the poem into English, "is always clear, always animated and buoyant, and often balladesque."[7] The presentation is spiced throughout with proverbs, and the author has adapted a half-colloquial diction that goes well with them.[8] Popular and learned at the same time, the book often applies to its subject matter a certain mocking tone of the sort cherished in students' farces, particularly in the retelling of classical history and mythology, a genre in which Brant himself makes quite a display. It functions like a sugar coating which makes the rather bitter moral pills of the songs easier to swallow. In spite of its serious errand, *The Ship of Fools* was light reading, and in those days people were not yet spoiled by such literature.

Quite likely the author's choice of title also contributed to the immdediate success of the book. *Das Narren-Schyff* has a ring that still today easily impresses itself on one's memory. Its two com-ponent words—"ship" and "fool"—were equally effective. In the time of the great geographic discoveries, the big overseas galleys must have spoken to the popular imagination almost as much as spacecraft do to ours today. It is true that Brant himself took a more skeptical, even deprecatory, view of this sort of adventure. Al-though he is known to have collaborated with his publisher in printing Columbus's letter about the discovery of the New World,[9] he considered it vain and useless for man to attempt exploration:

> If round the earth a man can fare,
> What men live here, what men live there,
> If underneath our feet below
> Men walk the nether earth or no,
> And how they hold their ground down there
> That they fall not into the air . . .[10]

In chapter 34 he again satirizes useless traveling:

> Fools often travel very far
> Yet never learn just where they are.[11]

The notion of the fool is, as we all know, an infallible source of fun, innocent or malicious.[12] Everybody enjoys hearing about someone else's slips and foibles, with little thought that he, too, might make similar mistakes. The latter consideration is, in fact, one of Brant's main points, and he does not fail to apply it even to himself:

> I know it, I confess to God
> Of folly I was never free
> I have joined the fool's fraternity.
> I pull the cap which I would doff
> Yet my fool's cap will not come off . . .[13]

By the time Brant wrote his book, the fool had long since become a time-honored figure, with an ancestry reaching back into the Old Testament and Greek philosophy.[14] In the Middle Ages, however, he took a more specific shape in the institution of the professional fool, the court jester and his amateur stand-ins, the Shrovetide revelers. Their fancy uniform, the main part of which was a cap with donkey's ears, ending in bells and with a further row of bells attached to the hood like a coxcomb, is how the fools are represented throughout the illustrations in Brant's poem, whatever their status in real life. High and low, young and old, even women (who were not supposed to take part in the Shrovetide pranks) appear in the woodcuts wearing this outfit.[15]

By applying the notion of foolishness to all sorts of people, Brant

has been able to draw a broad panorama of the society of his own
time, in much the same way as, in another century, the caricaturist
Daumier jested his fellow citizen. The historian who wants to
know what life was like in those days has much to learn from
Brant's poem and from the illustrations accompanying it. City life
and rural conditions, ecclesiastical and secular customs, labor and
leisure time pass in review, rendering with a keen eye the debility
of all human striving. As a professor *utriusque iuris* Brant was well
acquainted with the various misdemeanors registered in the normative textbooks of canon and civil law. The thirty-six *Causae* of the
Decretum Gratiani discuss the same number of typical departures
from the ordinances of the ecclesiastical legislation, and Brant's
The Ship of Fools actually resembles this treatise in the not very
systematic order in which both present the different cases.[16] We are
constantly thrown from one type of fool to another with little connection between them. The review of human weaknesses seems in-
exhaustible in its motley variety. "The reader wonders," as Richard
Newald wrote, "that after the twentieth chapter the book still goes
on, and when he comes to the end, he wonders that it ceases."[17]
The very artlessness of the composition has a purpose. It enables
Brant to give the impression that he covers everything in need
of scrutiny:

> For fools a mirror shall it be
> Where each his counterfeit may see,

he says in the prologue.[18] It all made the book captivating in the
same way as a good sermon. In fact, *The Ship of Fools* became the
text for a hundred and forty-two sermons preached in 1498–99 by
Johannes Geiler von Kaisersberg from his pulpit in the Strasbourg
Cathedral, an attention rarely given by an ecclesiastic to a piece of
secular literature.[19] Indeed, Geiler's sermons, when printed in
1513, had even greater reverberations in pre-Protestant Germany
than the original text on which they were based.

Brant's own influence on the developments that were to result in
Luther's open revolt against the Roman church was moderate. As
literature, *The Ship of Fools* had a quality characteristic of most best

sellers at all times: its outlook was neither too old-fashioned nor too modern. As a humanist, Brant belonged among the progressive writers of his time, but he was at the same time deeply committed to tradition. His book has been called "a ship passing into modern times with its sails filled by the last wind of the Middle Ages,"[20] and it would have been a paradox were this not the way one era quite often develops into another. Several chapters have an outspoken, critical tang, such as the one entitled "Of the Decline of the Faith," in which Brant takes the Western powers to task for not stopping the advance of the Turks (ch. 99). But mostly his criticism of the grievances of his time was not stringent enough to make those hit by it feel seriously smitten. In his own eyes Brant was a valiant combatant of hypocrisy and deceit, wherever they could be detected:

> Full often have I been maligned
> Because this ship I have designed . . .
> But I would let them freeze forsooth
> Ere saying anything but truth.[21]

Nevertheless, he is careful not to point his satire too openly toward any specific institution or party in power. Here and there he pleads for ecclesiastical or social reforms, but only indirectly and as a faithful son of the church and a loyal supporter of the Holy German Empire. In chapter 91, "Of Prattling in Church," for instance, he avoids mentioning the priests, nor does he in chapter 30, "Of too many benefices," blame the widespread misuse of pluralities on the pope.[22]

It is exactly by his allegiance to the Christian dogma that Brant fails to draw the full consequences of his humanist conception of man's mission on earth. In his time, two different systems of ethics were facing each other: the old theocratic system that put every act in relation to afterlife; and the pragmatic view that preferred to see human behavior in relation to prevalent social conditions and to how it could help each individual overcome his weaknesses. The former drew in no uncertain terms a fixed borderline between good and evil, reflecting the dualistic conception of the world underlying all religions, including Christianity. Man was the eternally disputed bone of contention between God and the devil. The chances of the latter were great from the beginning because of original sin. Basically, every human being was a sinner, and his sinfulness manifested itself most flagrantly through the seven deadly sins: pride, avarice, wrath, envy, greed, lechery, and sloth.[23] It did not matter what place you had on the social scale, the devil was always ready to throw your soul into perdition. In this fatal situation, man could hope for salvation only by being a faithful son or daughter of the church and by the infinite grace of Christ, who had taken all the sins of mankind on himself by his death on the cross.

The pragmatic view of ethics, on the other hand, did not admit so univocal a belief. The humanist idea of the dignity of man gave the conflict a different dimension.[24] The more manageable antagonism was that between wisdom and its opposite, human folly. Long before the rise of Christianity, wisdom had been featured as the supreme value by the pagan philosophers, and the humanists professed the same doctrine. Wisdom had, moreover, a less high-flown side—that practical wisdom for which another name was prudence and which aimed at helping man conduct his life to the benefit both of himself and his fellow beings. If you behaved like a fool, you deserved to be castigated, rather than punished. And there was for every fool a time-honored medicine, written over the entrance to the temple of Apollo in Delphi: γνῶθι σεατόν: know yourself!

The pragmatic notion of folly retained some relevance all through the Middle Ages. As early as the twelfth century, an English author, Nigellus, called Wireker, had in a *Speculum stultorum* ridiculed the monks and clerics who suffered from the desire to move around from one place to another.[25] But it was mainly at the very end of the medieval period that the idea of man's inveterate foolishness gained momentum in the thinking and writing of the educators and the pamphleteers, and in no other work with more imagination and consequence than in Brant's *Narren-Schyff*.[26]

Generally speaking, Brant sided with the more liberal ethics of the humanists by replacing the sinner with the fool. More than

anything else, this change of perspective must have been the kin-
dling spark that put him to work and inspired his rhyming effu-
sions. Notwithstanding the verses quoted at the beginning of this
essay, he did want to reach out to his fellow citizens and make
them realize their foolishness, not only through criticism, but also
through good advice. In preaching the virtue of prudence, some of
his poems even profess a moral below the standard of true humanism. The explorer's bold search to widen knowledge of the earth
had, as already mentioned, little to recommend itself in his eyes.
On the contrary, one chapter professes the belief, certainly not
heroic at all, that one should not take any risks. In defiance of
the classical motto, *Ut desint vires, tamen est laudanda voluntas*, he
recommends, "Better keep away!"

> 'Tis better never to attempt
> Than end with losses and contempt.[27]

Chapter 58 is about the foolishness "Of forgetting oneself." He is
a fool, the author says, "who thinks of others, not of himself," who
tries to

> quench a neighbor's blazing fire
> While flames around his barn mount higher.

For this frankly egotistical wisdom Brant refers with approval to a
classical playwright:

> Terence was right when once he stated
> 'I am nearest to myself related.'[28]

Openness and trust in dealing with friends and neighbors would
seem to be a good humanistic rule of life, but Brant in chapter 19,
"Of idle talk," recommends instead a cleverly reckoned reticence.[29]
His attitude toward "outlandish fools" (ch. 98), nonbelievers, mad
women, suicides, panderers, and so on—"so many worthless folk"
—is not very enlightened either:

> They can't be cured howe'er we try
> I'll keep my peace and pass them by.[30]

He is, furthermore, suspicious of cheating beggars, of loquacious and boozing messengers (ch. 80), of lawyers who either are ignorant (ch. 2) or who blindfold justice (ch. 71), of physicians who are quacks (ch. 55), and of journeymen who never properly learned their craft (ch. 48). He believes deceit is typical of the relations of servants to their masters ("Of cooks and waiters," ch. 81). Brant also reminds his readers of the many ways a woman can make a man unhappy—by committing adultery, by being quarrelsome and prone to gossip, as well as through the inborn vanity of the feminine sex (chs. 32, 33, 64, and 93).[31]

To a considerable degree, Brant's ethics focus on the social consequences of human actions and people's unwillingness to foresee them. If you are old, do not divide your possessions among your children before you die; they will only make bad use of them and show you no gratitude (ch. 5). It is pure folly to start building a house without calculating the costs (ch. 15), or to fail to provide for future needs, so that:

> In winter you'll have naught to eat
> And like the bear lick hands and feet.[32] [ch. 70]

Foolish behavior brings on its revenge automatically. Who "aims at birds' nests very high" is likely to tumble head first to the ground (ch. 36). It is in the nature of the fool to "want things that do more harm than good" ("Of useless wishing," ch. 26). In fact,

> Many pray for things so bad
> 'Twould irk them if those things they had.[33] [ch. 45]

This applies particularly to those who wish for a "protracted life":

> Who live too long, have great distress
> Accursed misfortunes them oppress. [ch. 26]

With merciless realism Brant describes their countenance:

> They are pale, misshapen, sick, and cold,
> Hollow their cheeks, their skin like crepe
> As though their mother'd been an ape.[34] [ch. 26]

Only the fool puts his faith in future happiness. The wheel of fortune keeps turning, and he who rises today will fall tomorrow (chs. 37 and 56). Some fools even invite misfortune by jumping with open eyes into perdition, as Empedokles did at Etna (ch. 45). Even without the chastisement of bad luck, the constantly fortunate person is also a fool:

> No greater fool was ever made
> Than one whose luck has never strayed.[35] [ch. 23]

Others take all the cares of mankind on their backs, for no good reason, and are not far from drooping beneath the burden; they are

> Fools who fret and falter
> Because of things they cannot alter.[36] [ch. 24]

In this manner, a gallery of human foibles is marshaled for scrutiny without any one of them properly qualifying as a sin.[37] But Brant does not reserve the notion of folly to these alone. Alternating with such minor manifestations of foolishness as bad manners at table (ch. 110a) and field sports (ch. 74) are quite as many faults of a more grave nature, and those committing them are likewise called fools. Even the seven deadly sins are put under the same denominator. They are, in fact, referred to in no less than twenty different chapters. Some are more precisely divided into separate variants, pride including self-complacency, vainglory, vanity, and boasting, lechery including carnal love, adultery, and obscene language.[38] Different acts of dishonesty, deceit, and uncharitableness are also featured in a great many chapters as foolishness only, to mention only usury (ch. 93), ingratitude toward benefactors (ch. 59), backbiting (ch. 7), and slander (ch. 101).

Thus, the sins, even the capital ones, may seem to be reduced to mere follies. But Brant's real conviction is the other way around. To him all fools are caught in the devil's toils, and this explains why matters that might be thought of at most as being heedless are judged severely. Although certainly not intended, a smile is evoked when men's new custom of shaving their faces is called a "quite disgraceful thing" (ch. 4)[39] or when Brant denounces the modern fashion of wearing coats so short "that almost the navel shows."[40] In fact, everyone who even approves of such costumes is a sinner:

> Woe's every man who rouses shame
> Woe's him too who condones such sin
> The wages will be paid to him.[41] [ch. 4]

Dancing, naturally, is condemned for the same reasons (ch. 61). The devil invented it, and therefore "dance and sin are one in kind." At Kermess—"where the fun is shared by priests and laity"—

> They swing their partners in the breeze
> Till girls' bare legs high up one sees.[42]

At night the peace is disturbed by serenading, another outrageous custom to which Brant devotes a chapter (ch. 62). Gambling, too, is a dreadful sin, particularly when exercised even by women (ch. 77):

> The distaff they should tend and wet
> And gamble not with men and bet.[43]

It all goes to show that Brant, in favoring the epithet of folly rather than that of sin, did not really intend to question the old theocratic order.[44] In full consistency with this outlook, we find among the passengers on Brant's *The Ship of Fools* quite a number whose unpardonable fault is thinking lightly of heavenly things, including the sacred service.[45] (Not just by chance was the publisher of the book, Johann Bergmann von Olpe, a Swiss archdeacon.) A chapter called "Noise in Church" (ch. 44) castigates men who come to mass bringing dogs and falcons, in the hope of seeing some attractive Lady Kriemheld. Equally reprehensible are failure to observe the holy days (ch. 95), chatting during service, and leaving immediately after it is over (ch. 91). But one may show contempt of Holy Writ in such other ways as placing credit in old wives' tales and reporting unattested miracles (ch. 11).[46] In these cases Brant speaks as an enlightened Christian and a humanist at the same time.

In applying the term "fool" to those who lack reverence for the ecclesiastical establishment, Brant reverts to the use of the word in the Old Testament that is equal in tenor to the term "godless," and his condemnation of these people resembles the austerity of the revenging God of the Israelites. There is no more evident sign of foolishness, he says, than to rely on the presumption of God's eternal mercy; people who read the Bible have not always seemed to have noted

> That punishment is always stated
> And retributions unabated.[47] [ch. 14]

And in "Of torture and punishment by God" (ch. 88), the Lord himself speaks straight to the point:

> "If my command you will not hear
> I'll send you plague and dread and fear
> Drought, hunger, pestilence and war,
> Heat, frost, cold, hail, and thunder's roar
> And make it worse from day to day
> And from your prayers turn away."[48]

It is characteristic of all fools that they take God's admonitions lightly:

> Though knowing well that they must die
> Where, when and how no one can know
> Till through the mouth the soul will go
> But that his soul to hell will fare
> No one believes until it's there.[49] [ch. 29]

The ultimate threat is the day of the Last Judgment, which will be preceded by the coming of the arch-fool, Antichrist.[50] To his appearance in the fullness of time, Brant has devoted one of his double-length chapters (ch. 103). It is headed by an illustration larger than the normal size (fig. p. 83). The ship of orthodoxy has capsized. On top of the bulging hull, Antichrist is enthroned like God on his rainbow. He is a beautiful young man with a purse in one hand and a scourge in the other. To deceive his followers, he

Albrecht Dürer, "Antichrist on the Capsized Ship of Orthodoxy and St. Peter's Lifeboat," Illustration to Sebastian Brant's *The Ship of Fools*, Ch. 103.

has laid off his fool's cap, which is resting beside him. He seems to enjoy having a huge devil puffing with a bellows into his ear. Some drowning fools are seen floating around in the water among useless books. In smaller vessels left and right, heretics come alongside the wreck to attack it and to help it perish. Only a few faithful in the foreground are rescued. Standing on a rock, St. Peter pulls ashore a boat with a handful redeemed, using his attribute, an enormous key. One of the saved, who may well be the author, turns toward St. Peter with folded hands. Of all the illustrations in *The Ship of Fools*, this one most clearly reveals the early mastership of Dürer and gives a premonition of the intense imagery characteristic of his first truly great work, the Apocalypse.

One may rightly wonder why an author as firmly rooted in the biblical belief that "many are called but few chosen" should have cared at all for the futility of people's strivings on earth. The answer is that Brant kept a stealthy affection for the fools he so severely condemns. Even the Lord loveth whom he chasteneth. Most of Brant's moral maxims are commonplaces, but the way he exemplified them has the freshness of the new sense of reality characteristic of the art of his days. Human folly was a manifestation of life itself in its misery and grandeur, and Brant took an obvious delight in depicting it in significant details. An example is chapter 75, "Of bad marksmen." The scene is a shooting range along a river, and the description of the way an archery competition happens leaves no doubt that Brant himself must have more than once tried his luck at it and knew all the excuses one could plead for missing the target:

> Some men will shoot too high and low
> They break the string or bolt or bow
> In bending bows some make a slip
> Or on the bolt they lose their grip
> Too soon the arrow's oft released
> Because the bowstring is overgreased.[51]

Similarly, the long chapter about gambling (ch. 77) makes one suspect that Brant was not unfamiliar with that sinful pastime either. His depiction of the next day's hangover after a night passed at the gambling table is exceptionally droll. In reading such passages, one has the feeling that Brant's keen eye for the characteristics of bourgeois life more than any missionary zest stimulated his writing talent. As so often is true in art and literature, the moralizing aspect functioned as a license for dealing freely with a subject matter that had not yet become acceptable in its own right.

Not that Brant would be a hypocrite to preach again and again the sinners' risk of being eternally condemned; he certainly believed in hell as seriously as any medieval domesday preacher. His was still the philosophy that taught the men of the Middle Ages "that they lived in a true middle age between the revelation of God's plan for man and the final execution of His judgment," to quote one of Charles Frankel's striking formulations.[52] But he could not help also looking with fascination at the people floundering in the devil's snares, and whereas the descriptions in the text only partially visualize their countenance and behavior, the illustrations, in the composition of which Brant no doubt took a part, come to the readers' aid congenially. Two souls were housed in Brant's breast, and in different ways they made his Ship of Fools steer its zigzag course toward the phantasmagoria of the land of Narragonia.

NOTES

1. Ch. 110, vv. 22–24, here quoted from Edwin E. Zeydel, *The Ship of Fools by Sebastian Brant*, translated into rhymed couplets, with introduction and commentary, Records of Civilization: Sources and Studies, 36 (New York: Columbia, 1944), p. 358. In the original, here and in the following notes quoted from the still normative edition by Fr. Zarncke (Leipzig, 1854), the verses run:

> Wem nit gefält disz narrenbuch
> Der mag wol lossen, das es louff
> Ich bitt keynen, das er es kouff.

2. For a comprehensive account of the different editions see Zeydel, *The Ship of Fools*, pp. 21f.; also *Gesamtkatalog der Wiegendrucke* (Leipzig: Hiersemann, 1930), pp. 5041f.

3. For a summing up see Barbara Könniker, *Sebastian Brant, Das Narrenschiff*, Interpretationen zum Deutschunterricht, ed. R. Hirschenauer and A. Weber (Munich: Oldenbourg 1966), pp. 8f., with bibliography.

4. Brant's *Narren-Schyff* was probably the first product of Bergmann's printing office in Basel, which in spite of its success lasted only a few years. See Ferdinand Geldner, *Die deutschen Inkunabeldrucker* (Stuttgart: Hiersemann, 1968), 1:128, and Horst Kunze, *Geschichte der Buchillustration in Deutschland. Das 15. Jahrhundert* (Leipzig: Verlag für Buch und Bibliothekswesen, 1975), pp. 390f.

5. Daniel Burckhardt, *Albrecht Dürer's Aufenthalt in Basel, 1492–1494* (Munich, 1892), was the first to ascribe the best woodcuts to Dürer. Rejected by some scholars, his assumption has been vindicated by Friedrich Winkler, *Dürer und die Illustrationen zum Narrenschiff*, Forschungen zur deutschen Kunstgeschichte, 36 (Berlin: Deutscher Verein für Kunstwissenschaft, 1951), so convincingly that a lingering hesitation among non-art historians seems unreasonable.

6. Although Lukianos is usually not mentioned among the classical authors with whom Brant was familiar, it is hard to believe that the first chapter of *The Ship of Fools* entitled "Of Useless Books" should have been written without knowledge of Lukianos's satire on "The Ignorant Book-Collector" (A. M. Harmon, trans., *Lucian*, Loeb Classical Library [Cambridge, Mass.: Harvard University Press, 1921], 3:173f.). It is not the only parallel. Like Brant, Lukianos also turns against slanderers (Loeb, 3:320f.), astrologers (Loeb, 5:348f.), and dancing (Loeb, 5:210f.).

7. Zeydel, *The Ship of Fools*, p. 17.

8. Zeydel rightly praises Brant's gift for coining pithy compound words and striking fancy names, such as *Klosterkatz* ("cloister-

cat"), *Sankt Grobian* ("St. Ruffian"), *Dr. Griff* ("Dr. Grab-it"),
Narragonia (from Narr and Aragonien).

9. Edwin H. Zeydel, "Sebastian Brant and the Discovery of
America," *Journal of English and Germanic Philology* 42 (1943):
410–11.

10. Ch. 66, vv. 11–17:

> Ob man hab umb die gantz welt fur
> Was volcks wone under yeder schnur
> Ob under unsern füssen lüt
> Ouch sygen, oder do so nüt
> Und wie sie sich enthaltten uff
> Das sie nit fallen jnn den lufft.

It has often been pointed out that in spite of its title, the ship
topos plays on the whole only a minor part in the book. In the
first half it hardly appears, and when, in the second half and in
the prologue (which, although referred to in chapter 64, must
have been written after the book was already more or less
finished in a draft), the ship is mentioned more frequently, it is
still only used as a setting for a few fools. This is not astonishing, however, because Brant describes and satirizes the human
fools one by one, and a ship provides a natural stage for a lot of
passengers. For the same reason, there are few ships included
in the illustrations, which instead depict the fools indoors, on a
street, or in a landscape. Apart from the frontispiece woodcuts
that do respond to the title of the book, one waits until chapter
48 before finding any ships among the illustrations at all. After
another twenty-five chapters, the next ship is sighted, at the
beginning of chapter 72, where a ship in the middle ground is
tied to the tail of a sow in the foreground—still a Medieval
space construction. Only at the end, preceding chapter 108, is
there a ship, overcrowded with happy and less happy fools on
their trip to Narragonia; whether a repetition of the second
frontispiece woodcut, or the other way round, is hard to
decide. There is also one of a fool alone in a vessel about to be
wrecked (chapter 109). The true meaning of the title is that the

book itself is the ship, and all the fools together are its passengers. This being so, it is hard to say whether the idea of a
shipload of fools originated with Brant himself or with the
illustrator who first drew them onboard a vessel.

11. Ch. 34, vv. 11–12:

> Eyn narr ist wer viel land durchfert
> Und wenig kunst, noch tugend lert.

12. The supreme testimony of this is Erasmus's *Praise of Folly*
(*Moriae encomium*), where Folly begins her oration by praising
her divine powers to "gladden the hearts of gods and men"
(quoted from the translation by Betty Radice [Middlesex,
England: Harmondsworth, Penguin Books, 1971], p. 63).

13. Ch. 111, vv. 71–76:

> Ich kenn das, und vergych es gott
> Das ich vil dorheit hab gethon
> Und doch jm narrenorden gon
> Wie vast ich am der kappen schütt,
> Will sie mich doch gantz lossen nytt

Similarly, ch. 110, vv. 27–28.

14. Karl Friedrich Flögel, *Geschichte des Grotesk-Komischen*, ed.
Friedrich Ebeling, 5th ed. (Leipzig: Barsdorf, 1888); O. Mon-
kemöller, *Narren und Toren in Satire: Sprichwort und Humor*
(Leipzig, 1912); Barbara Swain, *Fools and Follies* (New York:
Columbia, 1932); Enid Welsford, *The Fool* (London: Faber &
Faber, 1935); Barbara Könniker, *Wesen und Wandlung der
Narrenidee im Zeitalter des Humanismus* (Wiesbaden: Steiner,
1966).

15. Most conspicuous is the representation of the Five Foolish
Virgins at the beginning of chapter 105.

16. On *Gratian's Decretum* see Anthony Melnikas, *The Corpus of the
Miniatures in the Manuscripts of the Decretum Gratiani*, Studia
Gratiana, 16–18 (Rome: Studia Gratiana, 1975), of which there is
a critical review in *Zeitschrift für Kunstgeschichte* 43 (1980):
318–32.

17. Richard Newald, *Elsässische Charakterköpfe aus dem Zeitalter des
Humanismus* (Kolmar, n.d.), p. 96.

18. Vv. 30–31:

> Den narrenspiegel ich disz nenn
> In dem ein yeder narr sich kenn

The fifteenth-century sources of Brant's book have been well brought to light by Hellmut Rosenfeld, "Sebastian Brants 'Narrenschiff' und die Tradition der Ständessatire, Narren-bilderbogen und Flugblätter des 15. Jahrhunderts," *Gutenberg Jahrbuch* (1965): 242–48.

19. Johann Geiler von Kaisersberg, *Ausgewählte Schriften*, in freier Bearbeitung von Ph. de Lorenzi, 2 (Trier: E. Groppe, 1883). On Geiler see also the article by D. Wuttke in *Neue Deutsche Biographie* 6 (1964): 18.

20. Newald, *Elsässische Charakterköpfe*, p. 92.

21. Ch. 104, vv. 50–51 and 56–57:

> Ich bin gar offt gerennet an
> Wile ich disz schiff gezymberet han
> Aber ich liesz sie alle erfryeren
> Das ich anders dann worheyt seyt

22. See Aurelius Pompen, *The English Versions of the "Ship of Fools"* (London and New York: Longmans, Green & Co., 1925), p. 122, and the pertinent remarks on Brant's character by Newald, *Elsässische Charakterköpfe*, pp. 89f.

23. Morton Bloomfield, *The Seven Deadly Sins* (East Lansing: Michigan State College Press, 1952).

24. The topic is too extensive to be covered by any survey. See, however, Hans Heinrich Schmid, *Wesen und Geschichte der Weisheit* (Berlin, 1966), and Carl August Emge, *Der Weise* (Erfahrung und Denken, 22) (Berlin: Duncker & Humblot, 1967).

25. A. Boutemy, *Nigellus de Longchamp, dit Wireker* Université libre de Bruxelles, Traveaux, t. 16 (Paris: Presses Universitaires, 1959), and *Speculum stultorum*, with Introduction and Notes by John H. Mozley and Robert R. Raymo (Berkeley: University of California Press, 1960). *The Book of Daun Burnel the Ass: Nigellus Wireker's Speculum Stultorum*, trans. Graydon W. Regenos (Austin: University of Texas Press, 1959). For a summary of its

content, see Max Manitius, *Geschichte der lateinischen Literatur im Mittelalter* (Munich: Beck, 1923), 3:810.

26. R. Gruenter, "Die 'Narrheit' in Sebastian Brant's Narrenschiff," *Neophilologus* 43 (1959): 207f.; Ulrich Gaier, *Studien zu Sebastian Brants Narrenschiff* (Tübingen: Niemeyer, 1966); Barbara Könniker, *Wesen und Wandlung der Narrenidee im Zeitalter des Humanismus* (Wiesbaden: Steiner, 1966); and Joel Lefebure, *Les fols et la folie: Etude sur les genres du comique et la creature littéraire en Allemagne pendant la Renaissance* (Paris: Klincksieck, 1968).

27. Ch. 15, vv. 29–30:

Vil weger ist nüt understan
Dann mit schad, schend, gespöt ablan

28. Vv. 11–12:

Als ouch Terencius vermant
Ich bin mir aller nähst verwant

The reference is to Terence's *Andriae*, 4.1.12: *proximus sum egomet mihi.*

29. Vv. 10–20:

Ich halt nit für eyn wysen man
Wer nit syn anschlag bergen kan

Same in ch. 39, "Of open plans":

That person is in folly dyed
who confidential plans can't hide.

30. Vv. 5–6:

Und sint zu bringen nit dar von
Will ich still schwygend für sie gon.

31. Ever since Juvenal's sixth satire, the vices of women have been a favorite subject for (male) satirists, as pointed out by Pompen, *English Versions of the "Ship of Fools,"* pp. 178–87. The fools on board Brant's ship are with few exceptions all male; in the prologue, the author excuses himself for not having paid more attention to the women. Brant's French translator, the Lyonese humanist Josse Badius, considered this an important gap and thus wrote a supplement of his own, called *La nef des folles*, in which the foolish women are distributed among five ships according to the five senses. See Paul Renouard, *Bib-*

liographie des impressions et des oeuvres de Josse Badius Ascensius,
imprimeur et humaniste, 1462–1535 (Paris, 1908; repr. New York:
Burt Franklin, 1963), 1:159f., and Anatole Claudin, *Histoire de*
l'imprimerie en France aus XVe et XVIe siècle (Paris: Impr.
nationale 1900–1914), 2:128f. I intend to come back to this subject
in a book on Art and the Five Senses, on which I had the
privilege of working as a fellow of the National Humanities
Center.

32. The translation by Zeydel is a condensation of vv. 19–23:
> musz durch den Winter sich
> Behelffen ettwan schlähteklich
> Und an den dopen sugen hert
> Bisz er des hungers sich erwert

33. Vv. 31–32:
> Mancher jm gbett von gott begert
> Im wer leid, das er wurd gewert

34. Vv. 18–20:
> Sint sie doch bleich, sieck, ungestalt
> Ihr backen und hüt sind so lär
> Als ob eyn aff jr muter wär.

35. Vv. 33–34:
> Denn grosser narren wurden nye
> Dann die allzyt glück hatten hye

36. Vv. 33–34:
> Der ist eyn narr der sorgt all tag
> Das er doch nit gewenden mag

37. This is often pointed out in the literature about *The Ship of Fools*,
for example, by Charles Schmidt, *Histoire litteraire de l'Alsace*
(Paris, 1879; repr. Nieuwkoop: B. de Graft, 1966), 1:201.

38. I am here following the analysis of Brant's text by F. A.
Pompen, *English Versions of the "Ship of Fools,"* pp. 20f.

39. Brant may have changed his mind in this matter—he is shown
clean-shaven on the woodcut at the beginning of his *Nova*
Carmina (Basel, 1498), reprod. in Jaro Springer, *Sebastian Brants*
Bildnisse, Studien zur deutschen Kunstgeschichte, 87 (Strasbourg: Heitz, 1907), p. 15, and also in some later portraits, such

as that by Hans Burgkmayr of 1508 in the Karlsruhe Kunsthalle, overlooked by Springer.

40. Vv. 25–26:

> Kurz schändlich und beschrotten röck
> Das einer kum den nabel bdöck.

41. Vv. 32–34:

> We dem der ursach gibt zu schand
> We dem ouch der solch schand nit strofft
> Im wurt zu lon das er nit hofft.

42. Vv. 23–24:

> Do loufft man, und würfft umbher eyn
> Das man hoch sieht die blosszen beyn

43. Vv. 37–38:

> Sie soltten an der kunckel läcken
> und nit jm spyel byn mannen stäcken.

44. As documented by W. Gilbert, "Sebastian Brant, Conservative Humanist," *Archiv für Reformationsgeschichte* 9 (1955): 154f., Brant in his Latin poetry appears as a fervent devotee of the Virgin and of both greater and smaller saints, particularly St. Onophrius, the hermit. He may even have considered for a time becoming a hermit himself.

45. Most sharply in chapters 86 and 87 about "Despising God" and "On Blasphemy of God," one illustrated by a fool pulling Christ's beard, the other by a fool attacking the crucified Christ with a trident.

46. In some of his Latin poems Brant featured, however, certain saints whose claim to veneration does not seem too well established, such as Joachim, the husband of St. Anne, and one of St. Ursula's eleven thousand virgins who escaped the martyrdom of her companions by falling sick on the way near Basel, where she was reported to have been buried (Gilbert, "Sebastian Brant," pp. 149–50).

47. Vv. 14–16:

> Dar usz er doch nit mercken will
> Das allenthalb die stroff darnach
> Geschrieben stat, mit plag und rach.

48. Vv. 17–22:

> Wann jr nit haltten myn gebot
> Will ich uch geben plag und dot
> Kryeg, hunger, pestilentz, und dür,
> Hytz, ryff, kelt, hagel, tunders für
> Und meren das, von tag zu tag
> Und nit erhören bätt noch klag.

49. Vv. 18–22:

> Und weisz doch das er sterben musz
> Wo, wenn und wie, ist jm nit kundt
> Bisz das die sel fert usz dem mundt
> Doch glabut er nit das syg eyn hell
> Bisz er hin jn kumbt uber die schwell.

50. Hans Preuss, *Die Vorstellungen vom Antichrist im späten Mittelalter* (Leipzig: Deichert, 1906), and Will-Erich Peuckert, *Die gross Wende, das Apokalyptische Saeculum und Luther* (Hamburg: Claasen & Govertz, 1948), provide the proper background for understanding this particular chapter in Brant's *The Ship of Fools*.

51. Vv. 12–17:

> Vil sint die schyessen über usz
> Eym bricht der bogen, senw, und nusz
> Der dut am anschlag manchen schlypf
> Dem ist verruckt stul oder schypf
> Dem losszt das armbrust, so ers rürt
> Das schafft der wyndfat ist geschmyert.

52. *The Case for Modern Man* (New York: Harper, 1956), p. 13.

JOHN SITTER

❧ THE FLIGHT FROM HISTORY

IN MID-EIGHTEENTH-CENTURY

POETRY (AND TWENTIETH-CENTURY

CRITICISM)

THE MID-EIGHTEENTH CENTURY was a period of un-
certainty in the history of English poetry, and I believe an analogy
can be found between its uncertainties concerning the relation of
poetry to political events and modern uncertainties concerning the
relation of the study of poetry to public life. Most crudely, comparable doubts find expression as ambivalent alternations of defen-
siveness and aggressiveness regarding mid-eighteenth-century poetic and late twentieth-century critical projects. Thus Thomas Gray,
at the close of *The Progress of Poesy* (1752–54), describes himself as
"Beneath the Good how far—but far above the Great," in a context
where "good" means privately guiltless and "great" means politically consequential. There is no single remark of our own to
balance conveniently against Gray's; but there is the common
assumption of literary academicians that their work is far beneath
virtue but far above vice—in a context where virtue is likely to
mean social praxis or societal betterment or even some benign
kinds of science, and vice will mean political compromise, economic complicity, or, sometimes, simply success. More particularly,
there is in the criticism of poetry written by many academicians a

94

tendency to define true criticism in opposition to history, a tendency with more than incidental similarities to the implicit definition of "pure poetry" as poetry that is detachable and detached from the historical events around it.

The phrase "pure poetry" first appeared, as far as I know, in the middle of the eighteenth century in England, and it was an emblematic part of the reaction against the dominance of Pope that united many of the interesting if mainly minor poets who began to publish in the 1740s. It may be well to concede at once that the generalizations to be made here are not and probably could not be based on a representative sample of shared stylistic traits. But attempts to define a period style are likely to be most interesting when they are attempts to define, as Ernst Cassirer argued in *The Logic of the Humanities*, a "unity of *direction*, not *actualization*." "The particular individuals belong together, not because they are alike or resemble each other, but because they are cooperating in a *common task*, which we perceive to be new and to be the [era's] distinctive 'meaning.'"[1] Cassirer's apology is especially appropriate for the sort of generalizations needed to make sense of the shifts in poetic practice in the middle of the eighteenth century because the sense of history to which he appeals, history as a direction or force, first became powerful at just that cultural moment.

When Joseph Warton spoke of "pure poetry" in 1756, he was using the term as it has been used ever since, polemically. "We do not, it would seem, sufficiently attend to the difference there is, betwixt a MAN OF WIT, a MAN OF SENSE, and a TRUE POET. Donne and Swift were undoubtedly men of wit and men of sense: but what traces have they left of PURE POETRY?" Warton's *Essay on the Writings and Genius of Pope* is an attempt to put Pope in his place, which is clearly second place for Warton, and it elaborates the position he had taken a decade earlier in the Preface to his *Odes*, when he declared his intention to divert poetry from the recent fashion of moralizing in verse and to restore it to its "proper channel." Although Warton would hardly go as far as Arnold did a century later in relegating Pope to the province of prose, he shared the assumption that there is something essentially unpoetic about

Pope's subjects, that many of his poems are too didactic to enter the kingdom of "pure poetry."[2]

If we look at Warton's own poetry and much of what he praised in the newer poetry around him, we find that he could in fact tolerate quite a bit of didacticism and moralizing in verse, so that we need to push further to find the real dividing lines. We get a better idea from these remarks concerning a poem Pope planned but never wrote, a nationalistic epic, *Brutus*. It would have been a failure, Warton decides, because Pope

> would have given us many elegant descriptions and many general characters, well drawn, but would have failed to set before our eyes the *Reality* of these objects, and the *Actions* of these characters, [so] that it would have appeared . . . how much, and for what reasons, the man that is skillful in painting modern life, and the most secret foibles and follies of his contemporaries, is, THEREFORE disqualified for representing the ages of heroism, and that simple life, which alone epic poetry can gracefully describe, in a word, that this composition would have shown more of the *Philosopher* than the *Poet*.[3]

One of the interesting things about this passage is that it is entirely in the subjunctive: like many present-day critics, Warton expatiates most freely when unencumbered by a text. Interesting for our inquiry is the assumption that what disqualifies Pope for the epic is his modernity—his skill in "painting *modern* life." Warton views Pope as too historical, too much in history to rise above it. Warton does not put the emphasis squarely there and is not usually read this way; in fact, he argues that poetry is likely to be better if it is historical because "events that have actually happened are, after all, the properest subjects for poetry." But his examples of great works "grounded on true history" are revealing: *Oedipus, King Lear, Romeo and Juliet* as well as Pope's own *Elegy to the Memory of an Unfortunate Lady*, all works based on very distant, obscure, or private history. Anything recent, documentable, and public will not have enough "poignancy." Pope's later poetry will be judged inferior to his early work by posterity because it is more historically particular. "For Wit and Satire are transitory and perishable, but Nature and Passion are eternal."[4]

The oppositions are interesting—Wit versus Nature, Satire versus Passion—and of course sentimental. With too much wit and too little passion, Pope's writing presumably does not come straight enough from the heart. But more is going on here than the victory of bourgeois sentimentalism over Augustan satire. Satiric poetry is nearly always highly *historical* poetry, therefore the battle is in large part over whether poetry should be factual or fictional (that is, "romantic" in the old sense). When Warton says that Pope's epic would have shown more of the Philosopher than the Poet, he means, I think, not that Pope would have been too logical but too accurate, too verifiable, and the antithesis anticipates Wordsworth's later declaration that the opposite of poetry is not prose but science. Closer to Warton's own day, and to the terms of our discussion, we hear Adam Ferguson employing a similar distinction in *An Essay on the History of Civil Society*, published in 1767. The historian, he complains, who invokes a mythical state of nature to prove his points, "substitutes hypothesis instead of reality, and confounds the provinces of imagination and reason, of poetry and science." (Ferguson's zeal in exploding historical myths of social origins was his generation's counterpart to Locke's zeal in exploding innate ideas.) For Ferguson as for Hegel, history begins once myth and poetry have been cleared away.[5] History is prose.

And the poets apparently agreed. Whether by decision or default, from the 1740s on, most of the younger poets avoided direct historical treatment of the events of their day, even of their century. We can best appreciate how fundamental a shift occurred at this point by recalling that one of the deepest connections we can find between Dryden and Pope—and many of their contemporaries—is the shared sense of the poet's role as historian of his own times. That Dryden was for a time both Poet Laureate and Historiographer Royal was perhaps partially accidental, but it is also perfectly emblematic of his concerns from *Annus Mirabilis* to *Absalom and Achitophel* and beyond. Pope's historical commitment deepened throughout his career, though it was strong even in the resolution of Windsor Forest into past and present prospects or the engaged observation of *The Rape of the Lock*, which, like John Gay's *Trivia*, fondly records as it criticizes. Increasingly in Pope's later poetry, the historical role impresses with more urgency; the decision to name names becomes not only a matter of satiric strategy but a determination to leave a record—the true record—for posterity, a record often spilling over into footnotes meant to outlast the pseudohistories of Walpole's propagandists. The catalog of corruption is wearying and perhaps futile, Pope concludes by 1738: "Yet may this Verse (if such a Verse remain)/Show there was one who held it in disdain." The desire to reconcile poetry and history—which in the broadest sense is characteristic of most of what we think of as "Augustan" poetry from 1660 to 1740—is likewise the warrant for all those details of political history that Swift appended as footnotes for posterity to the *Verses on the Death of Dr. Swift*. Finally, the nightmare lurking behind the *Dunciad* is an Orwellian one of cultural amnesia: "O Muse! relate (for you can tell alone,/ Wits have short Memories, and Dunces none)."

The specter that seems to be lurking behind much of the poetry of the generation after Pope's and Swift's, however, is not the fear of the loss of history but of its crushing presence, a subliminal version of Stephen Dedalus's vision, where "history is a nightmare from which I am trying to awake." If this is a correct interpretation of the underlying motivation of much mid-eighteenth-century poetry, and I will try to argue it satisfactorily in what follows, it should be added at once that it is usually not conscious and that the poets frequently wake from history by turning to sleep. All of the symptoms of sleepiness that Pope attributed ironically to the dunces and to Dulness—lethargy, indolence, inertia, aversion to light, the blurring of perceptual and conceptual boundaries—began to appear quickly in the 1740s as positive poetic values. One aspect of this change was what Martin Price has characterized as a shift from the "light-centered worlds of Spenser, Milton, and Pope" to the "asylum of darkness."[6] Probably the most popular poem of the 1740s (and an extremely popular poem for another century) was *Night Thoughts*. Kindred but blessedly less sublime are the evening poems, of which Gray's *Elegy* and William Collins's *Ode to Evening* are conspicuously the best.

That an atmosphere of melancholy gloom was cultivated during this period by solitary poetic wanderers has been well known since Eleanor M. Sickels wrote *The Gloomy Egoist* nearly half a century ago. Not much has been explored in depth since then about what might be thought of as the politics of melancholy, or perhaps more accurately, the politics of sensibility, of which melancholy is simply the commonest form in poetry. We will need to derive such a "politics" in most cases without the aid of the poets' explicit political statements, which are generally either lacking altogether or run contrary to what seem to be the likelier implications of certain poetic decisions. To put these decisions into a context that clarifies their meaning, we need to consider them in continual relation to poetic procedures typified by Pope and Swift. A little later I will contrast Swift and Gray in hopes of illustrating different sets of assumptions about the relation of public history and "poetic" privacy, but here the most useful general context may be suggested by considering Pope's career again. As Maynard Mack has pointed out, the vantage point from which Pope was able to tell his modern history was one of retirement.[7] This is a very complex stance, not something achieved merely by living in the country but close enough to the metropolis to be part of it (a sort of Connecticut of the soul); it is something that must be achieved again and again in poem after poem, a vocal vision carefully and naturally "cultivated."

By the midcentury, retirement hardened into retreat. The poet longed characteristically to be not only far from the madding crowd, which Pope had wanted as much as Gray, but far from everybody. Accordingly, many of the poems most "of" the 1740s and 1750s are not epistles—that is, poems with an explicit audience and implicit social engagement—but soliloquies or lyrics, usually blank verse musings or odes addressed to personifications. Conventionality again gets in the way of taking this vogue as seriously as we might; but the fashion seems potentially revealing largely because it became so fashionable so quickly. Moreover, the melancholy poems seem merely to be a part of a larger turning away from the social-historical world to which poetry traditionally belonged, and the deliberate break with and from the past is sometimes just as evident in many of the more cheerful poems of the period.

When, from the late 1740s on, we find poems in praise of memory, they are likely to be in praise of private memory; thus, William Shenstone's *Ode to Memory* (1748) is largely an ode to childhood days and "innocence." Whatever other motives may be involved, the act of prizing private memory and childhood innocence allows the poet to declare his innocence of history, that adult world of public contention. The innocence of childhood is something of a mid-eighteenth-century invention, and we can best grasp its political content by considering what it is frequently opposed to, namely, "Ambition."

A few years before Shenstone's *Ode to Memory*, Gray wrote the first important eighteenth-century poem posing childhood scenes against the fallen world of adulthood, *Ode on a Distant Prospect of Eton College* (1742). Gray's nostalgic praise of childhood joys, the "paths of pleasure" from which the speaker is separated by time and space, is all the more interesting as a period phenomenon because Gray most likely had some miserable years on the edges of those celebrated playing fields. But after the gracefully awkward humor of pliant arms cleaving grassy waves and idle progeny urging the flying ball, the description of childhood is mostly in negative terms, contrasting its difference from the speaker's present condition:

> Gay hope is theirs by fancy fed,
> Less pleasing when possessed;
> The tear forgot as soon as shed,
> The sunshine of the breast . . .

Only a powerful need to simplify childhood experience could prompt a poet of Gray's intelligence to describe the child's tear as forgotten as soon as shed or to sum up the world that includes adolescence—Gray himself left Eton at seventeen—as a guiltless succession:

The thoughtless day, the easy night,
The spirits pure, the slumbers light,
That fly the approach of morn.

Gray's lament for the "little victims" soon to leave this haven would seem at first to be wholly apolitical in that the woes that await the children are envisioned as human rather than historical evils, resulting from the nature of things rather than the nature of the social allotment of things. The children shall one day be torn by "fury Passions," those "vultures of the mind" that Gray catalogs iconographically. Then Gray turns to a somewhat more social picture, though the images remain indistinct:

Ambition this shall tempt to rise,
Then whirl the wretch from high,
To bitter Scorn a sacrifice,
And grinning Infamy.
The stings of Falsehood those shall try,
And hard Unkindness' altered eye,
That mocks the tear it forced to flow;
And keen Remorse with blood defiled,
And moody Madness laughing wild
Amid severest woe.

Perhaps the most accurate interpretation of the politics of this particular melancholy is that Gray cannot or will not make a distinction between necessary and unnecessary human suffering, just as it is not clear a few lines later whether "Poverty" is as inevitable as "slow-consuming Age" or something that accompanies it because of human "Unkindness." Gray offers no political analysis, just as Samuel Johnson does not in *The Vanity of Human Wishes*. But what is politically significant is simply the fact that childhood and rural innocence are being used as new norms by which to measure the passionate tragedy of the world adults make. The prepassionate or innocent state attributed to schoolchildren is a kind of internalized golden age, a prehistory of the sort Adam Ferguson later complained of as belonging more to poetry than to truth. Accordingly, at the beginning of *The Seasons*, James Thomson lavishly describes the earliest stage of human life as a prepassionate childhood of the race. All was once springtime harmony and vegetarian plenty; now, however, "all/Is off the poise within: the passions all/Have burst their bounds," and the breeze of social feeling has given way to a psychic "storm" of "mixed emotions."

One secular version of history that had been available to poets who wanted to retain the idea of a golden age was a correspondingly secular version of the fortunate fall: being expelled from a cultural Eden (or, as Thomson puts it, out of "Nature's ample lap") leads man to exert his energies, learn, build cities, make laws, and so on. This is Pope's version of history in Epistle III of *An Essay on Man*, and it is compatible both with traditional Christian patterns of theodicy and the desire to posit a Lockean rather than a Hobbesean original state. But more emphatically toward the midcentury, the fall into society and history is seen not as a fortunate fall but just a fall, a catastrophe.

In mid-eighteenth-century poetry, history's metonymy was conflict. Very often it was the violent conflict of war, but it could also be the strife of competition. Not surprisingly, the retreat from history occurs in poems most dramatically when historical events and public actors are portrayed as hostile not only to the life of poetry (for example, as antithetical to the nature-loving solitary Thomson creates) but to the life of the poet himself. The very earliest major poems of William Collins and Thomas Warton the Younger are pastorals in which the youthful poetic speakers are victims of violence perpetrated by older, more public males. The speakers are fugitives from war, appearing in the poems at just the point where they are becoming refugees. The last of Collins's *Persian Eclogues* (1742) ends with two shepherds fleeing the invading Tartar army—

> when loud along the vale was heard
> A shriller shriek and nearer fires appeared:
> The afrighted shepherds through the dews of night,
> Wide o'er the moonlight hills, renewed their flight.

Warton's *Pastoral Eclogues* (published anonymously in 1745) are set "during the wars in Germany," and his young swains are continually retreating from the clamor of war to the protection of groves and caves.

But the best example of such a collision between a poet-speaker and the hostile force of history is *The Bard*. Gray's poem is based on the appealing tradition that Edward I executed the Welsh bards once he had conquered that country (an appealing tradition because it suggests the poets were once too potent politically to be ignored), and the poem happens as the bard stands high on a cliff hurling prophetic curses down on the king like so many verbal boulders. Finally he hurls himself:

> ". . . with joy I see
> The different doom our fates assign.
> Be thine despair and sceptered care;
> To triumph, and to die, are mine."
> He spoke, and headlong from the mountain's height
> Deep in the roaring tide he plunged to endless night.

To triumph and to die. The phrase feels more like a definition than a paradox in Gray's poetic world, where death, like childhood, can so readily become an emblem of innocence from history. The bard's suicide is both a badge of his sincerity (a poetic association we have since tended to take more literally) and a final exercise of the linguistic power the clergyman William Law had attributed to God: "What he speaks he acts." To end his poet's lyric and life in the same breath is Gray's sublime speech act; but we need to visualize as well as hear the dramatic moment Gray has frozen in the poem to understand the full significance of the encounter and the redefinition of death as triumph. The fantasy on which it turns is double. On the one hand, history must stop for the poet, because this king, unlike George II, must actually listen to the ode he has occasioned.[8] On the other hand, the forced march of history, embodied in Edward and his army, will go on and will kill the poet.

The collision between poet and history is less violent in the *Elegy Written in a Country Churchyard* but no less fatal. The poem ends with the imagined death of the poet himself, a death related in the subjunctive but converted into virtual fact in the Epitaph, which I take to be the poet's own. Once we think of the *Elegy* as a poem in which the poet imagines the reaction to his own death, a useful comparison comes to mind with Swift's *Verses on the Death of Dr. Swift*. The poems are so obviously different in intent and effect that it is not surprising that most readers would not draw the comparison; but it may help to clarify some rapid changes in poetry if we attempt to be explicit about some of the differences between these poems of the early 1730s and the late 1740s.

Both the *Verses* and the *Elegy* are poems of moral generalization. Swift's reflections are largely glosses on the maxim from La Rochefoucauld, which he translates in the epigraph as, "In the Adversity of our best Friends, we find something that doth not displease us," and versifies as, "In all Distresses of our Friends/We first consult our private Ends." Gray's "maxims," on the other hand, are "The paths of glory lead but to the grave," and "Even from the tomb the voice of nature cries." The moral position implied by the *Elegy* as a whole is almost an inversion of La Rochefoucauld: we are so sympathetic, so tenderly framed, that even the imagined distresses of total strangers affect us feelingly. Not everyone exactly, but surely the speaker and the reader will appreciate the moral sentiments carved in the stones and trees of the churchyard in innocent country.

Distance from town is an important part of the moral atmosphere of Swift's poem, too, and so is the relative solitude of the speaker. If Swift is not as explicit about locating his world "Far from the madding crowd" or isolating his speaker ("And leaves the world to darkness and to me"), the ethos of his *Verses* is quite as dependent on the impression that the speaker is far from the center of power and that he is insulated by his integrity. Gray's generation seemed to require more insulation, and the difference became one between partial and total solitude. The simple and supposedly neutral speaker who characterizes Swift insists upon his social life: it is a contracted society, to be sure, but the friendships are as essential a part of the man as his pleasant stories of whigs and tories. Gray's speaker speaks to no one, except the reader. For the hoary-headed swain who describes him (a nice counterpart to Swift's coffeehouse judge) he is the silent image of "one forlorn."

The sympathies of Gray's poet are generalized to the whole village and to simpler folk everywhere. He is "mindful of the unhonored dead." But he has no specific connection to anyone. The different attitudes toward the use of particulars give rise in fact to most of the other differences between the poems. For just as the expression of anger and humor in Swift's poem depends on the use of historical particulars, Gray's melancholy and solemnity depend on the generalization of emotions into a subjunctive world, a world where *"Perhaps . . . is laid"* some potential hero to be mourned by a poet whom *"Haply* some hoary-headed swain *may"* describe to *"some* kindred spirit" who comes by "chance" to ask. Swift's poem is wholly without despondency because its anger so clearly has particular limits; Gray's distress, like the melancholy it marks as its own, is grief without an object.

Whereas Swift's poem aims to make all of the people and events it names into part of the historical record, much of the most poignant musing in Gray's *Elegy* centers on the reflection that the simple villagers buried in the churchyard are not part of history. The "short and simple annals of the poor" are contrasted with the public "Memory" left by "Ambition," "Grandeur," and the "pomp of power." There is much melancholy in their obscurity as it is translated into the speculative subjunctive:

> Perhaps in this neglected spot is laid
> Some heart once pregnant with celestial fire;
> Hands that the rod of empire might have swayed,
> Or waked to ecstasy the living lyre . . .
>
> Some village-Hampden that with dauntless breast
> The little tyrant of his fields withstood;
> Some mute inglorious Milton here may rest,
> Some Cromwell guiltless of his country's blood.

But Gray insists upon having it both ways, as we have ever since the mid-eighteenth century: the pathos of unrealized potential is balanced emotionally by the triumph of rural innocence.

> The applause of listening senates to command,
> The threats of pain and ruin to despise,
> To scatter plenty o'er a smiling land,
> And read their history in a nation's eyes,
>
> Their lot forbade: nor circumscribed alone
> Their growing virtues, but their crimes confined;
> Forbade to wade through slaughter to a throne,
> And shut the gates of mercy on mankind. . . .

The conception of potential—unnurtured or thwarted talent—is what is most remarkable in all of these reflections. What, after all, is a mute Milton? The fact that we are likely to read the lines again and again without asking that question suggests how deeply the ideal of potential is embedded in modern thought. A blind Milton we know, a deaf Milton we could imagine; but to conceive a mute Milton we need to conceive of the poet in a different manner: not as one who writes but one who has a poet's soul. In the *Ode to Fear*, Collins prays not that he will be allowed to compose like Shakespeare but "once like him to *feel*," the presumption being that the rest will follow.

Just after the stanzas from the *Elegy* considered above, the villagers are idealized for living "Far from the madding crowd's *ignoble strife*," a phrase that suggests a vision much like the one available in Thomson's mirror of vanity in *The Castle of Indolence*. The emphasis is less on the crowd as an unruly mob—a traditional staple of satire—than on "strife," the competition and ambition of city folk as "ignoble" virtually by definition. Gray's poet is not made for such a world, and even the subjunctive intrusion of history into the village where he has sought refuge is enough to kill him. The mixture of defensive and superior feelings at being out of the public world and the historical mainstream crystallizes in the last line of a later poem with which we began: "Beneath the Good how far—but far above the Great."

A melancholy response to history is always possible, Hegel would write early in the next century, if we decide to lament the decay of kingdoms and contemplate history as the "slaughter-bench at which the happiness of peoples, the wisdom of states, and the virtues of individuals have been sacrificed." But, he insists, "we have purposely eschewed that method of reflection which ascends from this scene of particulars to general principles. Be-sides, it is not in the interest of such sentimental reflection really to rise above these depressing emotions and to solve the mysteries of Providence presented in such contemplations. It is rather their na-ture to dwell melancholically on the empty and fruitless sublimities of their negative result."[9]

Hegel is not but easily could be describing in this meditation on melancholy the "fruitless sublimities" of Gray's *Elegy* or Johnson's *Vanity of Human Wishes*. We have seen how the conflict and violence of public history as it is conceived metonymically by many of the poets leads to images of Retreat, images of shepherds fleeing as they sing, for example, hurrying toward the shelter of shady groves or the protection of caves, and we have seen that these images of seclusion are also metaphors for the solitary poetic imagination itself. In one of the most radical of retreats Joseph Warton imagines himself at the end of *The Enthusiast* secured from the ravages of historical reality, like Thomson's idealized sage in his distance from disaster but unlike him in that he does not even hear the disturbance:

> So when rude whirlwinds rouse the roaring main,
> Beneath fair Thetis sits, in coral caves,
> Serenely gay, nor sinking sailors' cries
> Disturb her sportive nymphs, who round her form
> The light fantastic dance, or for her hair
> Weave rosy crowns, or with according lutes
> Grave the soft warbles of her honeyed voice.

The imagined shipwreck is suggestive, for it is the image Hegel would invoke to characterize one response, an inadequate response in his view, to historical misery: "And at last, out of the boredom with which this sorrowful reflection threatens us, we draw back into the vitality of the present, into our aims and interests of the moment; we retreat, in short, into the selfishness that stands on the quiet shore and thence enjoys in safety the distant spectacle of wreckage and confusion."[10]

What is the nature of the world into which the poets retreat and which they pose as an alternative history? It is not in general a world of romance, although that is the term usually opposed to history in eighteenth-century criticism. The successful assimilation of romance material into psychological poetry really is a Romantic achievement. The post-Augustan poetic world first evident in the 1740s is typically less rich in narrative analogues and more abundant in detached images of seclusion and protection. It is a world that is often visually indistinct or darkened, and it is a world where consolation is prized over confrontation, stasis over strife.

The lyric extreme of such a world is the abstract ode, a lyric devoted to a personification or group of related personifications. The "plot" of such poems typically involves an encounter with timeless powers, and the encounter has—or is just about to have— the effect of finality, moving the experience out of a world of temporal process. The very lack of process excludes the abstract ode from some of the dramatic resonances of Renaissance lyrics and the resolutions characteristic of the great sonnets. For different reasons, the denial of process also separates the mid-eighteenth-century poems from the greater Romantic lyrics, which make much of their music out of the recognition that the timeless vision is timely.

But the "common task" (to invoke Cassirer again) of many mid-eighteenth-century poets seems to be a different one, an attempt to subsume personal and social change under unchanging but secular categories. When these categories take the form of personification they are capable of proliferating all too easily; but their proliferation is a sign of their commonality. These personifications can be multiplied more readily than Renaissance or Romantic "powers" because they are often neither deities nor forces of nature but avowedly human constructs. Pity, Solitude, Fancy, Liberty, and so on are more plentiful than gods and goddesses, west winds and skylarks. Yet when we think of these constructs collectively, we may begin to perceive something else, one more personification, as the common task of poetry of the period: the unconscious conversion of history into History. In the poets' various attempts to generalize the public past into War or Ambition or Luxury and in their attempts to dissociate themselves from it, we see glimmers of a new historicism, a crudely idealistic or "Hegelian" sense of history as a directive force—against which the poet must invoke forces of his own. Most of this is indeed less than conscious, and what we have is more like a photographic negative of the idea of history than the positive image of it. But we can in a sense develop the picture ourselves, seeing how History was beginning to be imagined by some of the people who, although by no means "world-historical individuals," tried to control it by abstraction or testified to its presence by trying to get out of its way.

What I have been referring to as the flight from history—an avoidance of particular external referents, especially political ones, and a preference for indefinite and static reifications—seems to be reenacted in much of modern criticism. The analogy may suggest something of the current imagery of academic seclusion and perhaps help refocus literary history.

Although contemporary critics of various persuasions routinely dissociate themselves from the formalism that attained its highest prestige in the 1940s and 1950s, the differences between New Critics and newer critics are often minor—differences, as Gerald Graff has recently argued, "between factions of the vanguard." Postmodernist perspectives have not, according to this view, demystified modernism so much as continued it. "The loss of significant external reality, its displacement by myth-making, the domestication and normalization of alienation" are all in Graff's view common features of earlier and later twentieth-century literature and criticism.[11] From a critical point of view, the continuity might be simplified this way. Modernist ideology tended to stress the conception of literature as self-referential: literature is autonomous, poems are about poetry. Postmodernist criticism has extended the ideal of autonomy to criticism as well: criticism is, if it is pure criticism, about criticism.

Most contemporary critics would not put that proposition so baldly, although in some circles such remarks are a way of establishing one's critical credit. So, in the pages of *Diacritics*, for example, it is possible to encounter one theorist congratulating another on having survived the "heroic labors of metacriticism." The vocabulary of muscularity and manliness is surprisingly common in current criticism. The assumption seems to be that the critic is either a wrestler or an executive. In the first case he will battle mightily with competitors dead and alive; in the latter case the critic is far too serious to deal with primary texts, much like the corporate president who rules so many people that he never actually sees anyone.

More representative of the situation of criticism, however, is the tendency to differentiate literature from mimesis and—by silent analogy—to differentiate criticism from commentary. In the 1940s, René Wellek and Austin Warren began their *Theory of Literature* from the position that in literature the "reference is to a world of fiction, of imagination. . . . Statements in a novel, in a poem, or in a drama are not literally true; they are not logical propositions. There is a central and important difference between a statement, even in a historical novel or a novel by Balzac which seems to convey 'information' about actual happenings, and the same information appearing in a book of history or sociology."[12] In the late 1950's, Northrop Frye underscored the distinction between a literary work—a "structure of words for its own sake," an "autonomous verbal structure"—and the "assertive" or "instrumental" use of language. "In all literary verbal structures the final direction of meaning is inward," whereas in "descriptive or assertive writing the final direction is outward." Frye's eventual goal is "pure Literature," a self-contained and self-consistent world, which "like pure mathematics, contains its own meaning." "We think of literature at first as a commentary on an external 'life' or 'reality.' But just as in mathematics we have to go from three apples to three, and from a square field to a square, so in reading a novel we have to go from literature as a reflection of life to literature as autonomous language." Criticism must have "some measure of independence from the art it deals with," and it must have its own "conceptual framework" if the "autonomy" of criticism is to be achieved.[13]

Neither Frye nor many of the critics who follow him could be called formalists. What is significant is simply that formalists and antiformalists have tended to agree on emphasizing the self-containment of literature; the difference is whether one argues for the self-containment of the individual work or the whole of what Frye calls the "literary field." In either case, the criticism that ensues will seek and find essentially static or "synchronic" works, detached from political events and the truths or falsities of public life.

For Frye and probably for many theorists interested in "autonomy," the analogy of music is important because music, like mathematics, comes closest to an ideal of "pure poetry" by being more coherent than referential. Perhaps for the same reason Stéphane Mallarmé tends to be invoked with uncommon frequency by French critics wishing to stress the nonreferential aspects of language. Frye attributes the formulation of the ideal of "pure poetry" to *symbolisme*: its conception of poetry as essentially centripetal in meaning successfully isolated the "hypothetical germ of literature." In other words, for all his interest in romance and myth and archetype, Frye's norm for poetry tends to be the lyric, an "elusive verbal pattern" that avoids statement but is held together by a "unity of mood."[14]

Whatever the problems of such a norm, the important point here is that its articulation was not, in England, the achievement of the later nineteenth century but of the mid-eighteenth.[15] It is not just the fact that Joseph Warton used the phrase in the 1750s that is revealing but the poetic practice of the period as well. The avoidance of history, controversy, verifiability, and political particularity are all parts of the ideal of poetry as essentially nonmimetic, evocative, and unified by mood rather than by a structure of descriptions or assertions. The world of a poem like Joseph Warton's *The Enthusiast* —with its final image of rosy crowns and according lutes undisturbed by the cries of sinking sailors—is as synchronic, as centripetal in meaning, and as autonomous as Frye or any critic arguing for the essential separation of poetry and history could wish.

Among the most popular poems immediately after the work of the generation of mid-eighteenth-century poets under discussion here were the "Ossian" poems, the alleged translations of ancient poetry that were actually written by James Macpherson in the 1760s. In addition to all the usual explanations for the immense popularity of Ossian (the poems' appeal to primitivism, to Gaelic pride, to notions of "sublimity," and so forth), we can add these further attractions: the Ossian poems tend to reduce history to family romance, reduce the external physical world to a cloudily subjective field of warring forces, and reduce the situation of the poet to that of a sensitive son of a strong father belonging to another era.

If Northrop Frye unwittingly echoed Joseph Warton, surely the Ossian of our generation is Harold Bloom. The connection is not one of forgery or even of anxious influence. The connection is the shared preoccupation with paternal predecessors, physical combat (determining who is the "strongest" poet), and the ghosts of dead bard-warriors. Since the proposition that Ossian begat Bloom may strike strangely upon some ears, I will try to establish the family likeness by means of three brief exhibits.

Exhibit A. Bloom: "A poem is not an overcoming of anxiety, but is that anxiety. . . . Every poem is a misinterpretation of a parent poem. . . . Poetry (Romance) is Family Romance."

Ossian: "Lovely were thy thoughts, O Fingal! why had not Ossian the strength of thy soul? But thou standest alone, my father! who can equal the king of Selma?

Exhibit B. Bloom: "Every poem we know begins as an encounter *between poems*. . . . The father is met in combat, and fought to at least a stand-off, if not quite to a separate peace. The burden for representation thus becomes supermimetic rather than antimimetic, which means that interpretation too must assume the experiential sorrows of a supermimesis."

Ossian: "Dimly seen as lightens the night, he strides largely from hill to hill. Bloody was the land of my father, when he whirled the gleam of his sword. He remembers the battles of his youth."

Exhibit C. Bloom: "The *apophrades*, the dismal or unlucky days upon which the dead return to inhabit their former houses, come to the strongest poets. . . . It is as though the final phase of great modern poets existed neither for last affirmations . . . nor as palinodes, but rather as the ultimate placing and reduction of ancestors."

Ossian: "'Raise, ye bards of other times,' continued the great Fingal, 'raise high the praise of heroes: that my soul may settle on their fame.' The dark winds rustled over the chiefs. A hundred voices at once arose; a hundred harps were strung. They sung of other times; the mighty chiefs of former years."[16]

(Of the Ossian poems Johnson remarked, "Sir, a man might write such stuff for ever, if he would *abandon* his mind to it.")

A fuller and fairer treatment of both the eighteenth and twentieth centuries would be needed to see in just what geometry these parallels would meet; but perhaps one or two readings may be taken. If the parallels are more than accidental, then the common view that modern literary attitudes are essentially an extension of Romantic ideas is misleading. Compared to the mid-eighteenth century, the Romantic period in England was one of significant repoliticizing of poetry, a resumption of the poet's public function. It is because of this recuperation of roles that, however different the terms, Pope and Blake often sound more like each other than either sounds like Collins or the Wartons and that Wordsworth objects less to the public voice of Dryden or Pope than to the refined withdrawal of Gray. (It was Arnold, contemporary of the *symbolistes*, who had the least tolerance for Augustan poetics.) In short, many of the modern critical premises concerning poetry are closer to the tendencies of "pre-Romanticism" than to Romanticism. An oscillation theory of literary history is no great boon, but until we do better it may represent the last two centuries of literary history with less distortion than a linear, evolutionary model.

The concern of this essay has been more with the eighteenth century than the twentieth, an attempt primarily to recreate and interpret the situation of a particular class of humanist at a particular historical moment. But I have also attempted to do partial justice to a question originally put to me by the man to whom this volume is dedicated. In the course of an informal humanities seminar, during which I and several other members waxed skeptical about the relation of our studies to contemporary problems, Charles Frankel asked, disarmingly, whether one would become interested in—"just to pick an example"—eighteenth-century poetry of solitude without believing that it had "something to do with now." The value of such a question is, I hope, not that it encourages scholastic imperialism (under which all things become colonies dependent upon the investigator's area of special knowledge) but that it may encourage one to discriminate between modesty and evasion.

If the resemblances between mid-eighteenth-century poetic and late twentieth-century critical responses are illuminating, it is because they exist not merely at the level of quaint resemblance or at the level of causes. Much of our present effort does not go into segregating poetry from history because a generation of minor poets attempted to do so two and a half centuries ago. But it is a fact that such a reaction is now part of the repertoire of responses available to students of literature and that to study its emergence and implications in various periods is to seek what we very much need—historical knowledge of our ahistorical impulses.

At present, claims for the historical study of literature tend to be made most loudly at the edges of the political spectrum, and there are limitations in both cases. Historical conservatives tend to make the case for reconstructing authorial intentions and the suppositions of a work's original audience; such literary history naturally tends toward the biographical and doctrinal (and, if sentimentalized, toward the reactionary, which in English studies is often a diffuse Christian Toryism). The history conceived by Marxist critics tends to be selective and impersonally mechanistic; few Marxist studies deal sympathetically with older literature or with poetry at all. Between these edges suppler possibilities exist but ahistorical procedures abound. It is easier of course to notice the gap than to fill it, but what is needed is a theory of the relation of public history and poetic production, one that does not begin by assuming that poetry is above or beneath other means of survival and celebration. Such a theory will need, I think, to be "liberal" enough in its individualism to be concerned with authorial intention and nonmaterial explanations and at the same time skeptical enough of bourgeois nostalgia to distrust any method that puts a proprietary fence around literary meaning.

NOTES

1. *The Logic of the Humanities* (New Haven: Yale University Press, 1961), pp. 139–40.
2. Joseph Warton, *Essay on the Writings and Genius of Pope* (London, 1756), Dedication.
3. Ibid., p. 281.
4. Ibid., pp. 253–54, 333–34.
5. Ferguson, *An Essay*, ed. Duncan Forbes (University of Edinburgh, 1966), p. 2, cf. pp. 6, 8, 10, 30. Hegel: "Myths, folk songs, traditions are not part of original history; they are still obscure modes and peculiar to obscure peoples. Here we deal with peoples who knew who they were and what they wanted. Observed and observable reality is a more solid foundation for history than the transience of myths and epics" (*Reason in History*, trans. Robert S. Hartman [Indianapolis: Bobbs-Merrill, 1953], p. 3).

6. Martin Price, "The Sublime Poem: Pictures and Powers," *Yale Review* 58 (1968–69): 194–213.

7. *The Garden and the City: Retirement and Politics in the Later Poetry of Pope, 1731–43* (Toronto: University of Toronto Press, 1969).

8. Similar fantasies of poets with access to or power over their kings are enacted in Thomas Warton's *The Crusade* and *The Grave of King Arthur*.

9. Hegel, *Reason in History*, p. 27.

10. Ibid.

11. Gerald Graff, *Literature against Itself: Literary Ideas in Modern Society* (Chicago: University of Chicago Press, 1979), p. 6.

12. *Theory of Literature* (New York: Harcourt, Brace and Co., 1949), p. 15.

13. *Anatomy of Criticism* (Princeton: Princeton University Press, 1957), pp. 5–6, 74, 351.

14. Ibid., pp. 80–81.

15. See M. H. Abrams, "The Lyric as Poetic Norm," in *The Mirror and the Lamp* (Oxford, 1953; repr. New York: Norton, 1958), pp. 84–88.

16. The quotations from Bloom are from, respectively, *The Anxiety of Influence* (New York: Oxford, 1973), pp. 94–95; *A Map of Misreading* (New York: Oxford, 1975), pp. 70, 80; and *The Anxiety of Influence*, pp. 141, 147. The first quotation from Macpherson is from *Carthon*; the second and third are from *Fingal*. The edition followed is *The Poems of Ossian* (New York: John B. Alden, 1883), pp. 226, 325, 354.

MURIEL BRADBROOK

♟ DOING LITERATURE ON

DOVER BEACH

''POETRY IS A DEED''; the Elizabethan stage clown Tarlton took his challenge from his patron, Sir Philip Sidney, the exemplar of humanist learning to his generation. In "setting forth and moving to well doing" poetry won the crown from philosophy and history. Aristotle had confirmed that "it is not Gnosis but Praxis must be the fruit"—so "poetry is the companion of the camps."[1] Praxis did not fail Sidney, who, as he lay dying at Arnhem of a shattered thigh, called for the song *La Cuisse Rompue*.

T. S. Eliot remarked that as bees make honey, poets make poetry. To its derivation from primal energies he could have called eminent witness:

> Our poesy is as a gum, which oozes
> From whence 'tis nourished . . .
>
> [*Timon of Athens*, 1.1.23–24]

If literature is not seen both as a derivative and a generator of energy, its study dwindles to a branch of cultural history or of the economic superstructure—or, as Geoffrey H. Hartman predicts, a service department to other disciplines.[2] Ezra Pound defined its function as "nutrition of impulse." Hartman fears it leads back only to more teaching; and a voice from Yale is not to be disregarded.

The relation between literature and literary history therefore differs from that between science and technology. Underlying such study is an unrecited confession:

> The nobleness of life
> Is to do this

or "The chief end of man. . . ." or "Here stand I; I can no other." The value implicit in such challenging demonstration, if extrapolated, is likely to be paradoxical or tautologous. The living principle is not abstract, and no contexts of theory could define it. It is apprehended, but indefinable.

The teacher, whether holy man, sage, expert, or technician, must nonetheless be prepared to distinguish between his own territory and neighboring territories. As Hartman pointed out, it is sometimes thought sufficient to say that "literature is *not* politics, *not* religion, *not* science, *not* rhetoric," and certainly not a "doing," but rather a secular state of grace.

In his *Defence of Poesie*, Sidney the humanist was defending Sidney the poet of *Astrophil and Stella* against a preacher of the Word, who as reformed actor and playwright grew overzealous for the exclusive claims of his new calling—invaded, as he thought, by the poets.

Three hundred years later, Matthew Arnold saw poetry as no usurper, but rather as a preserver of threatened religious values: "The future of poetry is immense because in poetry . . . our race will as time goes on find an ever surer and surer stay. There is not a creed which is not shaken, not an accredited dogma which is not shewn to be questionable, not a received tradition which does not threaten to dissolve. Our religion has materialized itself in the fact, the supposed fact, and now the fact is failing it. But for poetry the idea is everything. . . . Poetry attaches its emotion to the idea; the idea *is* the fact."[3] For, as in poetry he had earlier lamented

> The sea of faith
> Was once too at the full and round earth's shore
> Lay like the folds of a bright girdle furl'd:
> But now I only hear
> Its melancholy, long withdrawing roar
> Retreating to the breath
> Of the night wind. . . .[4]

Doing literature on Dover Beach replaced not lost dogmas, but daily habit and practice. What he advocated in the poem was truth in human relationships. (It was addressed to his wife.)

A little later he pointed out that the value of poetry is in the implicit nature of the judgments it forms, in those who live by it, "without any turmoil of controversial reasonings." It is the record of "the best that has been known and thought in the world"[5]—the world is there, but if (to revert to Sidney) poetry makes "this too much loved earth more lovely" the action takes place in the heart of man. Literature, attempting to reconcile the irreconcilable, to bring into the realm of the articulate what otherwise cannot be articulated, must include features that do not belong to the earthly paradise—not only Dover Beach, but King Lear's Dover Cliff, if not Dante's Inferno. Arnold hinted at this in his "touchstones," the great lines of verse against which to test the value of new poetry, "if we have tact and can use them." He quotes as one of the touchstones

> Io non piangevo; si dentro impietrai,
> Piangevan elli.   [*Inferno*, 33. 39–40]

To accept the *Inferno* is not to subscribe to a creed but to enter on a journey to the depths; in his recent translation of this same episode of Ugolino and Archbishop Roger, the best of poets now writing in English (he is an Irishman) has included a vision of something much nearer home.

> I walked the ice
> And saw two soldered in a frozen hole
> On top of other, one's skull capping the other's,
> Gnawing at him where the neck and head
> Are grafted to the sweet fruit of the brain,
> Like a famine victim at a loaf of bread.[6]

Events change the poet's terms; and to read this must now include "doing literature in Sligo Bay."

Fifty years after Matthew Arnold, the task of the critic appeared to be the reconciliation of science and poetry. This task, springing directly out of Arnold's work, was integral to the English studies of my youth in Cambridge, in a period now fifty years behind us. I. A. Richards used the passage from Arnold first quoted above as epigraph for his *Science and Poetry* (1926)—a book he rewrote several times and last revised, in 1970, at Cambridge, Massachusetts.

If I now attempt, in the light of Sidney and Arnold, to assess the dilemmas and paradoxes, issuing in action, of literature and the study of literature over this last half century, it must be in terms of the actions initiated by my teachers, of literature as "the actually loved and known."[7] The poetry of Heaney offers a contemporary example of how poetry is sustained by the past that is always present. So I shall return to it at the end of my assessment. The object of the writer's quest is "To conserve, to develop, to bring together, to make significant for the present what the past holds, without dilution or any deleting but rather by understanding and transubstantiating the material . . . neither pedantic nor popularising, not indifferent to scholarship, not antiquarian, but saying always, 'of these thou has given me, have I lost none.'"[8]

In *Science and Poetry*, I. A. Richards presented the psychological justification of poetry, as a deed. Poetry disturbs the mind and at the same time provides means by which disturbances can adjust themselves. "The poets are failing us, or we them, if after reading them, we do not find ourselves changed."[9] By concentrating on the psychology of the reader, Richards dissolved the reified poem and was consequently left with the questions of value and of communication. (Later he was to reestablish the autonomy of the poem as process.) He once went so far as to assert that "God's in his heaven, all's well with the world" might be read as "All's well here and now with the nervous system," and the diagrams to illustrate paths of impulses gave his first audience the exhilarated feeling that boundaries were really being crossed. Richards, however, combined the training of a scientist with the temperament of a poet. The immense sense of urgency was conveyed by his reading a passage from his friend T. S. Eliot or one from Joseph Conrad (at that time considered passé). The reading constituted analysis, with the peculiar attention that Practical Criticism enjoined. In his book with that title (1929) the experiment of giving his class unidentified poems and inviting comments had uncovered the ability to swallow nonsense—or to construct it—that passed for reading. In exposing the complexity of the transactions between writer and reader, Richards was to alter the way literature was taught. He did not regard this as merely a literary matter: "It is not true that criticism is a luxury trade. The rearguard of society cannot be extricated till the vanguard has gone further. . . . For the arts are inevitably and quite apart from any intention of the artist an appraisal of existence."[10]

Richards brought together in his own studies philosophy, psychology, and literary theory. He also expected his audience to have gained some knowledge of these areas and of anthropology and other literatures. He assumed that sort of audience; and in the small, intimate Cambridge of those days he refused to notice the demarcations of academic subjects. Some of the doubts expressed by Geoffrey Hartman about Practical Criticism or New Criticism as it became in the U.S.A. therefore do not apply to the English variety. If the pressures of social change sometimes involved dramatic predictions of doom,[11] Richards always remained confident. His social concern led to practical experiments in the artificial system of Basic English; his sense both of the difficulties and complexities of the language took him to Peking at the age of eighty-six to restart this simplified form of communication with the Chinese. (As if in compensation for those almost indecipherable annotations with which his later books were loaded; every word had to be qualified, examined, refused, or granted the status of a referent.) When at the age of sixty or so, he first took to writing poetry himself, encouraged by his friend Robert Lowell, he found himself "taken over" by language. He seems to have subscribed to the view Eliot put forward in *Three Voices of Poetry* (1953) that

> What you start from is nothing so definite as an emotion, in any ordinary sense; it is still less an idea; it is . . . a

bodiless childful of voice in the gloom
Crying with frog voice 'What shall I be?'[12]

for a section of his revised version of *Science and Poetry, Poetries and Sciences* (1970) was entitled "How does a Poem Know When it is Finished?" One of his own poems employed a metaphor from his private form of "doing"—the mountaineering that took him to Sikkim, Burma, the Western Hills of Peking, the Japanese Alps, the Diamond Mountains of Korea, the Tai Shan of Shantung . . . and always back to the Alps. The poem is "Lighting Fires in Snow."

Tread out a marble hollow
Then lay the twigs athwart,
Teepeewise or wigwam,
So that the air can follow
The match flame from the start
As we begin a poem
And some may win a heart. . . .
As the under cavern reddens
Leave well alone!
Cold fuel only deadens,
But pile across the smoke,
And give the dog a bone.
For it's life's sake, don't poke!
The wise fire knows its own.

The wise poem knows its father. . . .[13]

Robert Lowell wrote to him:

The imperishable Byronics of the Swiss Alps
change to a landscape for your portrait,
casual, unconventional, innocent, earned—
gratuitous rashness and serpentine hesitation . . .
you know you will move on; the absolute
bald peaked glare-ice, malignly beckons . . . goodbye earth.[14]

His friend and pupil, Sir William Empson, afforded him a new appendix of Practical Criticism for *Poetries and Sciences*, in the analysis of one of his Cambridge poems. Both Richards and Empson became involved in such a variety of public work, always maintaining amateur status in a very grand way, that in a sense they acquired no following, founded no school. They never looked for disciples, only for friends.

F. R. Leavis (an exact contemporary of Richards in years, but his junior at the university) began by taking his bearings from "Mr. I. A. Richards, whose opinion is worth more than most people's,"[15] and from Eliot and Empson. But his aim was always to show, to teach, as theirs were not. In the words of Isaiah Berlin, Richards was a fox and Leavis a hedgehog. The two men resembled one another in the high charge of nervous energy that, on encounter, gave a distinct shock and also in the air of being at once threatened and confident. Leavis's words of appeal, "That is so, is it not?" never seemed to anticipate the answer, "No, it isn't." Yet when describing his approach to poetry, a "kind of reverent openness," he resembled nothing so much as a fourteenth-century devotional writer, such as Julian of Norwich, on the act of prayer.

"Tentative in his movements, [Richards] always seemed able to come back without difficulty from any position, however experimental," wrote Mrs. Richards to John Holloway of her husband's climbing tactics. Leavis, too, assumed a tentative procedure, but his program was determined.

In *How to Teaching Reading, a Primer for Ezra Pound* (1933), the mapped exercises in Practical Criticism ("Test . . . do comparisons" and the like) were designed by Leavis to illustrate the historic development of English. Later he said, "Practical criticism means for me criticism in practice. It is hardly possible to insist too much on the training of sensibility as prior and irremissible. Literary study unassociated with it becomes, infallibly, 'academic' and barren—a matter of profitless memorizing, of practice in graceful or scholarly irrelevancies . . . or of discipline at the higher navvying."[16] "The training of sensibility" implies that the reader's self-criticism is being exercised; but this was often taken as judgment upon the work itself, and so provoked the kind of reaction that is shown in Helen Gardner's *The Business of Criticism* (1959): "To attempt to measure the amount of value, to declare or to attempt to declare that this poem is more valuable than that, or to range authors in an order of merit, does not seem to me to be the true business of criticism . . . to attempt to train young people in this kind of discrimination seems to me a folly, if not a crime."[17] Leavis developed the technique of Practical Criticism as an instrument of teaching the history of literature, for he thought that "the relation of the individual artist to others, to the contemporary world and to the past, to be grasped at all, must be grasped in limited particulars."[18]

But, because "it is only in the present that the past lives," (*English Literature in Our Time in the University*, p. 68) literature as the consciousness of the age demanded above all attention to the present. As Eliot, Yeats, Joyce, D. H. Lawrence, E. M. Forster, and Virginia Woolf were all then at work, this was not difficult. The energies released by World War I and its tensions dictated the revival of Donne and the metaphysicals in an attempt to include all the negative feelings that war had generated. For many, Eliot's *Waste Land* represented the first contemporary attempt to order chaos; if at first he repudiated the idea, saying this was a personal poem only, later he came to recognize that a poem may carry more significance to his generation than the author recognizes. It may be modified by its currency in the world. Richards went so far in *Poetries and Sciences* as to claim that poems correct their own mistakes and buy their own railway tickets. We are defined by "what we want," poems by what they may become.

Literature, according to Leavis, being the central subject in education, he evaded any statement of philosophic or political commitment—the complex language of literature alone being adequate for full statements. But he committed himself to practice in his educational program, for which the founding of *Scrutiny* was a prerequisite. This movement became concerned with teaching in schools, especially after the Butler Education Act (1944) opened new possibilities for "the meritocracy."

Leavis wrote, "In Education . . . the power of the Press, of the advertiser and of the literary racket can be challenged as nowhere else. Education, that is, is very unusually practical politics, and without a movement in education, it is difficult to take any kind of politics seriously."[19] Literature remained Leavis's world; he chose to feel exhilarated and threatened at the same time. (Even after fame had arrived, he remained in Cambridge for his working life, but for one who had spent the years between 1914 and 1918 in Flanders mud, this did not imply lack of experience as some of his bêtes noires, like the BBC, were apt to suggest.) He never spoke of those years; but their effect may be gauged by his extraordinary attitude to Milton (the only book he carried in his pocket during the war) and by his appalled rejection of systems, coupled with the manufacture of little ways to get round them (tips for examination technique). He was an excellent strategist, an intuitive one; literature was for him, as it had been for Matthew Arnold, David's sling with which he went out against the Philistine.

Literature, as offering primal order in a situation where no other order can be worked out, makes it still a "deed" in societies that are changing rapidly or that are in a state of internal conflict. A primal release of free energy, it is now polarised with political systems, for these have replaced the scientific systems of the nineteenth and the religious systems of the sixteenth centuries as limiting channels or categories. Poetry, still the companion of the camps, made World War I tolerable for Leavis; since World War II, smaller nations and ethnic groups under alien power have used literature in the manner first developed by the *Résistance*. In Russia an underground network of publication distributes writing from twelve national copying centers; in Prague a circulating library of books from the West is driven round in a van by an ex-professor, now a lorry driver. As a form of "internal emigration," literature supplies active self-defense against the dull uniformity of official "works of art," where the aim is to blanket response; it serves, in Pound's words, as "nutrition of impulse."

Its status as a world language and the richness of its literary heritage enable English to serve this purpose in regions where incipient nationalism might seem to dictate the use of local speech.

Although a second language for blacks in South Africa, it gains steadily against the strong local pressures in favor of Africaans. The combination of censorship and the small market in South Africa means that much of this writing first appears in London; for example, the essays of Steve Biko, the activist leader from the Xhosa, who in 1977 died in police custody. André Brink, an Afri-kaner brave enough to protest, continues to produce his novels both in Africaans and English, and the success abroad of *A Dry White Season* in 1979 forced the lifting of a local ban. Although Steve Biko's *I Write What I Like*, being political, remains banned, the oral nature of much African black culture restores power to the word. If in South Africa, literature is in Leavis's words, very practical politics, poetry remains here the most natural form of education, especially when combined with music and dance. In the urban centers there is much communal playing; local groups find here "nutrition of impulse" in Soweto and elsewhere. The great barracklike building that houses the University of South Africa deals by correspondence with forty thousand pupils, some of whom are in jail. They write in English, for the language has been appropriated and converted as the prison on Robben Island has become a shrine (English is after all a minority language now). Black poetry in English dates from 1968. If this conversion is only imaginative, yet it is affecting practice.

Poetry is still a deed, even if certificates in computer science have priority at Fort Hare.

> they know what they have lost
> they guess at what they've gained
> divining an innocent justice[20]

Perhaps the most articulate voice in English poetry today came out of Ulster where political and cultural tensions find in poetry their energies may be unchanneled. Seamus Heaney, son of a farmer, taught English at Queen's University Belfast; after a few years for meditation in the Wicklow Hills, he now teaches in a training college in Dublin.

The first poem in which he found a voice was written in 1964.

Here he felt "I had let down a shaft into real life."[21] It opens with the crack of a couplet, like a shot:

> Between my finger and my thumb
> The squat pen rests; snug as a gun.[22]

In affectionate and tender recollection, seeing his father digging a flower bed, he recalls digging on the farm

> The coarse boot nestled on the lug, the shaft
> Against the inside knee was levered firmly . . .
>
> By God, the old man could handle a spade.
> Just like his old man . . .
>
> But I've no spade to follow men like these.
>
> Between my finger and my thumb
> The squat pen rests. I'll dig with it.

"Heaney's spade" became something of a joke among his fellow poets in Ulster. He had "found a voice" for a new kind of "higher navvying." "To analyse the craft of putting feelings into words is inevitably, I think, to talk about poetry as divination, poetry as revelation of the self to the self, poems as elements of continuity, with the aura and authenticity of archaeological finds."[23] So the discovery of the self generally begins, Heaney thinks, with the "voice" in another who has "spoken something essential to you, some thing you recognise instinctively as a true sounding of aspects of yourself and your experience." Gerard Manley Hopkins, and later Wordsworth, gave Heaney "voices"; from Wordsworth he learned what he calls "technique" as distinct from "craft"— "the discovery of ways to go out of his normal cognitive bounds and raid the inarticulate." In Heaney this has been the discovery of dread, the unfocused form of fear. Fear, because it is recognized, may be controlled. Dread is unrealized, "a bodiless childful of life in the gloom." When "the killings" started in the summer of 1969, Heaney's poems on the prehistoric finds of ritual victims, dug up

in the bogs of Denmark, presented a horror appropriate to Bog-
side, "adequate to our predicament." He wrote, "I felt it imperative
to discover a field of force in which, without abandoning fidelity to
the processes and experiences of poetry . . . it would be possible
to encompass the perspectives of a humane reason and at the same
time to grant the religious intensity of the violence its deplorable
authenticity and complexity."[24]

In the North there have been layers of invaders, among them the
Vikings, who established a series of small kingdoms round the
Irish Sea. Where Heaney identified these invaders with the later
Scots, with the Orangemen, with Carson, and also went back to
their origins, in Denmark, he reached a level beyond the cognitive.
On the coast he found

> only the secular
> Powers of the Atlantic thundering

he heard out of the barrows another voice

> It said Thor's hammer swung
> To geography and trade
> thick-witted couplings and revenges[25]

So he went on a pilgrimage to Aarhus, to see the Tollund Man and
the Grauballe Man. The sensuous richness of Heaney's verse—described by one reviewer as "mud-caked fingers in Russell Square"
—found a new voice and a new image of action, comparable to
the great images of Yeats. The second poem is more completely
realized in the image than the first, which has a residue of commentary:

> As if he had been poured
>   In tar, he lies
> On a pillow of turf and seems to weep
>
>   the black river of himself
> the grain of his wrists
>   Is like bog oak . . .

The chin is a visor "raised above the vent of his slashed throat";
he lies

> with the actual weight
> of each hooded victim
> slashed and dumped.[26]

It is not known who killed whom. Cause and guilt become irrelevant; guilt is universal; anonymity shows "the doom of man,"
unreversed. On the prehistoric woman victim, the commentary is
again more explicit:

> I who have stood dumb
> when your betraying sisters
> cauled in tar,
> wept by the railings
>
> who would connive
> in civilized outrage
> yet understand the exact
> and tribal, intimate revenge[27]

Heaney had recovered myth, thus linking the immediate present
of dread with factual history. The Irish government refused to
allow the site of the old Viking city in Dublin to be preserved; they
bulldozed over it to erect an office block. Myth was meaningless
to bureaucrats.

Borrowing and twisting for his own use a phrase from Philip
Sidney, "Among the Romans a poet was called *a Vates*, which is as
much as a diviner," Heaney had used in his first volume the image
of the "divination." The man

> Circling the terrain, hunting the pluck
> Of water

with a hazel fork, till suddenly "the pluck came sharp as a sting."
The bystanders would ask to try.

> It lay dead in their grasp till nonchalantly
> He gripped expectant wrists. The hazel stirred.[28]

So in South Africa, "divining an innocent justice," the people themselves stir; they are the small living force that conquers the dead weight of earth, signaling hidden springs.

In times of stress the consolation lies in "the actually loved and known."[29] Killings are somehow consoled in the present by this.

> Who's sorry for our trouble?
> Who dreamt that we might dwell among ourselves
> In rain and scoured light and wind—dried stones? . . .
>
> And today a girl walks home to us
> Carrying a basket full of new potatoes,
> Three tight green cabbages, and carrots
> With the tops and mould still fresh on them.[30]

That could not be formulated as a political hope, yet it stands; for "The Unacknowledged Legislator's Dream" (the title of another poem) carries the power to change those who read it.

NOTES

1. This and preceding quotations are from Sir Philip Sidney's *Defence of Poesie* c. 1579, in answer to Stephen Gosson, *The School of Abuse*, which had been dedicated to Sidney.
2. Geoffrey H. Hartman, "A Short History of Practical Criticism," *New Literary History* (Spring 1979): 495–509.
3. Quoted by Matthew Arnold from his own earlier work at the opening of "The Study of Poetry," *Essays in Criticism*, 2d ser. (London and New York: Macmillan, 1888); see *Complete Prose Works*, ed. R. H. Super (Ann Arbor: University of Michigan Press, 1973), 9:161–88.
4. "Dover Beach," *New Poems*, 1867; probably written June 1851.

See *The Poems of Matthew Arnold*, ed. Kenneth Allott (London and New York: Longman's, 1965), pp. 139–43.

5. Introduction and Preface to *Literature and Dogma* (London, 1873; New York, 1883). See *Complete Prose Works* (1968), 6:151, 168.

6. Seamus Heaney, *Field Work* (London and Boston: Faber and Faber, 1979), p. 61; from *Inferno*, Canto 33, 124–29.

7. "Only what is actually loved and known can be seen *sub specie aeternitatis*"; David Jones, Preface to *The Anathemata*, (London: Faber and Faber, 1962), p. 24.

8. David Jones, *Epoch and Artist*, ed. H. Grisewood (New York: Chilmark Press, 1949), p. 243.

9. *Science and Poetry*, Psyche Miniatures, no. 1 (Cambridge: C. K. Ogden, 1926), pp. 18, 43.

10. *Principles of Literary Criticism* (London and New York: Routledge and Kegan Paul, 1924), p. 61.

11. Christopher Isherwood, *Lions and Shadows* (London: Leonard and Virginia Woolf at the Hogarth Press, 1938), p. 12.

12. T. S. Eliot, *On Poetry and Poets* (London: Faber and Faber, 1962), p. 98.

13. I. A. Richards, "*Goodbye, Earth*," reprinted in *New and Selected Poems* (Manchester and London: The Carcanet Press, 1978), p. 12.

14. *I. A. Richards: Essays in his Honour*, ed. Reuben A. Brower et al. (London and New York: Oxford University Press, 1973).

15. F. R. Leavis, *Mass Civilization and Minority Culture* (Cambridge: The Minority Press, 1930), p. 31. This was Leavis's earliest publication. In it he records his reservations concerning Basic English.

16. F. R. Leavis, *How To Teach Reading: A Primer for Ezra Pound* (Cambridge: The Minority Press, 1933), pp. 26–27.

17. Helen Gardner, *The Business of Criticism* (London and New York: Oxford University Press, 1959), pp. 7–13.

18. *How To Teach Reading*, p. 35. Cf. his last published work, *The Living Principle* (London: Chatto and Windus, 1975), pp. 13–14.

19. *Scrutiny*; from a manifesto issued c. 1933.

20. Guy Butler, "The Divine Underground" *Selected Poems* (Johannesburg: Ad. Donker, 1975), p. 88. Fort Hare is the black university college where men from all over Africa were educated; now it is confined to local people in one of the tribal "homelands."

21. Seamus Heaney, "Feeling into Words," *Innovations in Contemporary Literature*, ed. Vincent Cronin, Transactions of the Royal Society of Literature of the United Kingdom, New Series (London and New York: Oxford University Press, 1979). Subsequent quotations are also from this essay, given as a lecture originally in 1974.

22. Seamus Heaney, "Digging," *Death of a Naturalist* (London: Faber and Faber, 1966), p. 13.

23. See note 21.

24. See note 21.

25. Seamus Heaney, "North," *North* (London: Faber and Faber, 1975), p. 19.

26. "The Graubelle Man," *North*, pp. 35–36.

27. "Punishment," *North*, p. 37.

28. "The Diviner," *The Death of a Naturalist*, p. 36.

29. See note 7 above.

30. Seamus Heaney, "Triptych," *Field Work* (London and Boston: Faber and Faber, 1979), p. 12.

PART THREE

THE HUMANITIES IN

SOCIETY

ABRAHAM EDEL AND

ELIZABETH FLOWER

❦ ELITISM AND CULTURE

THE ANALYSIS OF such concepts as liberalism and conservatism, virtue, culture, and civilization that shape our perception of social reality and its problems is no easy task. Not only their present use is significant, but also their history, the context in which they arose, their interrelations with other ideas, the functions they served, and the consequences they encouraged. Often their history will leave, perhaps unnoticed, a mark on the present that carries a distinct coloring and affects their utility.

Such a concept is that of *the elite*. It has a historical career, it enters into historical events as participant. We are tempted to hold it responsible for benefits bestowed as well as havoc created. It cannot be evaluated in general terms, for it may have different consequences in different fields, and these consequences may seriously affect policy. Perhaps its continued use distorts our perceptions and blocks fresh and more creative approaches. We are led to wonder whether the concept of the elite has outlived its usefulness. Our strategy here is, first, to look at some aspects of the historical career of elitism, and, second, to review a recent situation in which it cantankerously exploded on the American cultural-political scene (which assures that it is not a dead issue). Thereafter we scan appeals to the elite in politics, education, and culture and offer a conclusion.

The basic distinction in elitism is between *elite* and *mass*. Elitism is an outlook (including a theory) that takes this distinction to be fundamental in understanding society and culture and in guiding social policy. It takes the elite to be the source of knowledge and culture, the guardian of quality, the preserver of standards, and the proper locus of leadership and authority. Populism is often regarded as the contrary or opposing outlook, believing vitality to lie in the mass. Populism would hold that policy should be directed to removing the shackles of tradition and authority that have bound it and that where a choice is necessary, resources should be directed to the education and liberation of the masses.

In earlier times the elite were an established aristocracy; the masses had no share in their activities. The lines were visible. Power and glory, as well as accomplishment, lay on one side. (Historians still have problems finding out what went on across the line.) The division was justified by theories of all sorts—theological and metaphysical, biological and social. Plato gave elitism a strong start with an underlying theory of human nature in which he saw the human psyche as composed of appetite (the dragon), will or spirit (the lion), and reason (the human). Appetite is demanding; lacking in self-control, it requires continual repression by reason with the aid of spirit. Assuming that reason is strong only in the few, Plato makes the central social task to be the need for restraint of the masses by the elite.

So blunt a theme admits of many variations in the history of aristocracy and elitism. Burke renews it for the modern world in the thesis that tradition is central to restraint, that respect and veneration for the traditional are essential bonds not to be lightly loosened, that if there are natural rights the most important is the right of the people to be protected against themselves, that it is better to retain any privilege however arbitrary than to precipitate the spirit of revolt against all privilege. In the nineteenth century, democratic advances in politics and democratic programs for education were opposed as diminishing respect for authority and opening the door to the passions of the populace. Even such a liberal as John Stuart Mill feared (in his *On Liberty*) that individuality was being swamped by popular conformity, while conservatives raised the slogan of liberty versus equality, suggesting the premise that the masses cannot achieve equality without ruining the liberties that support quality and culture.

In the early part of our century, the self-styled elite among our college youth could be reassured about their superiority by reading H. L. Mencken's column in the *American Mercury* in which he jibed at the American "booboisie" and depicted its antics. Or they could turn, in the academic world, to the humanism of Irving Babbitt and find democracy accused of lacking standards and engaged in "the irresponsible quest of thrills."[1] Babbitt analyzed the psyche more genially than did Plato or Burke; not simply the aggressive and the predatory but the sympathetic and the humanitarian could work havoc. The humanitarian goes astray, for example, by seeing in the college "a means not so much for the thorough training of the few as of uplift for the many."[2] Only an inner discipline (of which apparently few were capable) could maintain civilization. In the grim struggles of the 1930s under the shadow of fascism, there was despair about the impasse of democracy, even in the United States. The idea of government by the people was repeatedly attacked as leading to chaos. "Government by the consent of the governed" was interpreted as at most the right of the people to elect their rulers, not to participate in governmental decision making.

The advance of democratic ideas from the seventeenth century on had been slow, and from the beginning it was attacked as "leveling." When, however, political democracy became fairly widespread in the Western world, the concept of the elite could not survive by identification with aristocracy. It began to lose its immediate descriptive validity as a concentrated and isolated elite was dissipated. The opposition to leveling had then to move from an outside criticism of democracy as a whole to an inside advocacy of policy within an established democratic framework. The elitist response was not to abandon the distinction of elite and mass but democratically to open the elite to the best of the multitude. When all come to wear the same clothes and use the same language and even have a higher education (although the beginnings of mass higher education are not yet half a century behind us in the industrially advanced countries) it may be difficult to spot who are the elite. Aristotle had said that nature intended some for slavery and that if nature had not mistakenly given some slaves the appearance of natural masters we could tell at a glance which were which. Moderns have sometimes thought that if we could peer into the minds and hearts (and genes?) of men and women, we would know who was destined for accomplishment. In the absence of such an easy way, meritocracy is invoked: keep the doors open and let success make the choice.

Admittedly, such a democratic conception of an elite tends to yield a dispersed elite. But it firmly saves the concept. Indeed, by becoming democratized, elitism seems almost to purify itself of any concern but excellence. The once sinister distinction between elite and mass seems now a truism and harmless. It simply asserts that there are in every field some who are abler, and they usually go farther. Everybody, it may be said, plays baseball, but only a few make the teams and fewer yet are stars. They are the elite. Many people go in for acting, but only a few make it; they become the elite. In every field some are *chosen* (the root idea of "elite" —the elect). Culturally, the elite write the successful books, get the top jobs, edit the successful journals, are wooed by the aspiring young, and so on. Even after the spread of higher education, the total productive group in all disciplines—those who produce as distinct even from those who perpetuate—is relatively small. A Shakespeare, a Newton, an Einstein, a Freud, a Mozart, are scarcely of the rank and file.

Comfortably ensconced within democracy, then, the concept was untroubled as long as the meritocratic idea went unchallenged. The world of the elite has perhaps to acquiesce in some dilution of culture as the multitude are encouraged to enter that world. This, however, simply reinforces a distinction between the higher culture of the few and the popular culture of the many. But with the populist "revolt of the masses" under the banner of the equalitarian ideal, the elitist sees a real threat emerging in the challenge to the standards of excellence. As the elitist sees it, the belief that "vox populi vox dei" has been spreading from politics to culture. Standards of excellence are being rejected as expressing the aristocratic values of the establishment, and the emptiness that results is being filled by any populist wind that blows. The taste of the populace, anything that "turns them on," becomes the test of quality. Elitism is thus confronted by populism in one or another theoretical form, and the antagonism between quality and equality comes out in the open. The question is now far removed from aristocracy. In politics, elitism conceives the contemporary task to be control of the demos within the democratic framework; in education, to select from the many those who are most able; in culture —regarded as itself an elitist concept—to foster the creative few.

To have pushed such issues into the center of democratic attention is the triumph of the democratized concept of the elite, for the dichotomy of the elite and the mass is perpetuated in the very formulations. Even populism counterattacks with the same distinction. Yet there is a far different possibility—that the dichotomy as it has historically emerged is now outworn, that the issues packed away in the concepts should now be separated and analyzed in different terms and the dichotomy itself abandoned. This is the thesis we wish to explore.

The power of a categorial dichotomy is not to be underestimated. The history of thought is strewn with dichotomies in terms of which questions were formulated, theoretical energies riveted, and answers constrained. Take, for example, the twentieth century's obsession with the cleavage between fact and value. This involved desperate attempts to parcel out phenomena, linguistic forms, activities, disciplines. It isolated science from ethics and insulated ethics, thereby supporting a science without responsibility and an ethics cut off from the growing resources of science. Decades passed until the realization grew—it has not yet been fully grasped —that the presumed absolute dichotomy is a relative distinction, useful in some contexts, irrelevant in others where other distinctions are more fruitful and where to cast inquiry in this presumed absolute only creates intellectual havoc.[3] Similar problems can be found in the history of absolute dichotomies of matter and mind, body and soul, human and divine, objective and subjective, sense and intellect, cognitive and affective, and countless others.

Has the dichotomy of elite and mass now run its course? Will democratizing the distinction rescue it, or do our problems require some other mode of organizing the study of social and cultural differences?

Before we enter on the several fields, let us examine the contrast of elitism and populism at work in a public controversy that recently swept the journalistic reportage of culture.[4] Here, for example, are some headlines, largely from the Arts and Leisure section of the Sunday *New York Times* from 1977 to 1979: "Funding Culture, High and Low, and Calling it all Art" (16 October 1977); "Elitism, In the Arts, Is Good" (5 February 1978); " 'Elitism' in Arts and Humanities Units Is Debated" (27 April 1978); "A Populist Shift in Federal Cultural Support" (13 May 1979). The issue erupted when President Jimmy Carter considered fresh appointments to head the National Endowment for the Humanities (NEH) and the National Endowment for the Arts (NEA). Senator Claiborne Pell had criticized NEH for leaning to esoteric projects instead of reaching out to the length and breadth of the country; he called it a pale shadow in comparison to its sister arts establishment, which "generated more momentum" at the "grass roots." NEH was said to have an elitist image, and the taint of elitism seems to have been fatal to some candidates. NEH was also said to be serving a narrow academic constituency instead of a broader popular constituency. These criticisms—pursuit of the esoteric, elitism, narrow academic constituency—were usually packaged as if they were one or aspects of one defect. When Joseph Duffey was nominated to head NEH, *The Chronicle of Higher Education* had a story headed, "The Humanist Endowment: Elitist or Populist? Carter's Nominee as chairman says agency can be both."

It may be said that the exigency of headlining drives to sharp contrasts. Yet the stories themselves show that this was indeed the structuring of the issues. We find questions like "Are we really prepared to sacrifice quality for numbers?" Elitism in culture and the arts is also equated with "the influence of acknowledged achievement of a high order." Among other strong statements we find:

"Intellectual activity, of which the arts is one manifestation, is and always has been elitist. Demagogues and yahoos do not like this; they would like to drag us down to their own level." "On its highest level the appreciation of art is as elitist as the creation of art. Those listening to a Beethoven symphony, content merely to let the music wash over them, are operating at a very low level." "Elitism of the intellect should be a term of praise rather than disparagement." One participant in the debate was reported as offering a history of elitism defined as "concern for the best" and as contrasting Matthew Arnold's idea of a democratic culture with that of the minority culture of the highly educated advocated by T. S. Eliot. Another put to Senator Pell the contrast of Athens (which produced Plato, Aristotle, Socrates, Aeschylus, Sophocles, Euripides, Aristophanes, Thucydides) and Sparta (which produced military heroes) and asked whether money for the arts and humanities should go equally to both. Senator Pell said it should, for in that way the arts and humanities might be stimulated in the city that lacked them. Populist policies were taken to be putting support for education in place of support for creation, concentrating on making the humanities comprehensible and useful to the wider public. They were described as arranging "a marriage between popular access and professional excellence." There was fear that the attempt to navigate the treacherous waters between elitism and populism might yield a flabby populism.

The question is whether the formulation of issues in terms of elitism and populism had really tapped the problems that had to be faced, or whether it distorted the argument over real differences of policy. Perhaps the first task is to unpack the bundle of issues about the pursuit of the esoteric, outreach to a broader constituency, and the concept of elitism.

The matter of the esoteric may be disposed of briefly. A problem is esoteric if it can be understood only by a professional in-group, but not by a wider out-group. But the esoteric is relative to time and place. Einstein's theory of relativity was esoteric only at first when just half a dozen people were said to understand his mathematics. Whether in art or science or humanities, what is esoteric in one age may become in the future a prevalent style, unifying theory, or dominant theme. Hence it is not wisdom to avoid investing in the esoteric. Indeed, there is no general problem of the esoteric. There is no point in praising a project or condemning it because it is esoteric. Every esoteric project has to be judged on its own as a separate question. Thus to be esoteric is not necessarily a permanent feature but a changing historical feature. The scholar with an esoteric interest need not be elitist, for elitism deals with a quite different dimension.

The core of elitism, as the statements quoted suggest, is not the values, the excellencies desired, but the conviction that the few are the bearers of such values and that the people at large cannot participate in or create these values and perhaps not even adequately appreciate them. Elitism reflects thus a kind of club spirit or small-establishment spirit. It is not a matter of extent of outreach, but of quality. An outreach to the length and breadth of the country could still remain elitist in spirit. For example, an arts endowment could conceivably offer the objective of "every American child a painter," but if it attempted to do so by furnishing paint-by-number sets it would be an elitist outreach, keeping people inert. The question would be what kind of momentum was generated. Aesthetic feeling cultivates fine shades; it does not simply arouse gross (e.g., aggressive) emotions. Humanistic dialogue engenders deliberative discussion, not simply ideological rhetoric. Elitism takes many different forms in a democratic context. It can be found, for example, in the tendency to talk down to an audience and to render it inert rather than participatory. There is also that strange permissive elitism in which the mere quantity of talk engendered is taken to be the measure of participation, for the attitude to people is paternalistic. In any case it is important not to look for elitism in the wrong place. Elitism is not identical with supporting esoteric projects, and it is not to be identified with supporting the academic. Neglecting the nonacademic often reflects a straight struggle of different interests for support where there are limited resources, just as within education itself graduate and undergraduate and adult divisions vie for greater shares of limited funds. In the case we have examined, there was clearly the fear that wider support of cultural education would be at the expense of cultural creativity through established institutions; sometimes the elitist tone seemed simply added for good measure.

The issue of constituencies to be served by NEH and NEA—or for that matter, by the National Science Foundation—was a wider one than (as one press account put it) the bid of other colleges, junior colleges, labor, ethnic groups, other cultural institutions, against the eastern academic establishment. It was not surprising that the more established academic community got more of the fellowship grants where support for original research was the point involved, for the simple reason that they had more opportunity to store talent for that kind of research. The wider question was what other kinds of educational and cultural objectives should be carried out by the use of public funds and through what other kinds of institutions—museums, labor unions, local groups, informal community organizations, TV and radio, and so on. The language of constituencies concentrated on the fact of different pressure groups, but ignored that of meeting different needs that were neglected or of using different methods that might prove efficacious for the desired objectives.

The central formulation of the problems involved could therefore be carried out only by facing directly the specific tasks required in advancing science, art, humanities. These tasks are of three sorts, just as in the case of education or, for that matter, health. One is advancing original creation: research, investigation, production of an original work, by the professionally equipped. The second is imparting knowledge, communicating learning, offering occasions for appreciation, whether through lectures or performances or other methods, and as widely as possible. The third is developing skills and encouraging participation and practicing, whether in laboratory and scientific experiment, humanistic and scholarly inquiry and writing, artistic production and composition and performance. There will, of course, be some overlapping. Essentially these are the basic functional differences, and all are obviously necessary in an ongoing progressing society over the generations.

The question for any foundation or endowment, the difficult choice given limited resources, concerns distribution and emphasis among objectives.

In an obvious logical sense of "priority" original creation is prior, for if it did not take place there would be nothing to spread educationally and nothing to practice or participate in. There are also other kinds of priority. For example, experience has shown that a wide supporting and understanding public is necessary in a causal sense to stimulate creation and prevent its systematic thwarting and sidetracking. In an understanding, supportive atmosphere, eager spirits among the young turn to the field in greater numbers, audiences exhibit keener taste, and criticism can penetrate to deeper questions of structure and technique rather than be limited to impressions and gross affective responses of consumers. The story of science as well as of art offers evidence. Even when science began to bring large practical benefits in its technological applications, support long was limited to immediate practical gains rather than to underlying basic research. Moreover, the public attitude to the scientist as an elite mystery worker was a ready concomitant of the attitude to the field as esoteric. Both the overconfidence of scientists and technologists in facing the ecological and social consequences of their work and the readiness of a public to turn on science with a revived irrationalism reflect the isolation of science from the citizen and the lack of a general public understanding of science itself. Science education and science journalism and everything from attractive exhibits to mathematical games play a serious part in building a responsible, scientifically minded culture. So, too, in the arts it is not merely that a culture in which men burst into song is one in which opera is more likely to flourish, but that it is more likely to be sensitively appreciative of differences in the quality of singing. The same audience that Aristophanes lampooned hooted an actor from the stage, the story goes, for a subtle mispronunciation. The Spartans, on the contrary, regarded taciturnity as a virtue. Perhaps a National Endowment for Hellenic Art, in ancient times, would not have gone astray if it had invested part of its funds in encouraging ordinary Spartans to talk, for the love of talk is the first step to distinguishing good from sloppy talk.

Tocqueville is often quoted for the view that democracy has a leveling effect on culture, that low culture drives out high culture. It is well to recall that John Stuart Mill, in his long and careful review of *Democracy in America*, argued that commercialism, not democracy, was a cause of such phenomena and that although America was much more advanced in commercialism, Britain in his day was already beginning to show the same effects. Mill's thesis well merits consideration today when we hear tirades against popular low culture, particularly in the light of what is going on in television and in book publishing, where the desire for huge immediate profits is hemming in the "high."

In sum, of the three tasks—supporting creation, educating for wider understanding and appreciation, encouraging experimental practice—to concentrate only on the first is like watering the stronger plants without attending to the soil in which they grow and ignoring the struggling shoots. It may be added that without support for the third task as well as the second the older models of creation are likely to become tyrannical. Ample evidence of this can be found in the history of successive revolutions in modern painting as well as in the difficulties encountered by research in the humanities that goes counter to prevailing schools.

Such considerations justify public support for all three tasks, not merely the first, but do not provide a formula for partitioning support. The fact is that there is no formula. Decisions have to be made not by rule, but by careful analysis in context of circumstances and prospects. Consider the parallel of an educational system in a developing country. Shall it invest its limited resources in a primary school system that raises the educational level of the whole population, though in a rudimentary way, or shall it select the most promising to create an advanced core of highly educated professionals by sending them to advanced educational systems in other countries? Surely the answer depends on the economy, whether the professionals are now absolutely necessary for the productive well-being of the country, whether they will return when educated or enter the stream of a "brain drain" to more comfortable modes of life elsewhere, what mixture of objectives is possible, what are the longer-run aims of the country for development, and numerous other relevant considerations. Not least might be whether absence of education at the lower level at home might retard health and production and industrial advance and whether supporting a select core might create a middle class isolated from the people and likely to pursue its own advantage. The weighing of complex possibilities is a central and familiar feature of policy decision.

The situation in the controversy we have been exploring is parallel. It might be worth comparing the science and art and humanities endowments with respect to the three tasks distinguished. In scientific fields there have been fewer complaints because scientific research is the recognized prime objective; nevertheless, greater attention has been paid in recent years to advancing public science education and encouraging entry into scientific work. In the arts, although part of the resources went to fellowships for artists and composers and some to encourage Americans to engage in artistic production, not merely to appreciate artistic performances, the focus on the second task was probably the secret of popularity for it made performance much more widespread. The humanities endowment traditionally gave a considerable part of its resources for scholarly fellowships, doing for humanistic research what the science endowment did for scientific research. With regard to the second task it was in a different position from the arts endowment, for this area of educational work is traditionally part of the curriculum of the high schools and liberal arts colleges, whereas performance in the arts has much less place in the educational curriculum. The humanities endowment thus played more a stimulating role, for example, on fresh methods (such as newspaper courses), TV programs on special topics reaching a wide audience, programs for senior citizens, and so on. In its state-based public programs it tried linking the second and third objectives, encouraging the cooperation of the academic and the nonacademic in consideration of public policy. The underlying assumption here was not merely that academic humanists had something to offer for consideration of public policy but that the public experience would enhance their view of their own fields and their understanding of the full scope of their work.

Whatever the values of particular experiments and programs, there seems little place, in evaluating them or deciding whether to adopt to abandon them, for the concept of elitism and its general dispute with populism. Its only effect would be to foreclose experiment by an assurance that all experiment is bound to fail. To regard such assurance as the lesson of past experience would be naive, for the past was an aristocratic world, the world of an elitist establishment, or restricted education and restricted participation. The development of democratic political forms was faced with the same arguments, the same assurances, the same forebodings, the same neglect of critical points and revolutionary changes in human life and social institutions. Of course, there is no antecedent guarantee of success, but this calls all the more for experiment, not for fixed apprehension of failure.

Let us now look at the part that the concept of the elite has played in matters of leadership—in politics and political theory.

Politics is a natural home for elitist concepts. As long as aristocracy in one or another form prevailed, the ruling group was clearly set off from the mass, and it monopolized the power, the glory, the benefits, and the culture. The long rise of democratic forms appeared to fragment the power, scatter the glory, hand around the benefits. Culture, however, remained concentrated in the educated classes, and here the question was who had access to education and what kind.

Elitist political theory in the twentieth century rejects the appearances. It sees the liberal hope of a shifting pluralistic pattern of power as vain, and it turns against the Marxian dynamics of proletarian revolution with its dream of universal liberation. It is best seen in the modern Machiavellian tradition that speaks in the name of realism: whatever the formal description of government, it is said, every society has a ruling group and the masses follow. Revolution in the name of the masses is deceptive; it only means that a new ruling group takes over. Vilfredo Pareto underscores the irrational relations of the mass to the rulers, with its affective responses to charisma. Robert Michels studies the oligarchic processes in democratic society and indeed in socialist movements and formulates his iron law of oligarchy. Gaetano Mosca bluntly redefines democracy as a ruling class open from below. James Burnham looks about for the emerging new class and pinpoints the technical group that is taking hold in the managerial revolution.[5] All this occurred in the first four decades of the twentieth century when the dream of a spreading universal democracy began to be overshadowed by world war, the rise of communism, the emergence of fascism and nazism, and the consequent general feeling that democracy was in retreat and at an impasse.

The elitist stance not only invaded political analysis and redefined democracy, it also staked out a commanding position in the philosophical analysis of social concepts. It extended far beyond the Machiavellians; for example, Bertrand Russell at one point even hoped that power might play the scientific role in social science that energy played in physics.[6] He, however, sought to mute power, whereas the others took the power concentrations to be unavoidable. Yet the attempt to recast political science as the science of the distribution of power had a distinctive character. It was not simply pointing to the importance of pressure and pressure groups as a political phenomenon and urging that ideals be examined in the concrete context of their political functioning, as A. F. Bentley had done in his classic *Process of Government* (1908). Its tone can be seen in the title of Harold D. Lasswell's *Politics: Who Gets What, When, How* (1936) and his initial formulation of politics as the study of influence and the influential: "The influential are those who get the most of what there is to get. Available values may be classified as *deference, income, safety*. Those who get the most are *elite*; the rest are mass."[7] The distinctive character of this view, although evident, is hard to pinpoint: it is not just realism, and it need not be cynicism. Let us try to track it down.

Such power theories present the appearance of neutrality and a generality that could avoid commitment to any one type of ruling class. They realistically formulate laws of the location of power and the rise and circulation of elites. They usually see the important values of a society concentrated in the elite, and they resist any conception of a society without an elite. For example, Lasswell and Abraham Kaplan, in *Power and Society* (1950), probably the most analytically sophisticated of the studies of power, say, "If political equality were defined so as to exclude the existence of an elite, the concept would be vacuous."[8] In such a perspective, the analytic stance of power theory with its concept of the elite clearly is that of the ruling group, not the ruled. Every topic is formulated in terms of the struggle for the maintenance of power of the elite. Goals of the rulers are telescoped into power maintenance and power expansion, and their psychic expression is prestige and the claim of greater reward in values received. The aims and ideals of the ruled enter only as they provide firm or insecure bases for the maintenance and aggrandizement of power. Such a stance suggests that the distinctive character of the approach lies in its self-limitation: it can see nothing as important except what impinges on the power effort and registers on the power barometer. In short, it not merely studies elites but is an elitist outlook. It accepts the implicit presuppositions of the view that the mass is irrational, that it does not count in scientific study except insofar as it affects the power struggles. The borderline between counting for purposes of scientific description and prediction and counting in a value reckoning often becomes very thin.

What are the distorting consequences of such an elitism in political theory? For one, the aims and ideals of the ruled are robbed of authenticity in this way of understanding the needs, conflicts, and directions of striving of the mass of people of the society. Ideals, particularly, are seen as bases for manipulation rather than as the articulation of needs. The approach need not be undemocratic, but its interpretation of democracy as simply a ruling class open from below and coopting the ablest is at most the meritocratic version of democracy noted earlier. By tacitly assuming the disparaging view of the mass and focusing solely on elites, the approach has no tolerance for concepts of democratic leadership, for any forms of participatory democracy, or even for a condition of widespread checks and balances through devices that ensure a broader public deliberation and more persistent popular initiative in determining policies. Its analysis of leadership focuses on the measure of authority preserved or charisma exercised, on the skill in building up and organizing mass support, on the propaganda that is likely to take hold, and so on. Experiments in the democratic world today range from forcing publicity through sunshine laws and legislating by popular initiative to giving workers representation on boards of industrial corporations. There is no guarantee that such experiments will work, but they are not to be written off in advance as sure failures and not worth trying. Our major institutions up to this point have been so overwhelmingly authoritarian that any democratic experiment is hardly likely to get a fair try in the sense that all the variables are under control. The elitist approach would thus incline us to let such experiments go by default.

It might be objected that power theory in the sense described had its day in the midcentury and that political science has since moved away in many other directions. That is perhaps the case for the academic discipline, but it remains in much of practice—obviously in questions of international relations—and markedly in our present political culture. Political life as reflected in the media shows it clearly. Polls are constantly being taken, not about the merits of current measures to advance public well-being and resolve pressing problems of meeting needs, but about how these measures affect the standing of the president (or would-be presidents) in the eyes of the public. News broadcasts raise at every point the question whether a president's specific action will help or hinder his reelection. The net effect of this elitist mode of analysis is to reinforce the power struggle in motivation as well as understanding. In its theoretical as well as its practical impact, it imposes the ghost of the older aristocratic society as the categories of thought and action in a world that has been thoroughly transformed and is seeking to develop its own categories.

Although elitism in politics operates today largely in a framework of an accepted democratic outlook, attached to either a presumed picture of underlying realities or to the need for a special kind of leadership, an older elitism still marks the practice and outlook of education. The great advances since World War II in educational opportunity in Europe and America remain within a meritocratic framework of opening the doors to the best, even in servicing professional and industrial needs. Some attempts have been made to replace tracking with mainstreaming and to replace separate schools for the elite and the mass with comprehensive schools. The manner of grading and testing, which tends to turn schooling into the fashioning of an elite by the way it shapes student motivation and teacher attitudes, has also come under growing suspicion. The functional distinction between liberal and technical or vocational education is still often assimilated to a distinction of higher or lower status. The equalitarian ideal that would invite every student to partake of whatever education he or she can master, needs, or is interested in has only begun to be implemented. In the successive liberation movements of Blacks, women, the aged, the handicapped, children, and other groups, the demand for open education of quality has spread throughout the whole community, bringing in larger and larger masses of people. The pressure on services and resources has been great and confusion of aims and methods rampant. In the resulting complex social conflicts, the same fears we noted earlier have found frequent expression: the dilution of standards, the loss of excellence, the threat of a populism that rejects traditional quality as the ideological bias of an establishment. A few remarks on the issues of quality, popular capacity, and attitude to differences may therefore be pertinent.

It is a common mistake to assume that students or people generally lack a sense of quality or excellence and that it is imparted to them with great difficulty. Children engage in all sorts of physical activity—they run and fight, play ball and skate, and as they grow older drive cars or repair machines. The role of learning and of practice in acquiring skill is no mystery to them in at least one or another domain. In the commercialism of our culture they rapidly distinguish the shoddy from the well constructed—in tools, clothes, equipment. General attitudes to sport have almost a religious character with detailed attention to ritual and to correctness in performance. The vicarious enjoyment, even worship, of excellence belies the lack of an idea of quality; indeed, the idea is usually accompanied with the understanding of the part played by disciplined practice and hard work in achievement. The educational problem is thus not to impart a sense of excellence where one is lacking, but to direct that sense to additional worthwhile cultural pursuits.

Concerning popular capacity, the dispute is old and persistent. As against elitist assumptions of mass incapacity, critics of contemporary education (often explicitly populist) assign its failures to inadequate resources, outworn methods, entrenched bias against the new entrants to learning, social conditions that incapacitate, and so on. Nearly everyone has some capacity for learning. Did not a person learn to walk, to talk, to distinguish the real from the fantasy about him, to form relations with other people, to work in one field or another? If ways were found so that a Helen Keller could learn to communicate in spite of her disabilities, surely ways can be found to develop in anyone the tools and skills for entry into the community of knowledge and culture. Assumptions of incapacity only hinder the effort. Neither the matter nor the manner of learning need necessarily be that of present schooling, nor need it be glued to the aristocratic elements in the cultural tradition. The capacity to learn is not absent; the challenge is that obstacles bar its expression. The situation requires a rich overall social effort that is focused on people and their needs; for clearing the way to exercise what capacities and interests they have; for developing ways of teaching in the generic sense of helping others learn; and for all this on a far larger scale than the traditional schooling with its preset design. If it shares the optimism of the eighteenth-century Enlightenment and refuses to accept the disillusion of the last century, it can at least point to gains and educational progress. How far the ideal can carry us is for the future to determine; novel experiment should not be barred by the prejudices of elitism.

But surely, it will be said, there are acknowledged differences in ability. Genius is a fact of experience, not an elitist myth. The question is whether this constitutes an unbridgeable chasm or whether there is continuity in human capacities. In his essay "On Genius" John Stuart Mill saw "the act of *knowing* anything not directly within the cognizance of our sensing (provided we really *know* it and do not take it upon trust) as truly an exertion of genius, though of a less *degree* of genius, as if the thing had never been known by anyone else."[9] His point is that to know something for the first time is a novel discovery even if others have known it before, and that others have not known it previously is adventitious. The same active thought is involved, though the degree in the genius who makes the first discovery may be greater. The educational task is therefore to encourage activity of thought.

All sorts of differences exist among human beings without becoming the basis for distinct social groups or for privileged and underprivileged classes. How, then, should the fact of differences be regarded in education? Some parents, for example, object to their children being classified as "gifted children," not because they are displeased at learning of their high abilities, but because they do not want them set apart from their fellows as a special group. The recognition of their abilities has revealed that these children can advance in certain kinds of work with greater rapidity and that their performance will have a higher quality. To see them as having opportunities for advanced work along certain lines, whether or not it may involve some work in separate groups, even with an extra sense of commitment, is one thing; to make them an elite group by name and type of school life is quite another. A realistic attitude to differences focuses on performance and quality, on serving needs and interests. Students with an ability for advanced work should have the opportunity for it. Students with greater athletic ability are, through the institution of school teams, given the opportunity of special coaching. Students with special psychological problems are given the opportunity of psychological counseling, others of remedial work. All of these can be seen under the same rubric as efforts in different ways to serve needs and advance quality. If we track them in different ways because of possible future careers, then we are allowing a vocational orientation to enter into early schooling—an approach quite inconsistent with the usual educational objection to vocationalism as permeating even higher education.

The ideals we are projecting may be called utopian because competition and the desire for success are natural tendencies that slide over easily into admiration of the successful, hero and heroine worship, and rank ordering of people. It is true that the present structure of schooling helps to entrench these tendencies, particularly if they are tied together. Let us take each separately. Whatever the controversy about economic competition, it is surely agreed that aggressive competitiveness is destructive of rich interpersonal relations and of a sense of community. The more pervasive it is in some areas of activity, the greater the need for muting it in education and for developing cooperative and supportive relations. In the case of hero worship, doubtless role models play a part in the development of the person, but hero worship that emancipates by emphasis on the quality of the achievement has to be distinguished from hero worship that enslaves—as in familiar cult phenomena. Indeed, moral respect for persons dissolves when persons are identified with their successes. The social issue is how to preserve a general concern for quality and performance without forming elites.

It was, we think, the French utopian Saint-Simon who, under the enthusiastic view that changing social conditions could change human beings for the better, envisioned a France of thirty million people *each* of whom was not merely a Newton but also a Shakespeare. Doubtless he underestimated what makes a Newton and a Shakespeare, but one could have a worse dream for culture.

What captures first attention in considering this notion is its universality. Again, nothing less is dreamed of than each person being a Newton and a Shakespeare, not simply an entire people capable of fully understanding and appreciating Newton and Shakespeare or all youth having the opportunity to work in a laboratory and to write plays. Extent, maximum achievement, opportunity— these are identifiable components in the ideal of equality projected from the experience during the French Revolution of the magnitude of possible change, the upsetting of entrenched ways, the hope of the future. There is, however, a further aspect that may have escaped notice: the dream embraces both Newton and Shakespeare in a common concept of cultural achievement. Looking back from Saint-Simon's time this is commonplace. But by our time, with the growth of science and the isolation of the humanities, Newton and Shakespeare live in different worlds.

When science was natural philosophy it was part of the culture of a well-educated person. It furnished an organized conception of the world of nature in which human beings were set. By the latter part of the nineteenth century, however, an adversary relation had arisen between science and the older literary or classical culture. There is no simple explanation for the cleavage. (In the twentieth century, a growing technology shifted the popular view of science away from its philosophical import to its practical role.) Perhaps the confrontation of science with religion that came with the Darwinian revolution provoked an antagonism of the scientific and the classical-humanist culture which was linked with the religious view of man. Thomas Huxley's formulation in his lecture on "Science and Culture" (1880) is suggestive: he does not question Matthew Arnold's view that a criticism of life in the light of the best ideal is fundamental to culture; what he questions is that literature alone provides the material for such criticism. He argues that science can serve equally or even more as a source of understanding. By the middle of the twentieth century the antagonism had not been healed. If C. P. Snow's popular contrast of the "two cultures" elevated science to the status of a separate culture, it still lamented the separation. The last few decades have witnessed many efforts to recast the image of the scientist from that of practical controller of nature and human nature to that of an imaginative and sensitive explorer of the cosmos, engaged in an enterprise that falls fully into the spirit of the humanities. Many studies in the history of science and of thought show that Newton is rightly coupled with Shakespeare in a comprehensive view of culture.

The import of this history for our consideration of elitism is considerable. Elitism in culture today focuses on a narrow concept that equates culture with a traditional segment of the arts and the humanities. To exclude the scientific outlook and the awareness of what the progress of science has brought to the understanding and possibilities of man-in-the-world is to suggest entrenched and partisan rigidities in the concept of culture itself. Such narrowness has been noted in the history of the arts and the humanities—for example, in the successive broadening of what is aesthetically acceptable in music and painting. It is not implausible that in the contemporary world we are at a turning point in which we are almost overwhelmed with new possibilities and new directions. Fresh arts are springing up with the emergence of new technologies; older arts are being altered in significant dimensions. There are doubtless many attempts to make distinctions of primacy or to allege cultural superiority within all these: for example, of writing a drama over its theatrical production, of theatrical over film production, of film over television production. Such elitist claims are wearing thin. If we have not yet reached the limit urged by some philosophers, at which the aesthetic is regarded as a possible dimension of almost all experience rather than as tied to a specific content, we have moved very far in that direction in the current state of the arts.

The notion of "culture" packs many value attitudes with its theory. The narrow view that has been controlling in the humanities ties it to very specific ideals: culture is the property of highly civilized people who—to take Werner Jaeger's account—have consciously pursued the ideal of perfection, a creation of the classic Greek mind.[10] In contrast, the concepts that prevail in the social sciences are more inclusive.[11] The anthropological notion stemming from Edward B. Tylor's *Primitive Culture* (1871) refers to the capabilities and habits, the entire social tradition, acquired by man as a member of society. A more limited account, used by some anthropologists and sociologists, identifies culture with the symbolic aspects as distinct from social structure. It is not that these latter definitions are value-free while the humanistic is value-laden and honorific. At stake simply are different and opposed values. The social science view is that primitive societies have cultures, not only advanced or "highly civilized" societies. This recognizes that a complex, ordered way of interacting with nature and fellowman is a genuine social accomplishment, whatever the differences. This is but a step short of urging respect for all cultures, as Franz Boas and Ruth Benedict did in the anthropological battles against Nazi theories of racial superiority in the twentieth century. The social science definitions thus turn out to embed democratic values.

In breaking with elitist concepts of culture, it is important not to lose any vital impulse they contained, particularly the insistence on quality and disciplined excellence and the emphasis on the tie to the past in which the past is assimilated in present efforts. In such general form, however, these are pertinent to any area of craft or inquiry. They are not the marks of selection for a group. Of course, not every purpose, every activity, every enterprise upon which people expend energies becomes thereby an art, or every reflection upon it a part of the humanities, just as not every questioning of nature becomes thereby a science. The old descriptions, the old borders, the old restrictions, are going. What constitutes an art, what the humanities are about, what makes an inquiry scientific, are questions currently controversial. The controversy is itself the scene of older conceptions stretched to the breaking point by technological, social, cultural, and intellectual change. We should make no attempt here to resolve this intellectual ferment of our age by too ready dogmas. What we insist on rather is that the old formulation in terms of elite and mass in the understanding of culture is outworn.

Elitism, even in the democratized form, fails to address realistically the social issues in connection with which it is invoked. We need to turn now more directly to the issues themselves. These centrally include the cultivation of quality and standards, the need for discipline and self-mastery, the role of tradition and innovation, the place of individual differences in the social scheme, the extent of access and participation, and the range of abilities.

The ideal of quality and the pursuit of excellence are intrinsic parts of effort and achievement. A rich society or a genuine community depends on the pervasive cultivation of this ideal throughout the population. It pertains to varied endeavors—production and daily chores as well as art and science, leisure as well as work, appreciation as well as creation. Quality in the appropriate sense is not necessarily tied to prestige, grading, or reward, or other such fumbling devices to ensure it. Although we may not yet know how, surely the problem is one of the quiet development of the sense of personal worth and dignity and the growth of aspiration. In all this there is the need to cultivate self-discipline and self-mastery, hard work and the mastery of technique, which are constitutive of any art, any practice, any inquiry. Such features do not gain by being refracted through the prism of elitism versus populism.

Tradition and innovation seem, however, more directly related to elitism with its veneration of the past and populism with its embrace of change. But to force a commitment to the past or to the future misses the mark. The tradition that policy must reckon with is not simple piety (in Santayana's definition as loyalty to the sources of our being), or the use of past materials as the stones of an ancient castle might be reused, or even the obviously important preservation of well-tried values. Similarly, the innovation to be reckoned with is not sheer love of change for its own sake, or simple dissatisfaction with the old, or even the perennial hope of something better. What is critical, rather, is the attitude toward both past and future. It is, of course, a lesson of experience that more advances come from assimilating and then transcending the past than from always starting afresh. Appreciation of the past involves an understanding of the problems and their contexts as well as their efforts at solution and answers; but it is also an effort to elicit criticisms and rules of critique with which to face the present. Critique also involves alternatives and faces toward possible futures, toward experiment and innovation that will meet continually changing situations. How much change in fact is advisable does not depend on attitudes alone. It depends on existent structures and the pace of change.

The range of human differences has often been a bone of contention between elitism and populism. In the former, selected differences in leadership, in intellectual and artistic and athletic ability, in occupations, in wealth and family background, are exploited to generate pecking orders and to mold elites out of those who self-consciously share the differences and to monopolize prestige and acquire social benefits. Populism, in contrast, emphasizing the similarities of people, appeals to the democratic ideal of equality and moves to strike down the benefits of differences. The realistic problem, as we have seen in discussing education, is to recognize differences and share their benefits and problems. We must not lose the kinship generated by shared specific interests or the communality of professionalism and of occupation. Nor should we lose the sense of common purpose in our human identity. We need not lose either if we come to view differences as task-centered rather than person-segregating.

One of the consequences of this last would be to break down old and hardened classifications of labor along elitist lines—the contrast of head and hand, of liberal and servile. An automated technology has removed the material bases that earlier perhaps encouraged such divisions. The divisions linger on, determining job specification and roles and, by isolating initiative and authority, engender passivity and obedience. Clearly, this involves a radical change of attitudes that now appear entrenched—witness the familiar intellectual hierarchies of university departments (theoretical mathematics and physics in contrast to applied and either of these in contrast to language teaching) or the fine status lines drawn throughout the medical professions. Doubtless some occupations will always be more desired and some better paid, in virtue of the character of the work and the risks involved, and some, like the military, necessitated under given conditions. This seems a curious base for creating an elite, insofar as all useful labor merits respect. The argument for not turning differences in kinds of work into cultural deference is part and parcel of the respect for persons that belongs in any genuinely healthy society.

Most of the above involve changes of attitude and outlook. There are already signs that we are moving in such directions. On the other hand, access and the opportunities for participation in culture are more open to institutional intervention. Indeed, that, too, is the direction in which we have been moving. The common democratic outlook about the need for universal literacy and education and the surge to higher education in the last quarter of a century have broken many barriers to access. And there is no doubt that the complex character of our technology and society requires higher general levels of education and even broader participation. Where the elitist wants the breadth to secure rise of talent, the populist stresses raising the general basic level. Putting aside for the moment differing estimates of popular capacities and where responsibility for past failures should be assigned, the serious problem is how to allocate limited resources, for example, whether to gifted children or to basic literacy. As we have seen, however, these are problems whose solutions are not much advanced by invoking the general slogans of elitism and populism. They involve a weighing of the specific needs and conditions of the society at the time.

Finally, there is the question of the range of abilities and the possibility of increasing participation in the life of society and culture by larger and larger segments of the population without sacrificing standards or excellence. We have seen the elitist's dim view of human nature pitted against the populist's romantic faith in the people. The former view operates to block experiment, whereas the latter usually underestimates the difficulties. Many changes, however, have taken place in our understanding of human nature and capacities under the impact of psychological investigation and the advance of the social sciences. However inconclusive and controversial the specific results may be, they are enough to show us that the essence of human nature is not to be captured in those broad, age-old generalizations. At least in some important way human abilities at any time are functions of the material and social conditions (including aspirations) and institutions of the society in which they live. If the borderlines in the great heredity-environment controversy are unclear, and if even the formulations of the controversy are being challenged (notwithstanding the recent claims of sociobiology), then experiment or exploratory practice is certainly called for by our democratic commitments. Our understanding also of leadership, of authority, and of the roles they play in social conflict has been immeasurably increased by twentieth-century experience of a variety of social forms and changes.

Whether understanding in confronting these issues can be harnessed to meet the novel conditions that now face us, is, of course, an open question. The future is always chancy and the immediate future doubly so. We need not only understanding but will. At least we ought not to be hampered by conceptual tools that are inadequate to even understanding. As Charles Frankel pointed out in his *The Case for Modern Man*, "We need to have some sense of the crucial variables in our present situation, the handles that will allow us to deal with the clusters of problems together. . . . Clearly, the way to begin is to try to find out just where the outlook on history with which most of us grew up has misled us."[12] We believe that the deep elitist presuppositions of our culture have been one such source.

NOTES

1. Irving Babbitt, *Democracy and Leadership* (Boston: Houghton Mifflin, 1924), p. 242. Cf. p. 5: "This book in particular is devoted to the most unpopular of all tasks—a defence of the veto power."

2. Irving Babbitt, *Literature and the American College: Essays in Defense of the Humanities* (Boston: Houghton Mifflin, 1908), p. 78.

3. This lesson is a particular contribution of the pragmatic approach. Cf. Elizabeth Flower and Murray G. Murphey, *A History of Philosophy in America* (New York: Putnam's, 1977), chapters on James, Dewey, and C. I. Lewis.

4. In exploring this situation we draw on an earlier brief examination of it at the time it was taking place. See Abraham Edel, "Elitism and the Esoteric in the Humanities Endowment," *The Public News*, The Public Committee for the Humanities in Pennsylvania, No. 1 (Fall 1977), pp. 5–6.

5. For a revealing, if overenthusiastic, study of this tradition in the twentieth century, see James Burnham, *The Machiavellians: Defenders of Freedom* (New York: John Day, 1943). The specific works mentioned are Vilfredo Pareto, *The Mind and Society* (New York: Dover, 1963; original Italian publication 1916); Robert Michels, *Political Parties: A Sociological Study of the Oligarchic Tendencies of Modern Democracy* (New York: Dover, 1959; first English translation 1916); Gaetano Mosca, *The Ruling Class* (New York: McGraw-Hill, 1939; original Italian publication 1895, enlarged edition 1923); James Burnham, *The Managerial Revolution* (Bloomington: Indiana University Press, 1960; first published 1941).

6. Bertrand Russell, *Power: A New Social Analysis* (New York: Norton, 1938).

7. Harold Lasswell, *Politics: Who Gets What, When, How* (New York: Meridan, 1958; first published 1936), p. 13.

8. Harold D. Lasswell and Abraham Kaplan, *Power and Society: A Framework for Political Inquiry* (New Haven: Yale University

Press, 1950). For a critique of this work, see Abraham Edel, *Analyzing Concepts in Social Science* (New Brunswick, N.J.: Transaction Books, 1979), chapter 7.

9. John Stuart Mill, "On Genius," in *Mill's Essays on Literature and Society*, ed. J. B. Schneewind (New York: Collier Books, 1965), p. 89.

10. Werner Jaeger, *Paideia: The Ideals of Greek Culture* (New York: Oxford University Press, 1945), 1:xvii. Jaeger maintains that culture is properly so conceived and is unique: "We are accustomed to use the word culture, not to describe the ideal which only the Hellenocentric world possesses, but in a much more trivial and general sense, to denote something inherent in every nation of the world, even the most primitive. We use it for the entire complex of all the ways and expressions of life which characterize any one nation. Thus the word has sunk to mean a simple anthropological concept, not a concept of value, a consciously pursued *ideal*. In this vague analogical sense it is permissible to talk of Chinese, Indian, Babylonian, Jewish or Egyptian culture, although none of these nations has a word or an ideal which corresponds to real culture."

11. The social science uses are included in Alfred L. Kroeber and Clyde Kluckhohn's comprehensive survey, *Culture: A Critical Review of Concepts and Definitions* (Cambridge, Mass.: Peabody Museum of American Archaeology and Ethnology, Harvard University, 1952). Their comment on the humanistic usages is of interest: "The Arnold-Powys-Jaeger concept of culture is not only ethnocentric, often avowedly Hellenocentric; it is absolutistic. It knows perfection, or at least what is most perfect in human achievement, and resolutely directs its 'obligatory' gaze thereto, disdainful of what is 'lower'. The anthropological attitude is relativistic, in that in place of beginning with an inherited hierarchy of values, it assumes that every society through its culture seeks and in some measure finds values. . . . Incidentally, we believe that when the ultra-montane among the humanists renounce the claim that their subject

matter is superior or privileged, and adopt the more catholic and humble human attitude—that from that day the humanities will cease being on the defensive in the modern world" (p. 32).

12. Charles Frankel, *The Case for Modern Man* (New York: Harper and Brothers, 1956), pp. 45–46.

RICHARD M. DORSON

❦ THE VALUE OF

THE HUMANITIES:

A FOLKLORIST'S VIEW

ALL MY ACADEMIC LIFE I have listened to and read about justifications for the humanities. Two recent statements on the subject are "Why the Humanities?" by Charles Frankel[1] and *The Humanities and the Civic Self* by my colleague William F. May, professor of religious studies at Indiana University.[2] These two graceful and informed essays address themselves to the questions ever facing defenders and exponents of the humanities: how does one define their purpose; what use are they, especially in a computerized civilization; how can they compete with the practical, visible contributions to the public weal of the natural sciences and the social sciences? The authors respond eloquently to these questions, setting forth the role of the humanities in providing knowledge, interpretation, and criticism of special fields of learning.

I wish to add to these and other explanations of the humanities an ingredient that is seldom mentioned by humanists. I believe that much of *humanity* is left out of the humanities and that the case for the value of the humanities will be strengthened with the explicit inclusion and recognition of folklore as a crucial discipline. May enumerates the humanities disciplines as "history, languages, literatures, philosophy, religious studies, the arts, speech, linguis-

A version of this essay has also appeared in the *National Forum*, the journal of the Phi Kappa Phi society, summer 1979, pp. 23–28.

tics, and the so-called humanistic aspect of the social sciences." All these disciplines emphasize high culture, the fine arts, and the achievements of the past elite. The humanities have always stood for the best of what man has said and written and thought and composed and created and accomplished. As one consequence, scholars in the humanities sometimes face the charge of being elitists, and they respond, as does May, by declaring that excellence is not to be equated with elitism. I agree, but also I charge the humanities as presently constituted with elitism, because they ignore excellence among the nonelite. The function of folklore as a discipline is to furnish knowledge, interpretation, and criticism of folk artists, folk bards, folk musicians, folk historians, folk philosophers, whose names may have vanished but whose re-creations live on in tradition.

If the humanities continue to exclude folklore from the canonical list of their disciplines, I will still passionately believe in their worth. I teach not only folklore but also American intellectual history, the latter from a consciously high culture point of view. Yet at some point in my thinking, the American folklore and the American history came together, and I perceived that the dominant systems of thought in succeeding eras of our historical experience —Puritan theology, the natural rights philosophy, social Darwinism, the radical humanism of the counterculture—all found echoes and reflections in the ballads, legends, beliefs, and sayings circulating among the folk. This thesis I presented in *America in Legend*, where I suggested that historians vainly seeking ways to "rewrite history from the bottom up" and reconstruct the record of the common man and woman could profitably consult the materials of folklore. As folk history counterbalances intellectual history, so will oral literature counterbalance art literature, folk religion counter the great creeds, folk arts counter the fine arts, folk speech counter the king's English. And what the folk have bequeathed us does indeed form part of our tradition and heritage—words singled out by May in his assessment of the humanities' role in perceiving and sharing the human past. May counsels "openness to the *whole* human past'' (his italics), but our educational administrators and humanistic scholars do not always demonstrate this openness.

A gifted student at the University of California in Berkeley who had spent her college years majoring in English literature was thumbing through the catalog of graduate studies when she discovered a master's degree curriculum in folklore. All at once, she writes, a whole sequence of lifelong interests—Andrew Lang's fairy tale books, ethnic cuisines, folksinging and folk dancing, old-fashioned singing games, Bella Coola and Eskimo string figures, traditional embroideries, folk toys, and Chinese papercuts—fell into an academic place. The prospect of studying these forms, rather than plowing once more through Chaucer, Dryden, Milton, Spencer, and Shakespeare for her M.A., gladdened her heart. The program she enrolled in fulfilled all her expectations and more, so much so that she continued for a doctorate in folklore at Indiana University and has gone on to a highly successful career as teacher of folklore at the University of Pennsylvania. Yet one Berkeley English professor refused to write a letter of recommendation for her file, saying that she would be dissipating her energies on a trivial subject that could only end in academic suicide.[3] This professor's attitude, which I know from countless experiences to be widespread, derives from simple and understandable ignorance of the subject matter and discipline of folklore. Although firmly established with a professorial chair in most European countries, folklore studies in the United States lead to a doctorate at only three universities: Indiana University, the oldest, the University of Pennsylvania, and most recently the University of Texas. At many fine universities students are deprived of the opportunity to learn about their folk heritage for lack of a single course in folklore.

And what are the humanistic values in the study of folklore? They stem in the first place from contact with human beings and their expressive culture. The vast majority of humanities scholars study books and manuscripts and documents in the library and the archives. Professors of all stripes converse mainly with one another. Anthropologists take to the field, but they depart from their own orbits to observe the life patterns of distant cultures. Only the folklorist takes for his province the populace all around him. As a graduate student at Harvard pursuing a doctorate in the history of American civilization, I devoured with relish the readings in Americana pointed out by the famous scholars—Perry Miller, F. O. Matthiessen, Howard Mumford Jones, Samuel Eliot Morison, Arthur M. Schlesinger, Sr., Ralph Barton Perry—then opening the door to what is now called American studies. We journeyed through many pathways off the beaten track of familiar writings and found excitement in colonial sermons, Wild West dime novels, nineteenth-century American plays, the literature of local color and industrialism. And we savored new interpretations of classic Americans in Bernard DeVoto's Mark Twain, Perry's William James, Miller's Jonathan Edwards, Matthiessen's Emerson, Thoreau, Hawthorne, Melville, and Whitman. But in the midst of our enthusiastic seminars, lectures, and shoptalk, I sometimes wondered why we could not talk to Americans as well as read about them. I was not sure what we would talk about, but surely some discipline or its spin-off, perhaps from anthropology or sociology, could show us how. At that time Harvard lacked a folklorist, but by chance I made the acquaintance of a Celtic scholar who explained to me that a subject known as folklore did indeed exist and who gave me some private instruction.

The day came when I struck off for the field, now with something to talk about that would lead me into the lives of fellow Americans outside the university. In time I talked with many persons I would never have encountered in my ordinary academic routine: lumberjacks, lobstermen, miners, steelworkers, Indians, black cotton-pickers and laborers, Finns, Serbs, Greeks, Mexicans, Puerto Ricans, even Assyrians. Because the folklorist seeks out the locally celebrated storyteller, singer, fiddler, craftsman, chronicler, fortune-teller, healer, wit, sage, he meets talented and memorable individuals to whom he can immediately relate.

What a breath of fresh air to visit with Aunt Jane Goudreau, the regal French-Canadian, pipe-smoking raconteur of true stories about the roup-garou [sic] that changed from human to animal shape; James Douglas Suggs, a jack-of-all-trades, who spun 170 assorted Afro-American tales and sang twenty songs to me in an endless stream; Swan Olson, a mild old Swede whom I heard in a barber shop mention eating "fly-pie" and who subsequently poured forth wondrous swashbuckling exploits of his youth; Curt Morse, a waggish retired lobsterman of the Maine coast weaving stories about his comical misadventures; Frank Jenkins, a black steelworker in Gary who produced, directed, and starred in a homemade gangster film he shot with a Super 8mm camera; Chief Herbert Welsh and dainty Rose Holliday, who swapped Sioux and Ojibwa trickster tales from their respective tribal traditions; and many others who enriched my life and whose words, as now set forth on the printed page, can please larger circles than their own immediate audiences.

With his fieldwork the folklorist can perform a double service for the humanities: he broadens his own aesthetic vision by observing carriers and presenters of oral literature at firsthand, and he enlarges the recorded store of our tradition and heritage by his collecting and publishing. Consider, among the discoveries just in American folklore, the Child ballads unveiled in the southern mountains by Cecil Sharp, the Ozark legends recorded by Vance Randolph, the staggering volumes of hoodoo beliefs and rituals set down by Harry Hyatt, the corpus of American folksongs archived by John and Alan Lomax, William Wells Newell's games and songs of American children, the Mormon folk history reconstructed by Austin and Alta Fife, the Italian-American fetes observed by Carla Bianco, the oil driller's lore salvaged by Mody Boatright, the coal miner's lore reported by George Korson, the Afro-American toasts unearthed in Philadelphia's urban jungle by Roger Abrahams—and one begins to realize what stores of living literature the collectors have contributed to the record of our heritage and tradition.

Still we must face the question of what are the values in this enlarged view of the humanities that embraces folk as well as elite compositions. Let me suggest certain fresh glimpses of the human spirit's resourcefulness and versatility afforded through folklore.

One is the opportunity to view the tension between tradition and creativity, the variability within a stable form, that folk items display. The so-called variant provides the key to folkloric phenomena, the requisite proof that the folklorist needs to separate out his subject matter from popular culture and elite culture, which manifest themselves in standard or unique forms. But the folktale, ballad, proverb, ritual, artifact are neither unique nor mass-produced; each variant blends into the next in an endless succession of overlapping specimens. Alfred Kinsey seized on this principle in nature and human nature in his painstaking field studies of gall wasps and human sexual behavior. After relentlessly gathering multitudes of specimens of the one and manifold filing cabinets of case studies of the other, he concluded that seemingly distinct subspecies could be linked if thousands upon thousands of individual examples were strung together, like an endless string of beads. The apparent gap between sexual normality and abnormality, between the Indiana and the Mexican gall wasp, melted away as the collections mounted. Folklore collectors experience precisely the same thrill as they round up variants and perceive their infinite variety. Once in a folk museum in Rome I saw an exhibit of handcrafted cradles from adjacent regions of Italy, the first ones close to the ground, the next raised higher, until at the end of the row they swung from trees, as swamp and flood conditions caused their elevation clear of the earth. If one had looked only at the low-lying and the tree-top cradles, he might have believed they belonged to separate craft traditions.

I collected and printed side by side sixteen variants of an Afro-American tale known as King Beast of the Forest Meets Man. In the older forms a lion boasts that he can whip any other creature. A rabbit tells him he can't whip Man. What is a Man? asks the lion. Come, I'll show you, says the rabbit and leads him to the roadside. Along trudges a boy. Is that Man? I can whip him, roars the lion. No, that's not a man, that's a will-be, says the rabbit. Next an old chap dodders by, and the lion prepares to charge, until the rabbit informs him it is a have-been. At last a man in the prime of life, a gun on one shoulder, steps briskly down the road. Now that's a Man, and I'm leaving, cries the rabbit. The lion wants to know what Man carries on his shoulder. Oh, that's just an old dry fence rail, chuckles the rabbit and scampers off. The lion races toward the Man, who fires at him, and the king beast turns and limps into the forest, until he finds rabbit. Well, did you whip Man? inquires the rabbit. No, moans the crestfallen lion; that Man, he took that old dry fence rail off his shoulder, broke it in two across his knee, and thundered it in my face, and lightninged it in my rear, and filled my side full of splinters. Thus the tale in one form. Sometimes the ending will say, "and cut me a brand new ass." As the versions take on a more American flavoring, the lion yields to the bear, and Man becomes the Cowboy, and at the end of my sequence the alligator, after seeing the black man light a match and throw it into an oil spill, reports ruefully to the whale that Colored Man had scratched his ass and set the world on fire. Juxtaposed, the variants portray the glide across the Atlantic of the hardy tale, the most popular of all that I collected from American blacks, and its slipping on new hues.

Or still again, read through the sequence of texts in Francis James Child's classic compendium of 305 English and Scottish popular ballads and marvel at the changes wrought by each singer while remaining faithful to the story element of ill-fated lovers, border battles, Robin Hood's adventures, and murders most foul.

A second value for the humanities illuminated through folklore may be called appreciation of oral power. So long have we been confined by the traditional humanities to the written word that we have lost the savor for spoken, recited, chanted, rhapsodized, and versified forms of artistic oral expression. Several years ago, the editors of *PMLA* published an article by Jeff Opland on some types of South African oral poetry and in their editorial commented excitedly on this extension of their conventional concept of literary studies to the oral. But as some literary historians are pointing out, the literature of writing represents but a fraction of unwritten literature, not merely before the invention of alphabets but flourishing today, as we are still learning in our discovery of south Slavic, central African, and south Asian oral epics.

Even in our own print- and media-glutted culture the spoken

traditions still thrive. Storytelling remains a vital part of our daily life, in anecdotes, jokes, and experiences told on all kinds of public and social occasions, but only the folklorist pays them heed as a serious art form—and not too many folklorists at that, for most continue to look to the backcountry and byways for tale-tellers. But a professor, a politician, a preacher as well as a horse trader or hill man can spin a yarn. During a year of writing a book at the National Humanities Center in Research Triangle Park, North Carolina, on urban folklore I had collected in northwestern Indiana, I found myself reaching for my notebook during lunches and at receptions with my colleagues there as they interlarded speeches and conversations with witty jests. In March, 1979 I delivered a paper titled "The Pernicious Influence of the Grimm Brothers on American Folkloristics" in which I used several of their jocular narratives to make the point that we need not look to the Grimms to find folktales but could hear them in our own midst. And besides the anecdotal tales, we can find fresh sources of creative vigor in the metaphors, idioms, localisms, saws, and salutations of folk speech.

Certain oral subcultures coexist with the central culture, for example, among Afro-Americans with their history of enforced reliance under slavery on the spoken and sung word. Indeed the "man of words" has emerged from this suppressed culture as a characteristic Afro-American leader figure, a preacher, an entertainer, a civil-rights spokesman, an athlete, a bluesman, a writer, a hustler, usually playing several of these roles concurrently: we think of Muhammed Ali, Jesse Jackson, Dick Gregory, B. B. King, Alex Haley, Malcolm X, on a national level, but in any black community one can meet their local equivalents, individuals gifted with a natural eloquence, living, as Charles Keil puts it in *Urban Blues*, in an oral and tactile rather than a visual and auditory culture. From this verbal power emerges a host of folkloric forms: the formulaic sermon, the blues, the violent rhymed narratives known as "toasts," the vituperative "dozens," the holler, the lyric cry, the street vendor's palaver.

Another type of oral performer that the folklorist encounters is the folk historian, the self-appointed annalist of local doings, with golden tongue and spongelike memory. Such a one was W. H. Barrett, whose tales of the Fen Country and life story in England's Cambridgeshire folklorist Enid Porter committed to paper. The Fenman did not relate conventional folktales but rather family and village saga, compounded of neighborhood events stretching back to Cromwell's times and striated with folkloric episodes of hauntings and witchery. Cruel episodes from the past stay fresh in this saga, such as the crucifying of the wretch who stole a loaf of bread to keep his body and soul together. Fieldworkers have not sufficiently heeded these oral history traditions that storytellers can narrate as fluently as any märchen. A rich sampler of such traditional history can be found in *The Dewar Manuscripts*, recorded in the late nineteenth century by Scottish gamekeeper John Dewar for the great collector-organizer Campbell of Islay, but only published in 1964. These annals preserve stirring feats of the Highland clans, sometimes set forth with economy and force of the highest artistry, as in the death duel between a captive Highland stripling and a powerful English soldier, on the outcome of which depended the fate of the Scottish prisoners, a David and Goliath combat worthy of its prototype.

A third value for the humanities to which folklore contributes is an appreciation of cultural diversity. Most historians, literary scholars, even anthropologists necessarily confine their attention to limited areas and specialties. Although folklorists, too, identify with a region, an occupation, an ethnic group, a country, in their broadest reach they must operate on a comparative basis and sweep the world. The materials of folklore traverse the globe, and in their pursuit, in the library if not in the field, the folklorist continually stretches his horizons. I commenced my career as an American folklorist and explored different regions of the United States, but never contemplated getting to know other lands and civilizations. Circumstances have led me to reside for several years in England and write a history of British folklorists; to spend a Fulbright year in Japan and compile a book of Japanese legends and edit a volume of essays by Japanese folklore scholars; to traverse west and east Africa meeting folklore-minded teachers and writers in preparation for a conference on African folklore held at Indiana University in 1970, from which evolved a book of conference papers titled *African Folklore*; and most recently to visit four cities in India to talk with folklorists there about developing a volume on folktales of India. Participation in international folklore conferences in Stockholm, Kiel, Copenhagen, Athens, Bucharest, Budapest, Helsinki, and Santo Tirso (in Portugal) brought me acquaintances and friendships with overseas folklorists that led to my conceiving a series titled Folktales of the World, issued through the University of Chicago Press. The format called for a folktale expert to assemble a selection of traditional tales from his country, which were then translated into English and provided with comparative notes and other scholarly aids. From the twelve volumes in the series and original contributions from a number of other authoritative collectors, I prepared a compilation in 1975, *Folktales Told around The World*, representing forty-six countries on four continents and in the Pacific islands. Thus, from a small toehold in folklore commencing with almanac legends of Davy Crockett, I eventually gained familiarity with many folk cultures. No matter in what part of the globe he sets foot, a folklorist will always find customs, observances, manners, beliefs, and rituals for comparative study, and today, as the developing nations come to appreciate the discipline of folklore, he will also meet fellow folklorists who can lead him directly into the indigenous traditions.

From these foreign excursions I gained an education and enjoyed experiences that could never have befallen me had I remained a library scholar or a conventional tourist. I pluck out a handful of incidents almost at random. In County Kerry on the west coast of Ireland I spent three days traveling with a full-time collector for the Irish Folklore Commission, Tadhg O'Murphy, as he made his daily rounds to folktellers in those remote villages, and heard from his lips a prize story, "Seán Palmer's Voyage with the Fairies." Seán traveled by boat across the Atlantic one night with some strangers, who allowed him to visit friends and relatives in New York and Boston and brought him back the next morning, with a bundle of dollars, a box of tobacco, and a fine new suit as proof of his journey. This fantasy is told as a true happening and seems to embody a dream or wish construed as realistic by Irishmen desirous of visiting American kinfolk. Variants of this tale transport Irish folk to other countries.

In Tokyo I watched a Kabuki play based on the legend of Uba-suteyama, the Mountain of Abandoned Old People, showing a desperately poor, Tobacco Road-type family, so poor that, according to custom, the son takes his sixty-year-old mother to the cliff's edge to leave her to die, as one less mouth to feed, but after a desperate internal struggle, enacted on the board extending from the stage across the audience, he returns to fetch his mother and bring her back to the village. In the oral legend known in Asia, Europe, and Africa, the aged parent is hidden in the cellar or the attic and saves the kingdom from a neighboring invader by providing solutions to enigmatic, riddling questions, whereupon the king rescinds the decree of abandonment for those reaching sixty.

In the Bat Valley Restaurant in Kampala, capital of Uganda, I beheld a strangely familiar figure and, walking over to his table, remarked, "Dr. Selden, I presume." The animated talker looked up and cried out, "My God, Dr. Dorson!" It was one of my folklore students, Sherman Selden, who had come to Africa to teach in a Ugandan school in the interior. I altered my travel plans and accompanied him into the bush, to a no-place hamlet named Morote, which called itself "the heart of Africa," and there I beheld the Karamajong men wearing animal skins, or nothing, and the women with coils upon coils of necklaces compensating for their poor garments. I wandered into a hut and purchased a cowrie necklace as an example of African folk art, only to learn that the owner had purchased it in a five and dime store.

Recently I journeyed to India and in New Delhi at a small industries fair saw a folk performance I never knew existed. A scroll painter from Rajasthan was touching up a large colored cloth scroll depicting over 150 scenes from the folk epic of *Pābu*. An animated young singer recited the epic, a musician accompanied him on a stringed instrument known as a *jantar*, and a small boy danced in regular steps to the music. Such a combination of folk performances joined in one narrative complex (described by O. P. Joshi in *Painted Folklore and Folklore Painters of India*, [Delhi, 1976] filled me with delight and wonder.

Folklore studies have led me and other folklorists out of the university and into many lives and many cultures. But they have also taken us into unexpected corners of the library. After forty years of folkloring I see that the humanities encompass the artistic expression of common people as well as of the celebrated. Through knowledge, interpretation, and criticism of such expression the folklorist can enlarge our comprehension of mankind's bottomless tradition and heritage.

NOTES

1. *Ideas* 1 (Winter 1979):2–3, 13–14. A publication of the National Humanities Center, Research Triangle Park, North Carolina. This essay was first delivered by Dr. Frankel as an address at the Lyndon Baines Johnson Library on December 4, 1978. It is reprinted in the present volume.
2. (Bloomington: Indiana University Foundation, January 1979), pp. 3–15.
3. Barbara Kirshenblatt-Gimblett, in *Roads into Folklore: Festschrift in Honor of Richard M. Dorson*, ed. Richard A. Reuss and Jens Lund (Bloomington, Ind.: Folklore Forum), p. 37.

TORSTEN HUSÉN

🦌 ENCOUNTERS WITH THE

INTERNATIONAL EDUCATOR

MY FIRST ENCOUNTER with Charles Frankel occurred in Williamsburg, Virginia, in the mid-1960s, where he was serving in his role as Assistant Secretary of State. In the State of the Union Message the previous year, President Lyndon Johnson had announced the submission of an international education bill. Its architect was Charles, who eventually had to suffer the disappointment of seeing Congress refuse to appropriate funds. The meeting of some 150 leading educators from all over the world, which Charles had inspired the president to sponsor, dealt with what the main working document referred to as the "world crisis" in education. At that date, although the writing on the wall began to be noticeable, the crisis was conceived mainly in terms of imbalances between demand and supply of formal education and in lack of relevant curricula. The conference took place less than two years before student unrest shook many American and European universities and precipitated a change in the social and intellectual climate that was to have a strong impact on Charles.

A few years later we met again as members of an international team of "country examiners" invited by the Organization for Economic Cooperation and Development to review French educational policy. It was, indeed, a timely review. Hardly more than one year had elapsed since the convulsions at the University of Paris. We met with Alain Peyrefitte, who had been thrown out of office as minister of education by the events of 1968, and with his successor Edgar Faure, who was then also out of office but who had been the architect of *la loi d'orientation*, which was a brave attempt to save what was still left of the French universities by capitalizing on student participation.

Over a hectic period of site visits and interviews I had the opportunity of watching how Charles, who chaired the team, led our work with comfortable elegance and ease and who spoke fluent French. He was fascinated by the peculiar French system of higher education, where the elite sector, *les grandes écoles*, had been relatively unaffected by the 1968 events, while the mass universities that had exploded from overenrollment, had been completely reorganized in smaller units and with entirely new provisions for governance and administration. Paris-Dauphiné, which we visited, was a case in point.

I recall particularly the afternoon we met with Edgar Faure, who sat behind the desk in the big library in his apartment close to Bois de Bologne. Charles cautiously started the interview by asking Faure how he thought that the new university law had worked out during the year since its enactment by the Assemblée Nationale. Edgar Faure for a moment looked at the four of us sitting in front of him. He then raised his head and looked above and beyond us as if he wanted to catch a much wider audience and began a long *exposé* in three parts: *premièrement, secondement,* and *troisièmement.* It was very French in its formal structure and elegance—and fascinating to listen to.

I mention these encounters because I eventually realized how important they were in shaping my views and those of many of my colleagues on today's problems in higher education in old Europe. Charles simply made us aware of what we European academics were up to. Until then I had spent almost two decades as a university professor under very protected circumstances. The continental system of "professorial feudalism" prevailed. To be sure, in my corner of Europe, the universities had felt repercussions of the unrest on the Continent and in America, but we had not suffered any earthquake of the type that had hit France and the Federal Republic of Germany. Vociferous groups were demanding widened student participation in university governance. In 1968, Olof Palme, then minister of education, had appointed a government commission, u68, consisting of the director generals of the central agencies of the schools, the universities, and the labor market with the charge of reshaping Sweden's system of higher education. But, still, my colleagues throughout Scandinavia and I were not particularly concerned about problems of preservation of academic freedom and of our professional, and professorial, integrity. These had, however, early become matters of prime concern for Charles. The reader of our OECD review report on French educational policy will find that the section on higher education is written with a particular commitment and devotion. It was drafted by Charles.

Not very long after the French review, Charles was instrumental in establishing the International Council on the Future of the University (ICFU). This was a timely attempt by a humanist to encourage the world community of scholars to defend basic principles of freedom and academic integrity without which universities would lose their raison d'être. Inspired by ICFU and by the shortcomings of u68, I embarked on a study of the role of fundamental research at the Swedish university and its implications for university governance. The report was published in 1975, a week before the Higher Education Act reached the floor in the Swedish parliament. It was a legislation that, without regard for historic traditions and the international network of scholars, completely reshaped the structure and governance of the Swedish universities. Its purpose was to make them fit the model the central bureaucracy, the central federation of unions, and the political power center wanted to imprint on them. After a short planning and transition period the new system was supposed to go into effect, as if one could change an institution like the university overnight.

It was therefore highly appropriate for ICFU to review critically what had happened and what was about to happen on the scene of Swedish higher education. The initiative to such a review was one of the last actions that Charles took as chairman of ICFU. By then I had become a fellow at the National Humanities Center and participated in briefing one of the two reviewers, Professor Howard Hunter. The observations presented below are taken from a document that I prepared during my stay at the Center. After sketching the changes that constituted the "reform" (I hesitate to use the word here without quotation marks), I shall conclude by hinting at some consequences for the humanities that the changes have led to.

The Swedish system of higher education by 1945 consisted of four universities and eight separate professional schools, most of which were located in Stockholm. Together these institutions constituted a national system of higher education for which the state provided the funds. Appropriations were made by the parliament every year on the basis of a finance bill for higher education submitted by the government. Tenured faculty, which meant chairholders almost exclusively, were formally appointed by the king in cabinet session. For example, my appointment to the full chair in education at the University of Stockholm in 1953 was signed by the king and countersigned by the minister of education. Every year the government issued a regulatory letter to all institutions of higher education in which the institutional setup was spelled out in detail and which prescribed how funds were to be used for staff and operations in each unit, such as institutes and departments.

This was the formal picture. In reality the universities enjoyed great autonomy in academic affairs. The full professors constituted the various faculties, which were powerful bodies because departmental organization had not yet been introduced, and institutes after the German model did not exercise political power. Thus, the faculties were the real decision-making bodies. The rule was that each discipline was represented by a chairholder, that is, a full professor. Because scholarships were not available, graduate studies were seldom conducted on a full-time basis. There were no formal graduate courses but usually a graduate seminar met regularly. In it students presented thesis chapters for critical review. Most of the undergraduate teaching was done by the chairholders, who also conducted seminars where students taking advanced courses had to submit papers for discussion.

The professor in a given discipline submitted a curriculum outline, including a list of suggested readings, to the faculty, which in its turn had to submit it to the chancellor of the universities for approval. The chancellor was elected by a council of electors chosen by the full professors. He was expected to serve as their spokesman vis-à-vis the government. Even if the government formally had the last word in the appointment of professors, their collegial influence was so strong that the government deviated from their choice only in extremely rare cases of serious disagreement. The appointment of junior faculty, which always was for a limited time, for the assistants only for one year at a time, was entirely in the hands of the faculty, that is, the full professors.

This system, which has been referred to as "professorial feudalism," worked as long as the institutions of higher learning were small and provided the state with the people needed: teachers for the secondary state schools, ministers for the state church, and civil servants for the state administration. The research conducted at the universities was of limited significance. They had no separate research funds. Research councils were established in the 1940s in medicine, technology, and the natural and social sciences. A humanities research foundation had been set up earlier. Government agencies and royal commissions had not yet begun to commission research of a policy-oriented nature. It was part of the prevailing academic ethos that "pure" research was of a higher intrinsic value than applied.

The changes that have taken place in higher education in Sweden since the mid-1950s have, because they have occurred over such a short time, been more dramatic, not to say revolutionary, than those that occurred in American education. The involvement of society in university affairs in America has been part of American higher education from the time of the establishment of the land-grant colleges. Enrollment has been soaring ever since the late 1940s and not been concentrated to about one decade, as was the case in Sweden. There, enrollment in higher education increased almost tenfold over less than fifteen years. The most striking feature of the enrollment pattern in the 1970s has been the change in age of the students and the rapid increase in the number of part-time students. By 1977, when the university reform went into effect, more than half the students who enrolled at the University of Stockholm were twenty-five years of age or older. Those who went straight from upper secondary school to university became a minority, and their absolute numbers are dwindling.

Governance all the way from the department to the national level has been changed entirely. The era of professorial feudalism has passed. The most drastic change in governance is not the increased participation of students but the increased role played by the organizations on the labor market, particularly the central federations of unions, both the blue- and white-collar ones. For under the old system, students had a say, even if they did not have a vote, in matters of curriculum.

Changes in governance in higher education have taken place in two steps, the Higher Education Acts of 1963 and 1975. After 1963, the chancellor of the universities was appointed by the government and no longer elected by the full professors. In the same year, tenured junior faculty, the university lecturers, who had been introduced in the late 1950s to meet the increased demand for undergraduate teaching, became members of the faculty. Soon they were in the majority. They were not required to conduct research. Simultaneously, students got voting representatives on the curriculum committees. But final decisions were taken by the faculty, where still only tenured teaching staff was represented. The university boards in the 1963 model consisted of the rector and the faculty deans plus representatives of the students and the nonfaculty staff. The national system was under the jurisdiction of a National Board of the Universities, chaired by the chancellor, who was appointed by the government and was expected to act on its behalf. The central federations of unions was represented on the board. The institutions of higher learning had entered the era of corporative society.

In the 1970s, under the impact of student unrest, which, as was pointed out above, was rather peaceful in Sweden, the chancellor launched a pilot program with various models of student and nonfaculty participation in governance at the department level. In the most radical of the models, the department was governed by a board on which all categories of personnel working in the department were represented: professors, assistants, undergraduate and graduate students, secretaries, laboratory technicians, and others. Without any systematic evaluation of the models in the pilot program, the government in 1975 opted for this model, the most "participatory" of the four in the pilot program.

The faculty in its old role as decision-making body disappeared in the 1975 Higher Education Act. In the void between the departments and the governing board of the university, study line councils were established for each undergraduate program with a vocational profile. On these councils were represented not only teaching staff and students but labor market organizations as well.

As a substitute for the old faculty there is now a body named the Faculty Council consisting of all staff that is, or is supposed to be, involved in research; it includes professors, lecturers, and research assistants. In the Faculty of Social Sciences at my university, for example, this is a body of some 130 persons. The council meets a few times a year to elect a faculty board on which the various categories are represented. This means that the tenured professors can easily be in a minority. It has turned out to be difficult, in some instances even impossible, to get a quorum for these meetings.

Each university has a governing board chaired by the rector and with a membership consisting of both political appointees and representatives of the various staff categories: teachers, students, technical and secretarial staff. The latter are nominated by the central federations of unions and not by the local chapters, which should be noted because there has been much talk about "decentralization" and "grass-roots participation" in connection with the reform. This is typical of the increased corporatism in present-day Swedish society, where the central federations of unions has become the center of power that tends to outweigh bodies elected according to the rules of representative democracy.

In the administrative hierarchy between the local university board and the National Board of Universities and Colleges, the 1975 Higher Education Act established a regional board for institutions located in a given area. The regional boards were a product of political trade between the Social Democratic government and the Center party, which has been the main champion of decentralization. The regional board is supposed to plan and to allocate resources to the various institutions under its jurisdiction.

What impact did all these radical changes have? It is still too early, two years after the reform went into full effect, to draw the balance, but certain tendencies are noticeable.

But before dealing with the impact of the reform I shall mention recent legislation that has had important repercussions on the universities, namely, laws on participation in decision making at workplaces and on job security. Both these pieces of legislation are the result of a heavy pressure on the part of the unions, and they apply primarily to the workplaces in industry.

Regulations that require negotiations with the staff on any change in the working conditions that can be construed to be of major importance have been added to the new system of university governance. Regulations on job security can uphold the principle of "publish or perish" by downgrading scholarly merits in favor of other criteria of promotion, particularly seniority. Evidently, such regulations act as constraints upon creativity at research institutions.

If negotiations under the provisions of the law of codetermination are requested when it comes to the planning and implementation of a research project, there is a clear-cut chance of a clash between competence and participation, which, if the latter wins, can only adversely affect the quality of research.

Clashes between vested corporative interests and those of scientific integrity and autonomy can occur and have, indeed, occurred in governing bodies with union representatives, especially in instances when the latter run the risk of having their dirty linen exposed. On one occasion the representative of the central federation of labor unions attempted to stop a study that focused on difficulties of people at the grass-roots level to maintain their interest against the central union bureaucracy.

The new legislation on job security can easily have adverse consequences in a system where promotion has occurred according to scholarly merits. The research system is, indeed, insecure. Research both as an activity and as a career is by its very nature beset with a wide margin of uncertainty. The person who embarks on a research endeavor self-evidently does not know where he will end up; otherwise he would not be involved in genuine research. Nor can a person who ventures to embark on a research career look forward to a well-staked-out path soon leading to a tenured position. Research and the decision to enter a research career are in most cases a gamble with bleak odds. The principle that many are called but few are chosen applies to the research career more than to any other vocation. This has certain unavoidable consequences for how research positions are established and research should be governed.

The research career is a highly meritocratic pursuit. One is not trained as a researcher in the same vein as one is trained as a teacher, a plumber, or a programmer. It has been said that researcher is something you are, not something you become by training. Two basic qualifications are required for a good researcher: creative intellectual potential and strong motivation bordering on obsession.

Thus, both graduate education and subsequent pursuit of research are by their very nature something of a lottery with many blanks and few prizes. At the beginning of graduate training it is extremely difficult to identify the few who have the potential to make scientific breakthroughs.

A necessary complement to creative intellectual capacity is a motivation that expresses itself as an obsessed diligence that defies regular working hours and bureaucratic regulations. Research, particularly basic research, has always been associated with major sacrifices, not least material ones. The autonomy traditionally accorded to the researcher is constituted not only by the freedom to select object, method, and channel of reporting research findings.

The sovereignty in using one's time is also an indispensable feature of the research activity. This is another reason why research is allergic to bureaucratic regulations.

What consequences are noticeable on the Swedish scene as a result of the changes in university governance and administration and recent legislation on participation and job security? Because preparation of the university reform did not include any inquiry into the nature and conditions of research, the system has been designed to fit only undergraduate mass teaching with strictly vocationally oriented programs consisting of "lines" of study. At the undergraduate level, the universities have become huge course cafeterias, where people expected to have a pragmatic orientation make their choice. A minority registers to take a complete degree. Students limit themselves to specific courses that can be fitted into a career web.

The number of students who take courses of a more discipline-oriented nature in order to study a given subject in depth has decreased dramatically. This in its turn reduces the recruitment basis for graduate studies, which have lost attractiveness also because of dire employment prospects and loss of status.

The attempt to vocationalize undergraduate studies and weave them into career patterns under the label "lifelong" or "recurrent" education is a threat to the basic humanistic value of pursuing scholarship for its own sake. I have heard representatives of the technocrats behind the reform privately talk about "luxury studies." In the new system, studies in the humanities have to be justified by their utility on the labor market, for instance, as a preparation for schoolteaching and other "communication professions." The recent reorganization of the national research councils has led to a merger between the ones for the humanities and the social sciences. It remains to be seen whether and to what extent the humanities run the risk of being submerged in their new environment.

Students have reacted strongly against the university act, which they perceived as an entirely bureaucratic "reform" without reference to the role the universities could play in extending the frontiers of knowledge. In spite of the tightening labor market, which could be expected to work for a pragmatic study order, many highly able students tend to flock to studies where the employment prospects, to say the least, are dim, such as philosophy, history, and art. This to me is the most encouraging sign in a situation that otherwise, to an incurable academic, appears to be rather bleak.

WILLIAM BENNETT

❦ THE HUMANITIES,

THE UNIVERSITIES, AND

PUBLIC POLICY

THE MOST IMPORTANT contribution the study of the humanities makes to public policy is the sound education—the development of the minds and sensibilities—of the young men and women who will make public policy in the future.

The purpose of education in the humanities, as in the entire liberal arts, is the cultivation of large-minded amateurs. Education, William James said, is where a person learns the difference between what is first-rate and what is not. It has also been put another way: the purpose of a liberal arts education is to teach a student to know when a man is talking rot. Because of the amount of rot around these days, educating students to know it when they see it is no small achievement. Or, as Isaiah Berlin has pointed out, the world's ills are not to be ascribed to an oversupply of rationality. Similarly, today, the conception and direction of public policy are not to be ascribed to too great an influence of the humanities. Public policy is not suffering from a surfeit of the best that has been thought and known. But how and where should the humanities have more influence?

The humanities are not a technique, knack, or subbranch of

This essay was originally given as a lecture under the auspices of the W. K. Kellogg Foundation and published in the fall 1981 edition of the *Educational Record*. It is reprinted here with the permission of the *Record* and the Foundation.

188

public policy: most of the best work in the humanities does not address, and is not intended to address, issues of public policy as we normally think of it. Rather, the humanities address the conditions, the dreams, hopes, fears, disappointments, failures, and aspirations in the lives of those who make and who are affected by public policy. The humanities, particularly literature, normally speak not to legislation or to administrative decrees but to the heart, not to the external but to the spiritual circumstances of our civilization; and their focus is usually narrower than the purview of public policy. The humanities' subject matter is most often the elucidation of the quotidian, of the commonplace, rather than large political or social questions. George Steiner, writing of the importance of the novel, has put it this way:

> It is one of the responsibilities of the novel to chronicle small desolations. These are sold short in that harsh artifice of selective recall we set down as history. Whose birthday party was cancelled by the fires that leaped over Troy? Who, on the Friday after Robespierre's execution, paid the laundress who had kept the great man's linens starched? What notes of felicitation, bitingly missed, what letters of condolence waited for by the hurt, impatient heart went to oblivion in the mailbags of the Titanic? In the troves and vestiges of Pompeii, it is the form of a dog wide-eyed with terror, still chained to his post, that numbs the spirit. The skein of experience [is] woven of these threads, of the immemorial weight of the particular.[1]

And Wordsworth put it this way:

> Thanks to the human heart by which we live,
> Thanks to its tenderness, its joys, and fears,
> To me the meanest flower that blows can give
> Thoughts that do often lie too deep for tears.[2]

We must grant that this is not the stuff of which policy in Washington, D.C., is made; but what is its utility? Justice Oliver Wendell Holmes, Jr., was right to say that the place for a man who is complete in all his powers is in the fight. But it is true, too, that the man who lives only for pertinent action runs the risk of neglecting the development of the sensibility and intellect required to put these issues in perspective, to act wisely as well as pertinently. The difficulty with adjusting one's intellectual life to the measure of what is deemed important and to what is happening now is, ironically, that as a steady diet it foreshortens perspective. The humanities keep us from forgetting that, although the news normally embraces issues no smaller than the measure of a city's disaster or a national goal, the experience—the life—of the individual who will be affected or who will affect public policy is particular. As Yeats reminds us, "All the drop scenes drop at once upon a hundred thousand stages."[3] We should not trust the smooth, glib student of all the contemporary issues of the day whose perspective and opinions never take in anything less than the movement of ten thousand, but who is never the student of one. We should not want a nation's public policy framed by men and women whose only interest is public policy.

In the annals of public policy, there is proof of the humanities' potency. Some of the best and most effective makers of public policy America has known—James Madison, Abraham Lincoln, Reinhold Niebuhr, Martin Luther King, Jr.—were not students principally of what is called public policy. All were students of the humanities—religion primarily, and literature, philosophy, the classics, and history. They took their sights from Virgil, Aristotle, Shakespeare; they knew and told stories; and they thought about the shape, character, ambivalence, and destiny of individual lives when they spoke to matters of public choice. They had depth of sensibility: they did not suffer from dry rot, and they did not flog us with flat and neat and bloodless formulas for adjusting the lives of men.

There are ideas in the humanities to develop the sensibility and the intellect of the young, ideas that are not dry rot, ideas that should underlie public policy, ideas about man and about human nature that should inform students, who one day will inform public policy. For example, Tacitus at the beginning of his *Histories* instructs a sensibility that may in time be able to put a Watergate in perspective:

> I am entering on the history of a period rich in disasters, frightful in its wars, torn by civil strife, and even in peace full of horrors; rapacious men robbed and ruined in every direction amid universal hatred and terror. Things holy were desecrated, there was adultery in high places. . . . Yet, the age was not so barren in noble qualities as not also to exhibit examples of virtue. There were brave and faithful sons-in-law; there were slaves whose fidelity defied even torture; there were illustrious men driven to the last necessity, and enduring it with fortitude; there were closing scenes that equalled the famous deaths of antiquity.[4]

Arthur Miller in *Death of a Salesman* instructs about the one equality all men seek and need:

> I don't say he's a great man. Willy Loman never made a lot of money. His name was never in the paper. He's not the finest character that ever lived. But he's a human being, and a terrible thing is happening to him. So attention must be paid. He's not to be allowed to fall into his grave like an old dog. Attention, attention must finally be paid to such a person.[5]

E. M. Forster in *Two Cheers for Democracy* tells us of the value of certain elites, why some elites must be preserved:

> I believe in aristocracy, though—if that is the right word, and if a democrat may use it. Not an aristocracy of power, based upon rank and influence, but an aristocracy of the sensitive, the considerate and the plucky. Its members are to be found in all nations and classes, and all through the ages, and there is a secret understanding between them when they meet. They represent the true human tradition, the one permanent victory of our queer race over cruelty and chaos. Thousands of them perish in obscurity, a few are great names. They are sensitive

for others as well as for themselves, they are considerate
without being fussy, their pluck is not swankiness but the
power to endure, and they can take a joke.[6]

These are the sorts of notions that are ignored by public policy
at its peril. If not speed-read, they might do something for the
sensibility of a student.

Now consider the contrast with contemporary public policy. I
quote from one of America's most influential public and social
policy journals:

> This article develops a formal framework to aid political
> designers in the comparison of social choice functions. It
> generalizes earlier assumptions of "impartial culture" so that
> we may begin to investigate the effect of politically interesting
> variations on the probability that different social choice func-
> tions will satisfy given performance criteria. As an application
> of the framework, a detailed Monte Carlo study compares the
> ability of four different social choice functions to select a
> Condorcet winner when voter preference orders have been
> generated from a spatial representation of ideal points and
> alternatives.[7]

Another piece is on "committee games":

> This essay defines and experimentally tests a new solution
> concept for n-person cooperative games—the Competitive
> Solution. The need for a new solution concept derives from
> the fact that cooperative game theory focuses for the most part
> on the special case of games with transferable utility, even
> though, as we argue here, this assumption excludes the
> possibility of modeling most interesting political coalition
> processes.[8]

I submit that these are not thoughts that lie too deep for tears—
these are thoughts and exercises that do not irrigate. They may
leave a desert where there should be a sensibility. "Monte Carlo
studies," "n-person cooperative games," and "modeling" are inert

conjectures. They are less factual and more inert than what Miller, Forster, and *Ecclesiastes* say.

George Orwell has made abundantly clear this contrast between ideas and writing in the humanities and in the public policy arena by his translation of a well-known passage from *Ecclesiastes* into modern public policy prose. Thus, the passage, "I returned, and saw under the sun that the race is not to the swift nor battle to the strong, neither yet bread to the wise, nor yet riches to men of understanding nor yet favor to men of skill, but time and chance happeneth to them all," becomes "Objective considerations of contemporary phenomena compel the conclusion that success or failure in competitive activities exhibits no tendency to be commensurate with innate capacity, but that a considerable element of the unpredictable must inevitably be taken into account."[9]

Too often in public policy, too often in formulating public ends and means under the inspiration of the country's ideals, confusion of thoughts is presented in a confusion of tongues; there is impenetrable, unfathomable, unconscionable talk and writing, and with this, invariably, comes distortion of reality. The study of the humanities, the study of the best that has been thought and known, should make its students attentive to language and to the thoughts language is supposed to convey. Sound education in the humanities ought to immunize students from attaching undue importance to inert conjectures and from speaking dry rot for very long without coming up for air, which here means without coming up for meaning.

Albert William Levi has written that the humanities are the arts of communication (language and literature), the arts of criticism (philosophy), and the arts of continuity (history). By such a definition, much public policy fails to be any of the three and to be any sort of art at all. And what is the consequence? Not communicating and not providing continuity. Of itself only, it cannot go beyond itself. Linguistic and conceptual barrenness do not invite any understanding of the conditions of men and society which the humanities record and which it is the task of public policy to address.

The purpose of education in the humanities is to encourage

students to think, write, and speak carefully, critically, and sensitively, mindful of the human condition in its particularity, those small desolations and victories. Not merely do the humanities encourage such skills by what should be contagious exposure to good thinking, writing, and sentiment, but more, the humanities at their best fix our gaze on what matters; they testify to what deserves attention and to what does not. In this way they mediate between the sensibility of the student and the grasp of the significance of what is going on in our world and our plans and schemes about it. So doing, they refuse both the imperial ambitions of the preset category and the reduction of the difficult into what is merely the specious complex. If, like the Laws in Plato's *Crito*, the humanities could speak to us, they would insist that public policy, which aims at efforts to make better conditions for men, retain a respect for irreducible complexity, but represent this complexity with a human countenance, and, as much as possible, with a public meaning.

Although the humanities may not speak to us directly, some humanists do speak out; some complain that they are not listened to, that the domination of the social sciences in today's thinking in public policy is unfortunate. However justified these complaints, the obligation is on the humanist to do more than complain, but actively to bring the humanities to public policy planning. As Chekhov pointed out, a man does not become a saint through other people's sins. No man or profession achieves a worthy end solely by the cultivation of negative superiorities. If we argue for the study of the humanities against the unnecessary arcana of public policy, then we must teach by example, and this we do not always do. It is sad to say that much work in the humanities has erected obscurity itself into an achievement. By example, we must teach otherwise.

Most of the work done by humanists is not directed immediately, but mediately, to public policy, and that is how it should be; but too much of our work now is directed neither immediately nor mediately to informing or developing the sensibility. Too much of our work is directed only to a few other specialists and last of all to one's students. We can, and should, afford some of this, but not as much as has become our habit. Removed from its former task—the study of man and the spiritual circumstances of men—some of the current work in the humanities has even degenerated into another form of dry rot. The study of man has become the study of the study of the study of man, and from trenchant commentaries on human experience such as those quoted earlier, we have moved to untrenchant commentaries on commentaries on commentaries. As Charles Frankel put it, too many humanists have refused the public invitation and have settled for taking in each other's laundry. Nor is an excessive preoccupation with minutiae endemic only to contemporary social science. The humanities suffer from that as well as from other contemporary academic diseases.

The "highest function of history," Tacitus says, is "to let no worthy action be uncommemorated and to hold out the reprobation of posterity as a terror to evil words and deeds."[10] But much history today knows nothing of commemoration and reprobation. Mired in quanto- or psychoanalysis, it not only does not record "worthy actions" or chronicle "evil words and deeds," it denies them and ignores them. "Worthy actions," "evil deeds"—memorable particulars—are swept away in a torrent of unmemorable details.

Kant asks, and points to, the questions of philosophy: What can I know? What should I do? What may I hope? Plato asks: What is a just state? A just man? Is pleasure the good life? Aristotle says we study ethics "in order to become good." But philosophy today, or much of it, studies not these, but the study of the study of the study of these—so far removed from them that their ancient connection with these questions is indiscernible. Today, the interests of many philosophers are in the residue of the residue of these vital questions. But here is the hitch: although many paths of inquiry laid out now are more and more distant from vital matters, the needs of each generation have not, in parallel fashion, become more remote. In two thousand years the answers have become more and more ephemeral in Cambridge, Berkeley, and Ann Arbor; but the questions of the young men and women in those cities are as concrete, specific, and vital as they were in Socrates' Athens. In our educational institutions today young men and women, with blood in their veins, and uncertain in mind and heart, are too often met by practitioners of "ghost disciplines."

Of literature, Peter Shaw in *Harpers* has chronicled the abuses in the most influential of literary movements today—literary revisionism. Shaw speaks harshly, but truly, of what he calls the "literature professors' uncoerced embrace of absurdity and inconsequence." When the novel becomes not what Steiner described, but "a self-consciously fictive construction" that reflects not small desolations and immemorial particulars, but only "the word's unknowableness," the invitation to the nonprofessional student is not one to passion, interest, or action in the world the novel presents, or to study it, but only despair about both. We can hear our students, borrowing a rhythm from J. Alfred Prufrock, say, "I cannot hear the cuckoos sing; I wish they would not sing to me."[11]

A few recommendations and suggestions on how to deal with this problem may be in order. Although they are addressed directly to higher education, these are also recommendations for public policy. First, in regard to research, the professional community of humanists themselves can readjust and clean up their shop by inviting each other to speak more often about their own and public matters in responsible and understandable ways. We must, in other words, get the humanist-citizen out of the closet and encourage him to speak in the public classroom.

We may also encourage by reward. University presses can provide humanists with encouragement, inducement, and invitation to the public classroom. As the scholarly journals, witness Alasdair MacIntyre's comments about philosophical journals in *The Hastings Report*: "[P]art of the destruction of the generally educated mind [the mind of the large-minded amateur] is the sheer multiplication of professional philosophical literature. . . . [T]he increase in the number of philosophical journals—and the pressure to write that produces that increase—are almost unmitigated evils."[12] The recommendation should be obvious. Yet some faculty members who write for newspapers or nonscholarly journals on issues of general interest may not count these "nonscholarly" publications in their appeal for promotion or tenure. Thus, ironically, on some occasions the only contribution to public discourse a professor makes that is generally understandable, the only idea in circulation, does not count for him, whereas his indecipherable work assists him in getting a permanent slot in front of the young.

A third recommendation is that in thinking of the humanities the university must consider the needs of undergraduates for the humanities as not less but as more important than the needs of graduate students, who ought to be able to work more independently. Too often the opposite happens. A colleague of mine who was a teacher of philosophy in a large university was thanked in writing every year by the chairman of the department for his "sacrifice." This "sacrifice" was to volunteer to teach the freshman course every year. The chairman's choice of words clearly indicates his values. To the chairman the vital activity of the university was in the graduate school parsing of A. J. Ayer; to argue with eighteen-year-olds about why they should study philosophy, about what equality means, about why values may not be subjective, about why the rule of law is a mark of a healthy society, was to him a sacrifice, not the heart of a philosophy teacher's time.

If the most important contribution the humanities can make to public policy is in the education of the young men and women who will make public policy in the future, then efforts must be made in the places where education is supposed to occur. In a classic statement, *The Future of Teaching*, William Arrowsmith pointed to the arrogance of scholarship and to the fact that in some places the teacher enjoys no honor. The scholar has disowned the student who is not a potential scholar, and the student has retaliated by abandoning the scholar. In 1966, and it is still true, Arrowsmith pointed to the dangers inherent in this mutual abandonment. "If the university does not educate," he wrote, "others will. Education will pass to the artist, to the self-appointed intellectual, to the gurus of the mass media, the charismatic charlatans and sages, and the whole immense range of secular and religious street-corner fakes and saints."[13] Arrowsmith was, and is, right. We have reaped the whirlwind of mindlessness.

What, then, should a humanist be talking about if he is to inform us about proper public policy? To give a concrete answer, let's consider a concrete example: the *Bakke* and *Weber* cases and the version of affirmative action involved and what the humanities through higher education should have been doing in educating their students to improve knowledge, and debate, about these matters. The humanist, if he had been interested, could have instructed us about the spiritual circumstances of *Bakke* and *Weber*. Philosophers and those who work in the history of ideas could have explored with students and colleagues in the law schools the meaning of the promise of equality in America: Jefferson's understanding, the equivocation of the Founding Fathers at the Constitutional Convention, the arguments—full, heated, and passionate —between Lincoln and Stephen A. Douglas on the meaning of equality, debates that, as Harry Jaffa has taught us, determined the doctrinal foundation upon which American government and public policy rest. And historians attentive to what matters, by the example of John Hope Franklin, C. Vann Woodward, and Benjamin Quarles, obviously could have helped here by tracing the atrocities of Reconstruction and the rise of Jim Crow. People in literature might have joined with Margaret Walker and instructed us (and with us, the courts) on the persistent dream of equality recorded in the literature of slavery—on what the particulars, the very memorial perceptions, of the slave were like, as well as the desolations—moral, if not physical—of the slave master. Students of the American legislative process and of the biographies of statesmen and presidents could have told us and the courts of the efforts of Booker T. Washington, Martin Luther King, Jr., Harry Truman, Franklin Roosevelt, John Kennedy, Lyndon Johnson, and the first Justice John Marshall Harlan's efforts to erase the color line once and forever as a badge of servitude. All together on this critical matter of public policy, we might have made some difference, some contribution, at least might have had something to say for both sides in the debate.

But survey the briefs (the record number of fifty-five *amicus* briefs in the cases) and you will find very little of the humanities. And it is of no point to protest that *Bakke* was a narrow, legal, not a "humanistic" matter, for the good briefs on both sides are unanimous on one point: the *Bakke* and *Weber* cases were at bottom about the meaning of equality—about the nurture, quality, and substance, not of a mere law, but of an informing ideal, promise, and commitment. It was a case not about the form of logical consistencies, of John Rawls's "original position," or mere legal precedent, but a case about us as a people—our heritage, our ideals, our purpose, and an enormous history of small and large desolations. It was about the humanities. But where were the humanists?

If, as they did here, the humanists abandon the nurture of the heritage—the recall of the desolations and the victories, the dreams, the hopes, fears, disappointments, and aspirations of a people, and of all people—then they will abandon instruction about our spiritual circumstances. Abandoning this, they abandon their task of providing continuity, of educating each generation to the intellectual, spiritual, moral, and political birthright to which it is heir and out of which public policy in the end must flow. If we abandon this and yield to absurdity and inconsequence, then we will deserve the ignominy, and even the contumely, so many seem so prepared to give us.

In the end, there is no structure, no program, no technique, not even a government subvention that can by itself give to the humanities greater potency in the formulation and execution of public policy. That potency must come from inner vitalities of sensibility and intellect. Whether it is of an individual soul, of a whole society, or of the teaching of the humanities for the marketplace, rot is removed by regeneration, and regeneration comes from within. What we need is a few more good men and women who, through their own drive and excellence, will accept the always present public invitation, who will write good books, do well-considered and directed research that will put good ideas into circulation, and who, most important of all, will teach what the humanities can do, not merely by proclaiming what they can do, but by doing it.

NOTES

1. George Steiner, "Unsentimental Education," *New Yorker* (15 August 1977), quoted in C. Hugh Holman, *Windows on the World* (Knoxville, Tenn.: The University of Tennessee Press, 1979), p. 1.
2. William Wordsworth, "Ode: Intimations of Immortality from Recollections of Early Childhood," ll. 202–5, in *The Norton Anthology of Poetry* (New York: W. W. Norton & Company, 1970), p. 583.
3. William Butler Yeats, "Lapis Lazuli," ll. 22–23, ibid., p. 922.
4. Tacitus, *The Histories*, bk. 1, no. 2, in Mortimer J. Adler, ed., *Tacitus*, Great Books of the Western World, no. 15 (Chicago: Encyclopedia Britannica, Inc., 1952), p. 189.
5. Arthur Miller, *Death of a Salesman: Text and Criticism*, Gerald Weals, ed. (New York: Viking Press, 1967), p. 56.
6. E. M. Forster, "What I Believe," in *Two Cheers for Democracy* (London: Edward Arnold, 1972), p. 70.
7. John R. Chamberlin and Michael D. Cohen, "Toward Applicable Social Choice Theory: A Comparison of Social Choice Functions under Spatial Model Assumptions," *The American Political Science Review* 72, no. 4 (December 1978): 1341.
8. Richard D. McKelvey, Peter C. Ordeshook, Mark D. Winer, "The Competitive Solution for N-Person Games Without Transferable Utility, With an Application to Committee Games," *The American Political Science Review* 72, no. 2 (June 1978): 599.
9. William Strunk, Jr., and E. B. White, *The Elements of Style* (New York: Macmillan Publishing Co., 1972), p. 17.
10. Tacitus, *The Annals*, bk. 3, no. 65, in Mortimer J. Adler, ed., *Tacitus*, p. 60.

11. See T. S. Eliot, "The Love Song of J. Alfred Prufrock": "I have heard the mermaids singing, each to each./I do not think that they will sing to me" (ll. 124–25) in *The Norton Anthology of Poetry*, p. 999.

12. Alasdair MacIntyre, "Why Is the Search for the Foundations of Ethics So Frustrating?" *Hastings Center Report* (August 1979): 22.

13. William Arrowsmith, "The Future of Teaching," in Calvin B. T. Lee, ed., *Improving College Teaching* (Washington, D.C.: American Council of Education, 1966), p. 58.

NICHOLAS P. CHRISTY, M.D.

❦ THE PHYSICIAN AS CITIZEN

IN THE ORDINARY EXERCISE of his profession, the physician qualifies as a practicing, practical humanist: he has to be a student of human affairs, he is concerned with human welfare, he relies more on human capacities than on the supernatural. He is humane, perhaps not in the sense of being well versed in broad humanistic culture, but as long as he does his job even passably well, is touched with compassion or consideration for other human beings. The concerned doctor brings his learning to bear upon mundane problems common to all people. The more he is a humanist in this sense, the more he is a citizen. He carries out in his daily rounds the function that Charles Frankel envisaged for humanistic scholars. Frankel had designed the National Humanities Center to be a conduit between the sequestered scholar and a raw, populous, and needy society; a mechanism for intensifying the scholar's activity and impact as a citizen; a device for bringing him closer to the rest of the citizens, for getting him out of the closet.

Frankel was an ethician or ethicist. When writing an essay to commemorate him by furthering the work he started but did not live to finish, it is therefore natural for a physician to begin thinking about physicians as citizens. There is nowadays voluminous and bitter criticism of medicine. Much of the criticism has an ethical basis. Ethics is concerned with "right," "wrong," "ought," "ought not." The newspapers and television broadcasts are filled with complaints about what the medical profession "ought" and "ought not" to be doing. The exhortations are very public, very vehement, and very shrill. Some criticize the doctor's behavior toward individual patients: doctors ought to make more house calls, spend more time with each patient, be more compassionate, have a more "holistic" approach—that is, take care of the whole person in his family and social setting. Doctors ought not to manage just a small, isolated piece of the patient, ought not to treat the disease but the man or woman, ought not to be so specialized. Physicians should not be so greedy. Other exhortations, equally emphatic, are aimed at doctors' societal functions: physicians ought to be more active in trying to hold down the rising costs of medical care, in spreading the good word by teaching medical students and educating the public, in caring for the sick poor, in primary care and community medicine.

These criticisms of the physician's public function have two defects. The critics fall into the error, common through the ages, of imputing to doctors powers they do not have. Doctors are not omnipotent. In addition, the caveats leveled at the profession miss the mark. They urge physicians to become wide-ranging generalists and political activists. These are worthy aims, but they are beyond the capacity of most doctors. First, there is not enough time. Second, the problems requiring solution are large and general and cannot be successfully managed by any single group unaided. Third, doctors are not trained to do what is asked of physicians by their critics.

The two aims of this essay are to suggest that physicians may better carry out their humanistic functions by being better medical citizens and that the idea of the physician as a worker for the public weal is relatively new.

Exhortations to good individual conduct start in medical school. Most medical educators believe that such injunctions are most effective if the groundwork has been laid at mother's knee and are perhaps totally ineffective without that early tutelage. The exhortations continue during the long years of internship and residency training and never let up from then on.

"Oughts" and "ought nots" for doctors began in antiquity. In its cold and uninspirational way, the Hippocratic Oath (fourth century, B.C., not written by Hippocrates himself but by his school), usually administered upon graduation from medical school, is hortatory. Reduced to its essence, the oath instructs the beginning doctor in how to behave:

A. Be good to other doctors.
B. Be good to patients.
   1. Be honorable in your life and work.
   2. Be good to sick people; do your best; do not seduce patients.
   3. Try only to cure; do no medical act for a criminal purpose.
   4. Do not blab.

The order of presentation is interesting: kindness toward the profession takes precedence over good, some might say minimally good, behavior toward patients. This pledge, it should be remembered, is simply a kind of legal document, a code of rules. It suggests nothing about the physician's duty to the community.

Two later documents, rooted in religion, urge good conduct upon doctors with great fervor: the oath administered to novices by the sixth-century A.D. Hebrew physicians Asaph and Jochanan, and the prayer attributed to the twelfth-century doctor, theologian, and philosopher Maimonides. Asaph's first rule is negative: "Take heed that ye kill not any man with the sap of a root." Other "do nots" abound: do not commit illegal abortion; do not (as "Hippocrates" had enjoined earlier) commit adultery with your patients; do not give away medical secrets; take no bribes; do not ignore the sick poor; do not practice witchcraft or idol worship; do not manufacture poisons for people to kill their friends with, or shed blood, or cause sickness, or willfully give bad treatment to patients just because they are wicked. In short, do not kill, abort, seduce, gossip, cheat, do magic, conspire in murder, promote more disease than you cure. Most citizens would consider this a minimal standard of physician behavior. Many of Asaph's positive recommendations have to do with upright personal and religious deportment: "Be strong and let not your hands slacken. . . . Be ye pure and faithful and upright. . . . Put your trust in the Lord your God, . . . for He doth kill and make alive, smite and heal." Again, in their more emotive manner, Asaph and Jochanan are intent, like "Hippocrates," upon personal propriety and occupational probity. They offer no rules for the behavior of physicians as doers of the common good, as public health officials.

Maimonides, who was also a rabbi, says nothing to doctors about the public weal but places his "daily prayer of a physician before he visits his patients" in the larger context of the doctor as an agent of the Divine Will.[1] "I am now about to apply myself to the duties of my profession. Support me, Almighty God, in these great labors that they may benefit mankind, for without Thy help not even the least thing will succeed." Maimonides admonishes the doctor not to be led away by ambition or greed and not to pretend greater knowledge than he possesses. He emphasizes the need for continual expansion of study: "Let me be contented in everything except in the great science of my profession. Never allow the thought to arise in me that I have attained to sufficient knowledge, but vouchsafe to me the strength, the leisure and the ambition ever to extend my knowledge." As for the public health, Maimonides offers only one prescription: he entreats God to "remove from their [patients'] midst all charlatans and the whole host of officious relatives and know-all nurses, cruel people who arrogantly frustrate the wisest purposes of our art and often lead Thy creatures to their death." That sounds more like a wish to preserve the integrity of the medical guild than an unsullied measure to benefit mankind at large. Like "Hippocrates," Asaph, and Jochanan, Maimonides gives guidance for the individual and religious conduct of the doctor, but is silent on the subject of the physician's function in the community.

Only much later were broader charges laid upon the medical profession. Here are examples from the first code of ethics promulgated by the American Medical Association in 1847. This code took as a model *Medical Ethics: A Code of Institutes and Precepts, Adapted to the Professional Conduct of Physicians and Surgeons*, which had been published in 1803 by the Englishman Thomas Percival. The 1847 code contains three chapters: "Of the duties of physicians to patients, and of the obligations of patients to their physicians," "Of the duties of physicians to each other and to the profession at large," and (the shortest chapter) "Of the duties of the profession to the public, and of the obligations of the public to the profession." The code requires high moral standards; like the Hippocratic Oath it exhorts kindly behavior toward other physicians; like Asaph's oath and the prayer of Maimonides it counsels enmity toward quacks; it echoes Maimonides's injunctions to extend the bounds of the profession's usefulness and to continue enriching the science of medicine (not in a fiscal but a scholarly sense). The AMA code, unlike the earlier documents, adds many suggestions for fostering the public health: "As good citizens, it is the duty of physicians to be ever vigilant for the welfare of the community, and to bear their part in sustaining its institutions and burdens: they should . . . give counsel to the public in relation to . . . public hygiene and legal medicine . . . enlighten the public in regard to quarantine regulations . . . hospitals, asylums . . . drainage, ventilation . . . and to measures for the prevention of epidemic and contagious diseases."

As stated at the beginning of this essay, exhortations to the medical profession are now more public, more exigent, and more strident: Doctors should be less selfish, less concerned for the good of the profession and more attentive to the public; get interested in community medicine, public health, social legislation in general. The question then arises: how much can the community or society at large reasonably expect from physicians? Must they become political activists, social workers, lawgivers? In earlier, quieter times, it is probably that less was expected of doctors because they had less to give, at least from the technological point of view. It is not that patients expected physicians to perform fewer miracles then than now: that expectation has always been prevalent and is so still. I think that one of the main reasons—not the only reason—the medical profession is now in such bad odor with the public is that television and the newspapers have so unrealistically magnified the advances of medical science that ordinary people have come to regard miraculous performance on the part of physicians and hospitals as the order of the day. Such performance is not always forthcoming. People still die of diseases, and, because Americans are notably ill prepared for death as a fact of life, medical failures have become doubly unacceptable. Hence, in part, the rising unpopularity of doctors in this country in comparison to their erstwhile eminence as revered healers, godlike ministrants to the sick and suffering. Further, because everything connected with medicine costs so much, the public feels it has a right to lay upon the profession more forcibly the biblical mandate: "Of him to whom much is given, much shall be required." The people have the sense that "much" is not what they are getting.

In quieter times, in the eighteenth and nineteenth centuries, for example, it is also probable that doctors, practicing a less exacting profession than they do now, had more time to participate in community affairs, to be active citizens, to carry on such other activities as farming, businesses of various sorts, politics, even literature. In fact, the notability of the physicians of other eras seems in many cases to be in direct proportion to their involvement in matters other than the practice of medicine. There are many exemplars.

Antiquity offers us several men who were versatile: Galen the Greek (129–199 A.D.) was a philosopher as well as a physician and physiologist; Avicenna the Persian (980–1037) also combined medical and philosophical careers. We know little or nothing about their involvement in the public health. The same is true of Maimonides (1135–1204). Arbitrarily skipping to the seventeenth century in England, we find a number of physicians who were deeply involved in community health. Sir Samuel Garth (1661–1719), an early advocate for improvement of community medicine, supported free dispensaries for the poor of London despite the concerted opposition of the apothecaries. Garth wrote a satirical poem about his bitter experience: *The Dispensary* (1699). Without question, its aim was laudable; Samuel Johnson judged it not bad as poetry. A less praiseworthy medical man, Mark Akenside (1721–70), wrote bad neoclassical odes and some other poetry, was an active political controversialist and a greedy practitioner of medicine. In the reign of George III he turned Tory and, in a sense, carried out a public medical function: he became physician to the queen.

Several American physicians were many-sided public men who worked diligently in community and public medicine. In the eighteenth century, there are at least three outstanding figures. John Bard (1716–99) established the first quarantine station in America on Bedloe's Island, now the site of the Statue of Liberty. Bard was also the first health officer of New York City and first president of the Medical Society of the State of New York. His son Samuel (1742–1821) served as a faculty member and then dean of the medical school of King's College, president of the College of Physicians and Surgeons, was a founder of New York Hospital and the New York Dispensary, and wrote on midwifery, diphtheria, medical education, animal husbandry, and veterinary medicine. Benjamin Rush (1745–1813), a signer of the Declaration of Independence, started the first free dispensary in the United States (1786), made contributions to medical psychology, helped found Dickinson College, and was from 1797 until his death treasurer of the U.S. Mint in Philadelphia.

In the 1880s, Oliver Wendell Holmes, Sr. (1809–94), studied law, composed many poems, was a famous teacher of anatomy and physiology, founded the Tremont School of Medicine in Boston, was for a time dean of the Harvard Medical School, lectured on scientific and literary topics, and produced three anti-Calvinist "medical" novels (one was *Elsie Venner*) that were far ahead of their time in psychological understanding. Holmes also completed two important medical treatises on the evils of homeopathy and on the infectious nature of puerperal fever. Silas Weir Mitchell (1829–1914) pioneered in applying psychology to medicine. He wrote extensively on nervous disorders, one of his major works being on the detailed neurology of nerve injuries; much of his case material was drawn from military survivors of the Civil War. Like Holmes, Mitchell published several novels.

That brief summary of the careers of versatile and involved

physicians of earlier times leads us back to the question posed above: what can society reasonably expect of today's physicians? Must they rival Garth, the Bards, Rush, Holmes, Mitchell? That would be a heavy demand, probably an excessive one. The geometric growth of modern technology has made the study and practice of medicine so exigent and the mass of material to be mastered so vast that the doctor has little time or energy left over to pursue other activities, no matter how important or how pertinent to medical practice. Further, most would agree that physicians should probably not neglect their medical functions to enter directly into local and national politics, become congressmen, edit newspapers, write poetry, do archaeology, or compose string quartets to surpass Bartók's. Plainly, such accomplishments are beyond the training, energy, available time, or inclination of most physicians. No one would seriously ask them to do these things.

The question then is what more does the public want of doctors, who, as I have suggested above, are beginning to get tired of the spate of exhortations to do more and do better? It may be argued that a reasonable public expectation should be that doctors make an effort to be more active medical citizens. In that area, the following complaints are commonly aimed at the profession.

Doctors do not participate in hospital politics that impinge upon their very bone marrow. During a recent court action in connection with the bankruptcy and closure of a hospital in New York City, the judge castigated the medical staff for failing to get involved in the day-to-day management of the failing institution.

Most doctors do not take part in medical society affairs. In the recent malpractice crisis in New York State, the remedial action, which was of the closest concern to the profession at large, was taken by a group of no more than half a dozen physicians.

By and large, practicing physicians have little interest in primary care, community medicine, public health, health care delivery systems, or hospital management.

By and large, academic physicians do not pay much attention to the concerns of patients.

By and large, practicing and academic physicians alike pay lip service to teaching, but tend to elude teaching responsibilities. They are too busy.

There is some basis for these accusations. Here are a few of the reasons that I believe underlie the objectionable behavior of doctors as medical citizens.

The medical curriculum for most students is in lockstep. Everybody studies the same things. This identity of educational substrate fosters uniformity of thought and behavior.

A policy of admissions committees in medical schools is self-perpetuation. The schools take on the same kinds of students year after year: very intelligent people, good learners, conformists, young men and women with excellent academic records.

On an unconscious level, the prospective medical student knows what he is about to let himself in for. He may not have a grasp of all the details, but as long as he has not spent his first twenty-one years living in a barrel, he realizes that he will have to spend all his nights studying merely to pass the scientific courses. He knows that in the clinical years he will often have night duty and that as a house officer his time will not be his own. I used to think that the medical school and postgraduate curricula were at fault for cloistering the students and residents. Not true. The receptors for cloistering have to be there, in the bosoms of the trainees who are cloistered and allow themselves to be cloistered because they are ready to be cloistered. Medical students desire it. They crave it, of course, subconsciously.

To change all these things is difficult. The problems are basic, general, and numerous. The already voluminous criticism of the medical profession makes one diffident about further "do's and dont's" for doctors, but a few suggestions may be offered. The measures set out below are all intended to generalize the way doctors function.

A national service program, like that of Peru or Sweden, in which just after graduation a student spends one or two years carrying out a public health function in a remote rural area or an urban ghetto would likely imbue the "intern" with some sense of belonging to an entity—the state—larger than himself.

Somewhere in today's curriculum, either in college or medical school, the student needs to be taught a broader notion of what medical ethics is than that expressed sometimes by organizations that purport to speak for the medical profession. An official of the AMA, for instance, has equated medical ethics, that is, medically ethical behavior, with private, one-on-one, fee-for-service practice; prepaid, government-subsidized medical care programs are defined as unethical.[2]

New medical school admissions policies would be helpful. A changed emphasis is desirable, with less attention paid to grades and to the virtues of the obsessive-compulsive personality (all good doctors have to have some of this) and more to humanistic qualities pertinent to dealing not only with individual people but to issues beyond the end of the nose. This approach to admissions may have been adopted already; according to a recent Rockefeller Foundation survey, college students majoring in religion (speaking of the cloister) have the highest percentage of successful applications to medical school, 55 percent higher than majors in the other humanities or in science.

Any attempt to inculcate medicine's larger missions is more difficult still. This is a job for the medical school and the education that precedes it. Most people would like doctors to aspire to something more than a "powerless security and a respectable social position." As James Lawless has written, physicians, by virtue of their mastery over death, should long since have become "a caste of supreme influence, power, and importance. This has not happened, and indeed the influence and power of the profession in international, national, and public affairs have perhaps never been less. By and large we do not find doctors outside their surgeries, consulting-rooms, or operating theatres. In general they have rejected the responsibilities, and therefore the opportunities, of an élite," despite the fact that "the organization of man and nature is their business." He wants them to exert their influence in general ways.[3] I only ask doctors to keep their own house in better order—that is, to function more effectively as medical citizens—because, if they do not, the public through its legislative emissaries will do it for them in ways that doctors do not like and that may in many instances be bad for doctors and patients and the public health. Further, if doctors pay more attention to their own proper concerns—hospital management, community medicine, teaching, the high cost of medical care—without being too parochial and self-interested, the public perception of the medical profession will be more favorable. Such an improvement in public regard, together with a more realistic public expectation of what doctors can actually do (that is, recognition that modern medicine for all its miracles has limits) will have the inevitable effect of brightening the emotional climate between people and doctors. A better climate should be conducive to improved health all around: better public health and better individual relations between physicians and patients.

For such reasons, large numbers of physician-watchers believe that it is time for doctors to come out of the closet of techne. This will not be easy. That closet is a fine safe place to hide from all manner of unpleasantness generated by a restless and demanding society. The atmosphere inside is comfortable. The surgeon in his operating room, for example, is quite as unassailable as the priest officiating at his altar. There are many similarities: special room, funny language, funny odors, funny sounds, unbridled authoritarianism in the air, much of the activity too arcane for profane and public eyes, a touch of the supernatural. In any specialized branch of knowledge there will always be some taint of the cloister. Not all the information is accessible to most people, and there is no need for it to be. Still, I think there is now widespread agreement that doctors would do well to come out of the temple, not necessarily in such generally humanistic ways as Maimonides or Akenside or Holmes or Mitchell, but simply as functioning medical members of the community, citizens like Garth or John and Samuel Bard. To emulate them is to be enough of a humanist, and that kind of emergence from the closet by the scholar or the specialist is what Charles Frankel taught and what he did himself.

NOTES

1. Moses Maimonides (1135–1204), a Hebrew physician who practiced in Egypt, regarded as one of the greatest medieval medical authorities, was a codifier of Jewish religious law and a notable philosopher. The prayer quoted and paraphrased here is believed by some scholars to have been written ca. 1793 by Marcus Herz, a German physician who had been a pupil of Kant.
2. R. H. Roth, "Medicine's Ethical Responsibilities," *Journal of the American Medical Association* 215 (1971): 1956–58. At the time this paper was written, Roth was speaker of the AMA's House of Delegates. The point of view he expresses can therefore be taken as the quasiofficial position of the AMA in 1970–71.
3. James Lawless, "The Role of the Medical Profession as an Elite," *Lancet* 1 (1971): 543.

PART FOUR

THE HUMANIST AS

CITIZEN

JACOB L. TALMON

❦ THE HUMANIST AND

HIS DILEMMAS

THE HUMANIST has always had to face two not easily reconcilable challenges: one, to cultivate his own self, watch over his inner light, labor for self-perfection, preserve his authenticity, and thus hold the disturbing, polluting, and contaminating influences of the outside world at bay; the other, to make the world a better place, to take responsibility for it. As Chesterton put it, nothing in this respect fails like success. The dilemma of the humanist, and indeed of all movements aiming at rebirth and purification, finds a parallel with that of the Church in the Middle Ages. Too exclusive and intense a preoccupation with the salvation of one's individual soul or the integrity of the sect meant surrendering the earth to Satan. Too much eagerness to guide and to better the world led to too much mixing with unregenerate society, to the employment of all the instruments of power, wealth, and influence, the arcana imperii that erode the purity of the spirit, and thus, in the words of Charles Peguy, caused the mystique to degenerate into politique and to forfeit the moral right to serve as guide. It is no accident that intellectuals resign public office, as Charles Frankel did, very soon after taking it up.

The humanist should, in the language of Matthew Arnold, exude light and sweetness. In the modern world of egalitarian mass society, however, he has found himself an embattled warrior and a

Jacob L. Talmon died in Jerusalem on 17 June 1980. This essay is a revised and edited version of an address given by Professor Talmon in honor of Charles Frankel on 25 September 1979.

suspect citizen. His descent from noble ancestry—classical antiquity—has become a stigma and scandal in the eyes of the many.
In the ancient world and for long after, the humanist's communion
with the liberal arts was automatically and emphatically associated
with and conditioned upon a life of leisure, with the concomitant
that, the universe being finite, the many, even if not born inferior
as Aristotle believed, were doomed to labor to enable the chosen
and superior few to preserve and cultivate in leisure a sample of
culture, because in a world suffering from scarcity as our earth
does, any attempt at an equal distribution of the bounties of nature
was bound to result in general wretched poverty and barbarism.
As late as at the close of the last century, despite the wonders of
technology and industry and the phenomenal growth of production, Heinrich Treitschke, admittedly a ferocious reactionary and
militarist but no Malthusian, preached vehemently that hereditary
inequality was the unavoidable condition of civilization and the
natural order of things.

That is why, on the other pole of the political spectrum, Russian
revolutionary ideology—the crassest example and a case most
pregnant with consequences for mankind—went to such great
lengths to repudiate any form of idealism, mysticism, religion,
individualism, and theories of art for art's sake, and to deify the
exact sciences, materialism, atheism, utilitarianism, and social realism in the arts. Thus its suspicion of or even contemptuous hostility to the humanities. The prophets of revolution were horrified
by any suggestion of the existence or desirability of superior and
esoteric truths, values, or experiences that were accessible only to
the chosen few and barred to the many, the ordinary men. The
very thought of a kingdom of pure ideas, hidden meanings, higher
import, gave in their view legitimacy to elitism and inequality. It
offered rationalization to privilege and divided mankind into those
few born to be served and the vast majority destined to serve—
rulers and ruled. Materialism was egalitarian because it taught that
we were all made of the same stuff, matter, and that all pretended
refined, noble ideas and sentiments were either deliberate mystification or other forms of sensuous energy and combinations of

sensations and reactions to outward stimuli. Extreme utilitarianism was again a guarantee of equality, for it went to show that we were all conditioned and guided by the same motives, the desire for pleasure and the recoiling from pain—in short, self-interest. All people were selfish and self-seeking, but when conscious of it, they were honest and candid. An acquired understanding and ability to discern between short-run and long-term advantages and our eventual comprehension of the ultimate identity of enlightened self-interest and the social good, makes us less selfish and more idealistic than those beautiful souls who are guilty of deception and self-deception, when boasting of altruism, patriotism, chivalry, disinterested service, and sacrifice. According to Csernyshaevsky, whom Lenin adored as his master, even a loving mother or bereaved wife is driven by self-love, the wish for emotional satisfaction, and the desire to flee deprivation. The possibility of quantification of pain and pleasure, profit and loss, provided a safe, impartial yardstick to measure merit and apportion due reward or punishment.

The exact sciences, above all the natural sciences, were democratic and progressive by nature, whereas the humanities invited mystification, pretentious claims, and esoteric attitudes. This is why the famous nihilist thinker Pissarev preached that the salvation of Russia was in the dissected limbs of the frog. Here was tangible proof of the unity of nature, of deterministic laws, embracing also man. The effort of unveiling, unmasking of arrogant pretense, led the revolutionary believers to defy and profane sanctified symbols. They relished a provocative coarseness of appearance and manner. They used every opportunity to defile ceremonious pomp and circumstance and public decorum—all in order to strip the king naked and to undermine the feelings of respect, awe, mystery—in short, to loosen the invisible spiritual chains, which church, divine-right kings, ancient authority, and class domination had allegedly imposed upon the hearts of oppressed men to make them more readily bear the material yoke with greater humility. For, as Marx put it, "Once the realm of imagination has been revolutionized, reality can no longer hold out." The first task was therefore to liberate the oppressed from the feelings that held them back from daring—to teach them to dare.

Similarly, literary and artistic formalism as well as preoccupation with personal idiosyncracies, morbidity, and pessimistic melancholy were not mere escapism, but a service to privilege and a libel on life as lived by the common run of normal, healthy, but suffering humanity. Not the migraine of a moody lady with delicate limbs and imaginary aches and pains, but the full-bosomed, hefty wench should form the subject of poets. Not erotic adventures, but social phenomena and economic developments should attract attention. A pair of boots interested the muzhik more than a Shakespearean sonnet or a Beethoven sonata.

Is the humanist's dilemma the need to choose between culture and justice? Must he be the jealous defender of a precious heritage bequeathed by (let us face it) a fundamentally aristocratic tradition against the barbarian, uncouth masses overrunning the ramparts of civilization, and close his ears to the call, "Cain, where is thy brother Abel?" This was the attitude of an unquestionably very great humanist, Jacob Burckhardt. With the sensibility of a most erudite, accomplished, and discerning aesthete, he was capable of striking the harshest accents when gleefully rejoicing at the rejection, by the Swiss patrician authorities, of the pretentious plebeian demands for public funds for universal education and social services. Burckhardt's targets were, in Edmund Burke's terms, the swinish multitude, the poor and the rising. He looked for salvation from the mounting tide of barbarian democracy in a retreat to secular monasteries that would, as in the Dark Ages, safeguard the holy flame.

The *Angst* of Burckhardt was not alien to Alexis de Tocqueville, who was truly resigned to the fact that the modern aspiration for equality was wholly irresistible, but who, in his *Recollections*, spoke of the fear that gripped the possessing classes of France before the onslaught of the proletariat. He compared it to the fear of the civilized late Romans in face of the barbarian invasions. We know how apprehensive John Stuart Mill was about the fate of cultivated minorities and individuals under the tyranny of majorities. Nor should we forget to mention Schopenhauer, Nietzsche, Ortega y Gasset, and T. S. Eliot.

The essence of humanism is indeed the sustained endeavor to appropriate and internalize the distilled and pruned legacy of the ages, the ability to roam about the vast expanses and the diverse paths and byways of past and present civilizations. It is permeated by a sense of awe for the achievement of the human spirit and motivated by the strenuous effort to fathom, follow, and comprehend the process of that spirit's beginning, growth, and varieties. It has a particularly tender love for the early stages, both because they help us understand future evolution and because the early samples were shaped by fresh revelatory inspiration and were created not as commodities for an anonymous mass consumer, but, as it were, as special onetime creations for the chosen. With all the respect for the ways and forms of old, for style and procedure, method and manner, law, discipline, and tradition, the humanist is constantly straining to avoid cliché and commonplace, platitude and generality, and is bent upon working out and practicing an idiom authentically his own, upon making his responses as direct, individual, and personal as possible.

Yet, the dream of an orderly world, the revulsion to squalor, the deep feeling for decorum and the drapery of life, the vision of the majesty of history and, above all, the dignity of man—these are the bridges that span the distance from the cultivation of the arts and the self to the quest for a civilized, orderly, and just society.

The humanist who feels committed to both the humanist heritage and the cause of social justice badly needs the reassurance accorded by a generous and optimistic estimate of human nature. He must cherish the hope that one day all Israel will become prophets. There was a time before the messengers of nuclear and ecological doom had seized the forum when people rather dreaded what men, with life expectancies vastly prolonged by modern medicine and made idle for most of their adult lives by automation, would do with their free time to avoid dying of boredom or escaping into vulgar pleasures or even crime. The glimmer of hope was that we could impart to all men the curiosity and the ability to commune with the things of the spirit.

All these dilemmas have acquired new dimensions as a result of the most important developments of the second part of the twentieth century, namely, the exodus of the white man from Asia and Africa, decolonization, and the emergence of the Third World. On the face of it, the vast transformations were the result of Western, and we may even say Western-humanist, inspiration and models. When the great English historian Macaulay was commissioned to prepare a curriculum for the schools of India, he devised a scheme entirely based on the European cultural legacy. Critics objected that surely it was absurd to bring up India's children on Western, and not native, traditions. Moreover, because Western literature was to a large extent a literature of revolt against tyranny and oppression, a European type of education would incite the natives to rise against their white overlords. Macaulay's reply was that all the literatures of India, Asia, and Arabia were not worth a single shelf of Western books—a claim full of hubris that no white racist would dare to make in public today. As to the second objection, the historian proclaimed that Great Britain's most glorious hour would be that when the colonial peoples had learned the lessons of European civilization so well as to rise and expel the Western powers. The English liberal took it for granted that the colored races were the future recruits of European civilization, just as the French regarded their own subject peoples as *candidats à la civilisation française*. Up to a point they were right. All leaders of colonial national liberation movements and all African and Asian elites eagerly imbibed Western teachings and then turned them against their imperial masters. From this point of view, the historian may soon sum up the significance of the age of imperialism not as the apogee of Western capitalism, but as a preparation of the subject races for independent statehood and industrial civilization.

But in the most recent past we have been receiving bewildering lessons that show that, far from wishing to join us as disciples or partners in shaping a new and perhaps ecumenical type of humanist synthesis, large masses of emancipated subjects of colonialism are on the crest of a wave of defiant and militant assertion of their authentic or imaginary traditions. It could be said that in a sense even this contemptuous rejection of Western models is also a form of imitating European nationalism.

Western man, and perhaps especially the humanist, finds himself on the defensive. Liberal and socialist doctrines left him with a bad conscience about Western imperialism and Western prosperity. The most conspicuous representative of that mood has been Arnold Toynbee, the castigator of European hubris and of the white man's sin of pride as it has been demonstrated for centuries by the West's arrogant and aggressive attitude toward the colonial races. Toynbee sometimes traced this attitude back to the influence of the Israelite claims to chosenness and to their divine right to inherit the land of the Canaanites.

In any event, these mighty developments may provide a new slant to the humanist's dilemma of culture and justice. In the last few decades, the classical socialist caesura between capitalists and proletarians, bourgeois and workers, exploiters and exploited, oppressors and oppressed has been somewhat overshadowed by the more obvious and steadily growing identification of social with racial differences. The distinction seems to be increasing between prosperous societies and foreign guest workers, old imperial countries and colored immigrants from the former colonies ("we are here, because you were there"), whites and Blacks in America, above all, the rich white North (which may soon come to include even Russia) and the poor colored South (with some of the Arab oil countries in what may prove only a temporarily ambiguous situation). The vast multitudes of the starving poor of Asia, Africa, and Latin America—Toynbee's "external proletariat"—are certainly strangers to Western humanism to an infinitely greater degree than the "internal proletariat" of the West. The Western humanist is thus being torn between the sense of guilt toward the colored races and the burning anxiety about the fate of Europe's ancient humanist legacy.

Humanism has been and is being besieged from many other

quarters. By way, perhaps, of historic justice, its own fixities and certainties have been shaken by the very means humanism lent centuries ago to the assault upon the dogmas of the Church: history and philology, the combination of which comes close to anthropology. It was the seventeenth-century English jurist John Selden who coined the beautiful phrase: "scrutamini Scripturas: these two words have upset the world." "Scrutinize the Scriptures": the medieval order collapsed when men, dissatisfied with clerical ignorance, made indignant by the poor morality of priests and monks, and shocked by the power politics of the Church, turned to the Bible and, by careful reading of the text in the original languages and aided by some knowledge of history, began to discover forgeries, interpolations, errors in translation, discrepancies, improbabilities, which put Church traditions in doubt, suggesting that they were not the Word of God but the historic contrivance of men.

At the height of its expansion and influence, history, the subject, prop, and pride of humanism, is doing something similar to its only begetter. The last two centuries have been the age of Pan-history, as we may call the flowering of the vertical sciences, which in one way or another have a historical dimension—geology, astronomy, biology, psychology—in contrast to the horizontal sciences—mathematics, physics, chemistry. They have made us acutely and obsessively aware that everything has a history, came about, or was contrived or shaped by conditions and circumstances. The paramount truth is not being, but becoming. What seems to matter most is not so much the question, Is it true or false, right or wrong, but How did it come about, evolve? The question focuses variously upon economic-social conditions and interests, anthropological or psychological data, the Darwinian struggle for survival and power, racial uniqueness, and indeed history all-encompassing. Man ceased to be the maker of history; he became a function thereof. No longer the Kantian legislator of nature and autonomous proud source of his own morality, he came to be seen as a product of collective impersonal forces—society, nation, race —or even as a bundle of irrational drives, instincts, impulses, urges, complexes, and obsessions; in any case not a free, conscious maker of rational choices. His sharply outlined contours of a self-contained, responsible being and his unique status in the universal scheme of things became suffused by the assimilation of man into the all-embracing determinism of nature.

The cultural despair spread by theories that have been dethroning man from his exalted position as the sole vessel of consciousness, creature of reason, holder of objective truth, and bearer of the eternal moral laws in the universe was bound to deny the existence of a rationality that was the exclusive, independent, supreme, objective, and safe guide of humankind.

The crisis of values was immeasurably deepened by the disaster of World War I, when at the end of a century of unprecedented stability and progress, in an orgy of carnage and destruction, the most enlightened part of mankind appeared to have completely lost its intellectual and moral bearings and the deep, centuries-old inhibitions that kept savagery repressed were swept away. This was followed by the ravages of inflation and then mass unemployment in the Great Depression that destroyed every type of credibility and predictability and the last shreds of the faith in the existence of a benevolent, hidden hand that secures social-economic harmony. In their longing for meaning and purpose and for compensation commensurable with the untold suffering undergone, men sought refuge in all-encompassing salvationist creeds, which in practice amounted to an abdication of feeble, discredited reason in favor of omnipotent would-be saviors, the terrible simplificateurs.

The Holocaust in World War II, the appearance of lethal nuclear weapons, followed by the ecological threat, spread an apocalyptic dread of a doom, which human reason, morality, or ingenuity seemed too weak to avert. In their exasperation, the young came to view the existing political and social order as a colossal sham and deception, behind which sinister, occult vested interests were manipulating society. Those among them who had a hankering belief in the power of totalitarian messianism of the Left to bring an end to human alienation and to every sort of oppression were shattered by the discovery that a salvationist message had given rise to a centralized bureaucratic establishment. The result was anarchism in both its forms, escapist hippie and drug culture and desperate terrorist revolutionism against the massive hypocrisies and the standing plots of the ruling castes. On the other end of the spectrum, the quest for some fixities and certainties produced a resurgence of doctrines of naturalistic determinism, social materialism, and sociobiology, based on the allegedly implacable and unalterable facts of hereditary inequality and eternal competition—nature versus nurture—with or without the aid of environmentalist social engineering. They amount to an apotheosis of hereditary inequality and of the eternity of competition and strife—hardly a vision of reconciliation, concord, and stability at the end of days. Faith in a theodicy, however, had been the polar star of all the Western creeds and ideologies from the Judeo-Christian beginnings till Marxism, the great heresy of the West. In the eighteenth century it found its lofty expression in Germany in the ideal of *Humanität* of Herder, the poet of ethnic diversity, in the famous saying of Schiller, "Nur deutsch sein ist nicht deutsch sein," and in Kant's vision of eternal peace. It was left to Hitler, the prophet of paganism, to proclaim defiantly in this century that man was simply an extension of nature, had never conquered nature in anything, and at most had discovered only some laws and secrets of nature, but what man discovered above all was the aristocratic principle of nature, the eternal privilege of power and strength and the right to lord over those other living creatures who lack this knowledge.

In his writings, Charles Frankel tried to come to grips with these dilemmas. His critique of the critics of liberal humanism was refreshingly characterized by an explicit or implicit employment of the adversaries' arguments in order to refute their case. A sweeping, all-denying relativism exposed itself in his eyes as itself another expression of relativism and not a conclusive verdict upon all other creeds. The fact, for instance, that materialism was used in the past by the Left as an argument for equality and in our days as proof of hereditary inequality showed not that the scientific theory was the final judge, but that the advocates of this or that interest were eager and able to harness it and to turn it to their respective uses. In the words of Fichte, it was the character, temper, and values or interests of the philosopher as a person that determined what kind of philosophy he would espouse and then develop a vested interest in. The weak and unsure person feels confirmed by relativist historicism in his wobbling confusion and despair, in his permanent crisis of identity; the robustly self-confident man, such as Charles Frankel, is inspired proudly to proclaim, "This is what I am and how I am," without shame or apology. Prophets of doom were, by way of self-fulfilling prophecy, prone to develop a dread of and hostility toward betterment and remedial reform and progress, in brief, a stake in evil and misery.

Frankel certainly would not have banned research because it might lead to uncomfortable discoveries that could undermine the ideals of equality and equity and, in the language of Nietszche, prove that the truth sustained neither life nor democracy. In the spirit of Kant, he seemed to hold the view that, as in the case of Kant's famous antinomies, whatever the compulsions of logical consistency, men have to act as if the moral order were the supreme categorical imperative among those who have the freedom and ability to make choices. Difficulties, complexities, and antinomies were to him not a blank wall, but a challenge to the human genius and man's resilience. He would have endorsed the mathematician Poincaré's dictum that "those who crave for certainty above all do not love the truth," but instead seek relaxation and comfort. As I. A. Richards has said, "Mysteries are the food of the mind, and all the fundamental mysteries are necessary to sanity."

WILLIAM E. LEUCHTENBURG

CHARLES FRANKEL: THE

HUMANIST AS CITIZEN

THREE DAYS AFTER he resigned as Assistant Secretary of State, Charles Frankel received a call from Admiral Hyman Rickover about a paper he had written for an International Philosophy Year symposium. Rickover said that he liked Frankel's paper, which argued that both intellectuals and the public would benefit if philosophers took a more active role in affairs of the world, but he did not agree with it. He also stated that he was glad that Frankel was no longer in the government. "Thanks," Frankel replied. "No, I don't mean it that way," the admiral responded. "I know what you've been trying to do. You're trying to be a citizen, and you think it's a good thing to try to inject some ideas into the government. But it won't work—the government isn't ready."[1]

The episode is instructive, for it indicates the difficulty Frankel encountered in getting others to go along with him in pursuing the goal that was the leitmotif of his career: the humanist as citizen.[2] Not only was the government not ready for him; many scholars, sometimes with good reason, were reluctant to follow him on the path he blazed. Furthermore, he had to clarify certain obscurities in his own thought. Yet, for all the vicissitudes, he succeeded perhaps more than any other American of his generation in personifying the ideal of the man of letters who is active in the world of great affairs.

Though Frankel had the kind of exceptional intelligence that might well have left a mark on his own discipline, philosophy, he chose a different course. At Columbia College, from which he was graduated at the age of nineteen, he made an impressive record. His teacher, the Columbia philosopher James Gutmann, remembered him as "not always the easiest student to have, but very bright, very keen. Very much a youngster still. If I'm not mistaken, I referred to him as the representative of the kindergarten in the class, because he was—not exactly boisterous, but full of high spirits. Full of ideas, too. Wonderful spirits."[3] At twenty-one, he was already a member of the Columbia faculty. Years later, the pioneer social psychologist Abram Kardiner, who had witnessed one of Frankel's performances, commented: "He's brilliant. I saw him take Niebuhr and Toynbee apart. He tore them to shreds and tatters. Did a brilliant job. And he walked away with all the honors."[4] But Frankel decided not to pursue an orthodox career in his own field. True, he wrote or edited seventeen books, published a great many articles, and delivered countless lectures. Yet he made no significant contribution to the scholarship of philosophy and got a cold shoulder from some of the members of his guild.[5] In his last years at Columbia he found a home not in Philosophy Hall but in the Law School.

The esteemed philosopher, Ernest Nagel, who knew Frankel for more than twoscore years, has reflected:

> The main focus of Charles's strictly professional concerns was social, political and moral theory, and eventually included the philosophy of law. He did not view philosophy as just another specialized discipline that deals with technical problems of prime if not exclusive interest only to its professional practitioners. To be sure, he recognized that professional philosophers explore many technical questions having a narrow scope, which are legitimate and often unavoidable subjects of study, and there can be no doubt that he himself knew how to play the game of creating and resolving such technical and esoteric puzzles. However, he maintained in consonance with the great tradition of philosophy that phi-

losophy is basically a reflection and commentary on the nature
of things, and especially on human aspirations and patterns of
human behavior.[6]

Frankel made no effort to conceal his contempt for bookish lore,
and he was forever hectoring his colleagues to relate their scholarly
endeavors to the everyday concerns of their countrymen. His first
book, a revision of his 1946 Columbia doctoral dissertation on the
philosophes, started a lifelong romance with those great thinkers
who were not content to confine themselves to the study. In 1972,
he was still writing, "The true successors of Descartes were those
who translated his philosophy into deeds. A philosophy is there to
be lived out. What goes into the word dies, what goes into the
work lives."[7]

He stressed the importance of political commitment by the humanist not merely because he thought it would benefit society, but
because he was certain it was in the intellectual's own self-interest.
"The right not simply to dissent but, if one pleases, to be indifferent; the right to be private; the right to be useless from every
respectable point of view; the right to be irreverent about what is
officially sanctified—when have these rights ever been safe from
the crowd?" Frankel asked. "When have they been safe even from
other intellectuals?" Strangely, the scholar could maintain his precious right to be idiosyncratic, he wrote, only if the government
intervened actively to preserve the independence of the university
campus where most intellectuals made their abode. "If government does not support intellectual independence, it will not be
supported very well," he contended. "This means that the relationship of scholarly independence to political power has changed," he
went on. "It may once have been possible for scholars to guard
their independence by keeping their distance from power. It may
be possible for individual scholars to do that still. But it is not
possible for the scholarly community as such to maintain its independence by running away from government. For key decisions
that affect scholarly independence will be made in any event. And
if they are made without the participation of men and women who

know something about the nature and necessary conditions of scholarly and intellectual life, they cannot be expected to be the right decisions."[8]

In his own conduct Frankel set other humanists an example of civic involvement. He served in a variety of posts such as director of the New York State Civil Liberties Union, president of the board of trustees of the Rockland Country Day School, and, with the law professor Louis H. Pollak, as co-chairman of the National Assembly for the Teaching of the Principles of the Bill of Rights. But he took a particular interest in those functions that intersected with the humanities or, more broadly, with higher education. Hence, he agreed to chair the committee on professional ethics of the American Association of University Professors and headed the committee that examined the "brain drain"—the migration of scientists and engineers to the United States. With the aid of a Carnegie grant, he studied democratic development in times of transition. This project took him to Mexico in the summer of 1961, and in the summer of 1962 he chaired a month-long conference of political, business, and education leaders in Japan to explore how and why democratic ideas and institutions emerge. Increasingly, he became engrossed in transnational cultural relations, an interest that culminated in his appointment as Assistant Secretary of State for Educational and Cultural Affairs. When he returned to Columbia from his tour of duty in Washington, he was elected chairman of the Council of Tenured Faculty of Columbia University, established in 1970 to oppose campus violence; and, alarmed by the deterioration of academic freedom in other lands as well as in America, he, together with Paul Seabury of the University of California at Berkeley, called an international conference to meet in Norwich, England, in September 1970. Two months later, scholars at press conferences held simultaneously in Rome, Berlin, and New York announced the formation of the International Committee on the University Emergency (subsequently the International Council on the Future of the University) of which Charles Frankel became chairman.

Still, Frankel did not abandon his devotion to the humanities when he immersed himself in public affairs. Indeed, it was second nature for him to refer to the classics when he spoke about modern-day issues. Invited to comment on Watergate at a service on the state of the nation at the Cathedral Church of St. John the Divine, he reflected on Plato's "The Laws." Asked by *U.S. News and World Report*, "Do democratic processes attract people to the superficial and to the charismatic rather than to substantive qualities of candidates?" he responded:

> That's always been a danger in democracy. Plato thought it was partly what had killed Athenian democracy. So did Thucydides. The Athenians had a great and moderate leader, Pericles; yet demagogues unseated him. Plato wondered how Athenian democracy could be saved in view of its tendency to such missteps. The guiding thought behind his idea of letting philosophers rule was to get away from demogoguery, which he thought was the disease of democracy.[9]

In short, if it was imperative for the humanist to be a citizen, the citizen did not cease to be a humanist.

In the summer of 1965, Frankel got the opportunity to act out his views on the civic responsibilities of humanists on a larger stage when he was approached about becoming assistant secretary of state for cultural and educational affairs. He had gained this consideration after conducting a study for learned societies and the State Department of the government's educational and cultural programs. "I said that the premises of official policy were largely wrong and the government's mode of operation outlandish," he later recorded.[10] Given the opportunity to improve this situation, he hesitated, but his friend J. Kenneth Galbraith helped win him over. Johnson is "an old school teacher," Galbraith told him. "He ought to like the kind of thing you represent. Maybe you can give him something more constructive to think about than Vietnam." Besides, a stint in the State Department would be good experience. "You'll find that it's the kind of organization which, though it does big things badly, does small things badly too," he added cheerily.[11]

Those who put forward Frankel's name for the post easily carried the day, for his performance as head of the investigatory committee had gained him admiration in powerful quarters. "I spoke with Dr. Frankel at some length and am much impressed by his personality, his appearance, his ability to articulate, and his understanding of the program which he would administer should you see fit to nominate him," Senator J. William Fulbright wrote President Johnson. "Field Haviland, the Director of Foreign Policy Studies for the Brookings Institution who is most familiar with the recent study done by Frankel, states that he is an intellectual leader, a great public speaker, and very realistic in his appraisal of the cultural exchange program. He has said, in addition, that he has great influence in the academic world and is influential in his dealings with foreigners. I have had similar comments from other persons who know Frankel well."[12] On 16 September 1965, Charles Frankel was sworn in as assistant secretary of state.

Frankel began his tenure in the State Department with a fundamental premise: intellectuals are politically important. "It didn't occur to me then, and it doesn't occur to me now," he wrote subsequently, that they were superior. "They aren't more responsible, more humane or necessarily more intelligent than people in other walks of life, and the way in which they govern their own institutions gives no reason to suppose that the world would be substantially better governed if they took over."[13] Nonetheless, intellectuals exerted power, and he wanted the government to become aware of that fact in the conduct of its foreign policy. "Education and cultural cooperation are not the most visible parts of foreign affairs, but they have the same relation to foreign policy that vitamins have to the human diet," he contended.[14]

Intellectuals, he maintained, constituted a world community of their own. In the eighteenth century, he noted, Voltaire had said that *les honnêtes gens qui pensent*, no matter what their nationality, "share the same principles and constitute a single republic." That was not altogether true either in Voltaire's day or in our own, he conceded. Still, there were "common problems and standards of workmanship that tie chemists, musicians or economists together, whatever their national origins or ideological affinities."

234 WILLIAM E. LEUCHTENBURG

The United States, Frankel held, should not only adapt to that fact in carrying out its own foreign policy, but should work actively to encourage the growth of this international community of savants.[15]

Frankel sought to conduct his office in a spirit different from that of the "hard-nosed psychological warrior" who thought that cultural activities were simply propaganda instruments for serving the national interest. Such an attitude struck him as "more than crass"; it was also naive. After all, "the advancement of the arts and sciences and the promotion of international understanding" were in the national interest. Beyond that, intellectuals simply would not permit themselves to be used as tools of *Realpolitik*.[16] He wanted to give intellectuals an enhanced sense that they had a public role to play. He would do so not by treating them as people to be exploited for national ambitions but by developing government enterprises that would win their respect. He hoped to create new patterns of international cooperation—an international teaching corps drawn from many nations that would be dispersed through different countries; universities that would share faculties with counterparts in other lands; an international review board of scholars who would attempt to reduce national bias in textbooks. By so doing, he would close the gulf between them and their government, a matter of great concern to him for he believed that a country whose intellectuals were alienated from the State was a country that was badly governed.

Even under such benign auspices, a number of intellectuals balked at associating themselves with their government and, indeed, raised doubts about the very notion of the humanist as citizen. It was not merely that they thought that scholars should be independent of government but also that they were unpersuaded that scholars ought to be activist. In response to one of Frankel's papers, Walter Kaufmann of Princeton objected that there was already too much "splintering" in philosophy and insufficient "rigorous Socratic questioning." Frankel's prescription, he feared, could easily become faddist. "Philosophy of practice is the kind of label that may win respect from the foundations and some deans and chairmen," he commented. "Indeed, it sounds as innocuous as 'philosophy of education' or 'ethics.' But what if the new field should turn out to be just as innocuous as is most work in the philosophy of education and in ethics?"[17] Another critic dismissed Frankel's *Education and the Barricades* as "this pompous little essay" whose "not-so-novel ideas belong (as one suspects Frankel does also) to a bygone era."[18] At the most extreme, Frankel was seen as the kind of intellectual Julien Benda had warned against in *La trahison des clercs*; he was regarded as a purveyor of the dangerous doctrine that humanists should put their talent at the service of the State.

Such a perception did less than justice to the complexity of Frankel's thought. It failed to acknowledge the extent to which citizen participation was only one of a number of values that Frankel held or to recognize the fact that he saw a tension between or among these values. Furthermore, Frankel understood that even ideas and institutions that he regarded most highly held elements that were not admirable. When he presented his four-part television series, "In Pursuit of Liberty," in 1977, he did not characterize liberty as an unmitigated good but began by emphasizing that privacy, "the right most cherished by civilized men," was "an ambiguous liberty."[19] Far from being single-minded, Frankel, throughout his career, was fascinated by ambiguity,[20] and, far from being a zealot who insisted that every humanist must spend all his energy in civic good works, he treasured the privilege of the scholar to scrutinize a text in solitude.

Though he was preeminently an example of *l'homme engagé*, Frankel had a skeptical view of the public scolds and self-conscious ideologues who preached the gospel of engagement. "For the existentialist stress upon the necessity to be committed, to be 'engaged,' is, after all, a slight redundancy for most of us, who, even in this age of alleged catastrophe, are already engaged as lovers, parents, job-holders, and citizens," he once observed. "To make such a point of 'engagement' in the abstract bespeaks a very special kind of isolation. Despite all its associations with the characteristic moods of a postwar world, one cannot help but feel that existentialism lacks balance and catholicity, and that, in the end, it is the metaphysics of the emotionally unemployed."[21]

"Nor should a fetish be made of the genuine democratic value of participation," he wrote on another occasion. "There are limitations, after all, on the time and energy of most citizens. . . . There is no magic in universal participation. From the point of view of the organization, there are always some people who are simply nuisances. From the point of view of the individual, there are surely gentler forms of torture than an unremitting round of meetings. Indeed, if an unhurried pace, a chance for contemplation, and an opportunity to pursue purely private interests are among the elements of a good life, and if they contribute anything to the quality of a culture, a good case can be made for the view that many middle-class citizens of the United States are suffering from an excess rather than a scarcity of 'participant activity.'" He even went so far as to say, "The conventional image of the ideal democratic citizen—the man who is an eager, active member of all the groups to which he belongs—has in fact some dangerous implications." The eighteenth-century philosophes had valued moderation as well as civic intensity, he pointed out, and the less involved provided a useful element of restraint in the political process. "A church could not exist if it consisted only of saints," he observed, "and the perfectly interested and forever active citizen is not the only kind of citizen that keeps an organization on an even keel."[22]

Frankel saw an inevitable tension between private and public values. If he believed in a duty of citizenship, he also set store by the freedom to be left alone. If he prized communion, he also had a high regard for solitude. He cherished "the intimacies and intensities that are only possible for rational people when they choose their company and keep the prying world away."[23] The intellectual, he wrote in 1956, "may live in the practical world and be committed to its fortunes; he may and should take sides in the political struggles of his time. But there is likely to be an edge of irony or regret in his attitude when he does so. For so long as he also lives the life of ideas, he will be unable, in this less than perfect world, to commit his entire heart and mind to any cause." It was improbable, he thought, that any intellectual would be "completely reconciled to any society, no matter how fine it may be. . . . Whatever his political persuasion, whether he is a conservative or a liberal, the intellectual is likely to feel himself at least a little the citizen of two worlds, a man with a loyalty to something that is not fully realized in any party or program or social order."[24]

As early as 1952, in an address to students from secondary schools at a Columbia University forum, Frankel distinguished between the roles of politicians and intellectuals. Intellectuals could never compromise their ideals, whereas, in a democracy, it was incumbent upon political leaders to seek compromises. Intellectuals, he affirmed, found a democratic political order the most hospitable, but they served democracy best by retaining their independence and, although this might engender suspicion, by being vigilant critics.[25] Toward the end of the next decade, he again acknowledged that "there is, if not a conflict, at least a certain discordance between holding ideas and holding public office."[26] Nor did he stress the importance of a public role for the intellectual because he was enraptured with the omnicompetent state. Indeed, he deplored the tendency "to neglect the importance . . . of secondary associations in between the individual and the State, and to overlook the possibility of any kind of collective action for the achievement of broad social purposes that is not State action."[27] Of all such associations, none was of more moment than the university, which, though it afforded an opportunity for "explicit discussion and debate about what it is that we think a better society would be," should function as "a center of abstract thought, abstract criticism."[28]

Though Frankel believed that scholars should take part in the actions and passions of their times, he cautioned that any participation should be based on thoughtful preparation. On one occasion he commented, "It is remarkable how many learned men there are, men who enjoy the ambiguities of John Donne's poetry or who spend their lives refining the refinements of Wittgenstein's philosophy, who nevertheless sail into the middle of social contro-

versies with all their answers ready and all their powers of qualified judgment put aside."[29] In a paper delivered at Brockport, New
York, in the fall of 1967 on the occasion of the International Philosophy Year, Frankel urged philosophers to take a more active role
in public affairs, but only after they had troubled to learn something outside their own field. If they expected to dissuade the
movers and shakers that intellectuals were "naive or irresponsible"
and hoped to "give the practitioner the illumination of a disciplined outsider's point of view," they must be prepared to gain
training or experience in fields germane to the world of affairs.[30]

Even when philosophers showed signs of heeding his counsel to
concentrate less on narrow academic preoccupations, Frankel expressed misgivings. The parochialism of "the vested interests of
the philosophic profession" had long distressed him. "The prospects of philosophy are dim when it feeds only on what philosophers say to one another," he asserted. "Plato was interested in
education and politics, Hume in history and economics, Kant in
religion and science." One might have supposed then that he
would have been delighted when, as a consequence of campus unrest, philosophers who had previously been oriented exclusively
toward their own discipline began to evince an avid concern about
such burning controversies as Vietnam. In fact, he had mixed feelings. This new attention, he was pleased to note, would invigorate
the philosopher's craft and might elevate the level of public discourse. But, he warned, neither would happen "if philosophers
reserve their intellectual caution and discipline for discussing questions such as the real existence of physical objects and throw all
their intellectual standards to the winds when they talk about
problems of social justice or international peace." If they did, "the
old separation of philosophy from practice, of reason from passion," would go on, "but in a more virulent form." He concluded:
"We have yet to see whether philosophers, having recovered an
active moral concern and a confidence in their powers of generalization, will contribute to our civilization's store of judiciousness
and reflectiveness or to its fanaticism and dogmatic ideologies."[31]

In 1970, he prepared a sagacious paper for a meeting of the

American Academy of Arts and Sciences that raised searching questions about the proper relationship of the scholar to political involvement. What was the status of Weber's concept of *Wertfreiheit* and of the distinction between science and politics as vocations? Was a researcher ethically bound to publish his results even if they might well result in policy consequences that were regrettable? Was it possible to define principles as to when it was legitimate for a scholar to become politically involved? The tone of the memorandum suggested that there were no easy answers to such inquiries and that a humanist had to be prepared to examine his own performance as a scholar and as a citizen with self-critical detachment.[32]

Instead of contenting himself with emphasizing that humanists should be in the service of the state, Frankel insisted that government should cater to the needs of intellectuals. "In our kind of society it is not the function of artists and intellectuals to serve the conception of the national purpose set down by the powers that be," he wrote in 1960. "It is their function to see things for themselves."[33] Similarly, in his report for the Brookings Institution on the government's educational and cultural operations, Frankel stated that "a too eager emphasis on the political purposes of these programs can discourage participation by artists, scholars, and students who come from private life, and can put American education and culture in precisely the wrong light by making them appear to be simply the servants of politics. In the eyes of most civilized men, the reverse is the appropriate relationship."[34] Even when he became Assistant Secretary of State and spoke for the government, he sounded the same note. In a lecture to the Fletcher School of Law and Diplomacy, he said somewhat whimsically: "The dangers are plain. Government officials, even professors of philosophy on leave of absence, should be carefully watched at any time, and certainly when they suggest that they have an interest in matters that belong above all to private taste, judgment, and conscience, or to the free community of scholars and teachers."[35]

If Frankel had any illusion that the path of a humanist with a highly developed sense of civic duty would be an easy one, his experience at the State Department would have been enough to disabuse him of it. A month after he went to Washington, a friend asked him how he liked power. "I like it," Frankel replied, "but I hope it likes me."[36] He discovered:

> To be an Assistant Secretary of State is to be in a situation in which other voices speak through you, and you speak through other voices. The letters you sign you usually haven't written. The most important letters you write are those which others sign—the Secretary of State or the President. If you are at a meeting, the chances are that you are quoting from a memorandum that has been prepared for you. When you give a speech, three or four other people, and sometimes thirty or forty, have worried about that speech, often more than you have. Even when you use words that are entirely your own, surprising things happen to them. They go reverberating down corridors, and in and out of other offices, where they become cables to embassies, press releases, policy statements. And although the sound of your voice has been amplified, somewhere along the line it has also been flattened out.[37]

Attempts to cooperate with the people's representatives in Congress could be even more disconcerting. After Frankel labored for months on his plan to create a corps of education officers, a House subcommittee disposed of the proposal in no more than five minutes without indicating that it had read one of the documents that scores of people had painstakingly prepared. Even when he achieved some successes,[38] they had a way of not working out as he had hoped. He could take pride in getting Congress to approve the International Education Act of 1966,[39] but then Congress failed to appropriate money to make the law meaningful.

Far more consequential, the Vietnam War became Banquo's ghost at the feast. As early as June 1966, Frankel noted in his diary: "My job, though I enjoy almost every minute of it, is like a small pinpoint of light in the surrounding gloom. The war is on my mind almost every minute I'm not at my desk. It's on everybody's mind, and nervousness about the cities and the prospects for the federal budget aggravate the situation. This has become a sullen, mean-tempered city."[40] At a plenary session of the general conference of UNESCO in Paris in October, 1966, the Soviet delegate denounced the "barbaric war" of the United States in Southeast Asia and asked, "How is it possible to speak of cultural exchanges, of educational development, while destroying schools?" It fell upon Charles Frankel, as chief American delegate, to respond. "It seems to me unnecessarily provocative to make remarks in this forum which everyone knows do not belong in this forum," he replied, not unreasonably. But he felt called upon to go beyond that to charge that it was the USSR "which has constantly refused to agree to take up the peaceful settlement of this conflict."[41]

After a time, he came to wonder whether, because the war was "steadily more hideous," he should remain in Washington. But he did not want to leave after so short a stint. The crucial consideration was not the war. He confided to his diary, "I've made up my mind, and have told Helen, that my staying in the government will depend on whether I can get the White House and the President himself to put on steam in relation to international education." However, the conduct of the war disturbed him, too; unless Johnson's policy changed drastically, he resolved not to remain longer than the end of 1967.[42]

Late in 1967, he informed the White House of his intention to resign, a decision that had more than one source. "The reasons for my departure are ambiguous because the situation is ambiguous," he said.[43] He had come to feel that, by remaining in a government with whose policy on Vietnam he disagreed, he was "fronting a fraud."[44] But that was not the only pertinent issue. In a telephone interview from Honolulu early in December, he made clear that his resignation was not solely a gesture of protest against the Vietnam War; indeed, he refused to confirm (or deny) that this was, in fact, why he was leaving. Rather, he chose to stress that, quite apart from the war, there was insufficient recognition either in the government or in the intellectual world of the international significance of education, and he asserted that the State Department was not the proper place to locate the supervision of America's educational and cultural commitments abroad. Even the rumors circulated by his friends indicated less that he was outraged by the general consequences of the Vietnam disaster than that he had become exasperated by the difficulty of trying to carry on an educational and cultural operation in the bleak atmosphere of the war in Southeast Asia.[45]

Moreover, as he departed from the Johnson administration, he took pains to see that no damage was done to the state by his action. When he granted two interviews to Richard Dudman of the *St. Louis Post-Dispatch* while he was still in office, he stipulated that they could not be published until ten days after he left the State Department. In addition, he made clear that he was solicitous for the welfare of America's political institutions. "I don't want people to feel that the Government is the enemy," he told Dudman. "The division in this country is terrible, and it could be lessened to some extent if people were more moderate in what they said. I don't want to contribute to this division. I want to help get some warmth back into the situation."[46]

Not even the Vietnam experience dissuaded Frankel from the belief that the humanist might carry his citizenship to the point of service in Washington. He had never anticipated that the state would be guided by the same standards of behavior that he hoped would prevail among people. He was fond of saying that, "as Spinoza observed, no one should expect that a government can act in accordance with the moral code appropriate to the conduct of individuals. Its problems are different."[47] In his first book, *The Faith of Reason*, originally published in 1948, he had come to the defense of "the belief in human betterment through the use of intelligence" by pointing out that "the philosophers thought that reason and humanity were one."[48]

If his optimism was tempered over the years, it never died. Nearly two years after his departure from Washington, he wrote:

> According to Pascal, "the most unreasonable things in the world become most reasonable because of the unruliness of men." Government is a product of unruly men trying to control themselves while they govern other unruly men. As a

consequence if they behave in peculiar ways, and surround themselves with astonishing rules, and produce decisions that have the clarity of *Finnegans Wake* read in a thunderstorm, one shouldn't be surprised. Their confusion is the world's confusion, and there may even be purposes, sometimes good purposes, that are being served. One chooses to work inside a government, believing that some good may come from doing so, and one finds, after a while, that a certain rationality shines through.[49]

However, while continuing to believe in these years that scholars should participate in the public arena, Frankel viewed with increasing dismay the politicization of the intellectual realm. For all his interest in involving humanists in affairs of state, he stoutly resisted the imposition of political criteria in academic matters and fought off efforts, however well-meaning, to transform the campus from a domicile for scholars to a launching pad for diffuse social purposes. Hence, he took a central role in the creation and leadership of the International Council on the Future of the University that sought to prevent the debasement of the university. He warned: "A university cannot be asked to harness all its separate departments of learning and all its people to the service of any single vision of the good society. It cannot be turned into the instrument of any particular political purpose, official or unofficial, except the purpose of general freedom and pluralism. If 'relevance' means the politicization of the university, then the word stands for the abandonment of free inquiry and criticism, and the negation of individual rights."[50]

Frankel advanced these concerns in a different form in his novel, *A Stubborn Case*, which depicts events resembling the Columbia uprising of 1968. In reflecting upon the nature of education, the protagonist says: "The question is whether we can turn the university into a hotbed of togetherness, a fine, large, pillowing, old-style family. Not the kind of family, of course, that ever gets in your hair, or with a grandparent who's sick that you've got to take care of. A family without obligations, not even with any clear business, except to love one another, and communicate. Well, I don't think the university can be turned into that, and I don't think it should be."[51]

Nonetheless, Frankel did not reach the conclusion that the way to deal with the difficult relationship of intellectuals to social obligations was to divorce the two. He continued to hold fast to the belief that the humanist must move beyond the minutiae of his discipline. "When the study of human experience turns entirely inward upon itself, when it becomes the study of the study of human experience, and then the study of the study of that study, it does not achieve greater objectivity; it merely becomes thinner," he wrote in an article published at the end of 1977. He added: "In every generation in which the humanities have shown vitality, they have refreshed their thinking by learning from other disciplines, and they have looked beyond their books to the primary materials that have made these books. They have performed an essential public, civic, educational function: the criticism and re-integration of the ideas and values of cultures dislocated from their traditions and needing a new sense of meaning. This is what humanistic scholars did in fifth- and fourth-century Athens, in the thirteenth century—miscalled an age of unity—in the Renaissance, and in the nineteenth century."[52]

It was such considerations that led Frankel to the last great venture of his life: the presidency of the National Humanities Center, an endeavor that brought to fulfillment his conception of the humanist as citizen. The attempt to define a central purpose for the new center united those humanists who thought that a research institution ought simply to provide a haven for philosophers, historians, literary critics, and others to pursue their scholarly interests and those who believed that professors should address critical societal subjects. Frankel, convinced that intellectuals had a civic responsibility, set as a goal for the Center "the imaginative understanding of public issues."[53] The humanistic disciplines, he declared, "have usually been at their best and most vital . . . when they have had a sense of engagement with issues of public concern." Yet at the same time he insisted: "Scholarship cannot and should not be shackled to problem solving. It must be free to follow crooked paths to unexpected conclusions."⁵⁴ As a consequence, the Center moved in both directions. Fellows were at liberty to carry out their individual projects as scholars, but they were encouraged to participate in seminars on public matters and to ask themselves whether their work might not have a broader audience.⁵⁵

Though others might question whether the life of the scholar and the career of the activist could be reconciled, Frankel saw no inconsistency. Asked about his own dual roles, he said, "I don't think of them as separate. Philosophy involves reflection on one's commitments, and teaching involves bringing ideas to light. So my interests as a teacher and philosopher flow naturally into practical action, and this in turn plays back into teaching and philosophy."⁵⁶ Giovanni Sartori, who holds the Schweitzer chair at Columbia, has written that to Frankel "the contemplation of the good life was, all in one, the promotion of the good life. To Charles, like the *philosophes* of the Enlightenment, the ivory tower was sterile: wisdom and action had to go together."⁵⁷

In his final years, Frankel, at the same time that he worked hard to make the achievements of scholars accessible to the American people, fought strenuously to preserve the independence of the intellectual in a democratic society. It was singular, he thought, to have "government doing business with humanists," for this was "to set before ourselves the task of maintaining a *modus vivendi* between politicians and poets, accountants and admirers of Kandinski, bureaucrats and followers of Thoreau." Five months before his death, he affirmed: "We have to keep the Humanities clear from taint by politics. Not that any of us is free from political beliefs, but when we're being scholars or humanists we ought to be aware of those political beliefs and try in some way or other to lean over backwards to keep them controlled." The humanist scholar, Frankel observed, "detaches himself, as it were, from that in which his fellows engage with passionate commitment." It is, he stated, the capacity of the humanities "to maintain involvement and detachment in equilibrium that is always on trial and it is the larger society's capacity to tolerate and appreciate such a state of precarious balance that gives the measure of its level of civilization."[58]

These emphases opened Frankel to the accusation that, despite a lifelong effort to relate the humanities to public concerns, he was an elitist. The charge was not altogether groundless. At a conference on public broadcasting in 1969, he served both as chairman and as devil's advocate in asking, "Wasn't it better to inspire a handful of influential viewers to pragmatic action on a social issue rather than waste time on the multitudes who in the evening had greater interest in a cold bottle of beer and 'Bonanza'?"[59] When he was Assistant Secretary of State, he received a message from President Johnson: "You're not going to make a program just for those Ph.D.'s are you? I want to do something for that little boy at the end of the line who can't read or write." Frankel reflected: "As one of the President's assistants has told me, there is a difference in emphasis, and probably in fundamental philosophy, between the President's approach and mine. The President's interest in international education is the interest of a man who has known children who couldn't go to school. I am thinking mainly of the need to strengthen a community of intellect and imagination, and specifically of strengthening communication among the most highly educated people in the world."[60]

This issue exploded at a conference on government and the humanities at the Lyndon B. Johnson Library in December 1978. In response to a paper by Charles Frankel, Elizabeth Carpenter, who had been Mrs. Johnson's press secretary, drew applause by saying:

> I don't know why I take Mr. Frankel's remarks personally, but I do, and I think you really are talking about women and minorities. I was thrilled yesterday when you said you wanted to embrace new issues in life, but I find a very standoffishness and I think that the people in the humanities really live in a dream world if they think they can stonewall it against the trends of the minorities and women and people who have been left out for more of the action. They want a piece of the

action and they want to be on your Boards and they want to
have something, because we are a part of humanities. . . . I
mean any administration that is subject to the public, and God
knows it ought to be, is certainly going to be tossing some
bones to the yowling dogs because we've been left out, and I
think it should be. And if it's going to be reelected, it damn
sure is.[61]

Frankel in turn was shocked by the pervasive philistinism he
encountered at the conference and by the dismaying prospect that,
in the name of democracy, the humanities would be laid waste by
pressure-group politics.

Furthermore, Frankel had good reason to resent the implication
that he was an elitist. It was not merely that he had given so much
energy to activities like television aimed at reaching the broadest
possible audience, for he had demonstrated that same desire as
Assistant Secretary of State. "Our efforts in educational and cultural fields," he had declared, "should have in view the many-
sidedness of man, the many-sidedness of poor men as well as of
the well-to-do."[62] As Assistant Secretary, he had wanted to make
it possible for ideas and information to be disseminated more
equably. If one could not go so far as to create an international
knowledge bank, the United States might at least take the lead in
seeing that less advantaged nations had greater access to the resources of knowledge that America and a few other great powers
had in abundance. Nor was this simply an exercise in paternalism.
Frankel insisted that the relation of the superpower, the United
States, to smaller nations must be on the basis of parity, that
cultural programs should "reduce the tutelary relationship that
mars our contacts with foreign countries."[63] Americans should not
think that they had a monopoly of knowledge and had nothing to
receive from others, he said. "The great thrust of the American
colossus is endurable elsewhere only if Americans can escape their
provincialism, and only if they give indication of a willingness to
learn as well as to teach."[64]

Still, at the time of his death, Frankel did have some sorting out and synthesizing to do. In truth, it was not clear that the role of humanist was always congruent with that of citizen, and one would have liked to have seen Frankel, who had thought so much about this association, delineate his own conception of what the appropriate relationship ought to be. Furthermore, he sometimes gave, or seemed to give, contradictory signals. After serving for years as a colporteur of the gospel that the humanist should be active in public affairs, he was nonetheless capable of writing, "It is, I think, good advice to give to intellectuals that they should be careful about serving inside a government because they may do it harm and it may do them harm. Most intellectuals probably are unfit to perform the jobs which they might be interested in taking in government."[65] Finally, it remained to be seen how an institute for advanced study would manage both to foster humanistic scholarship and to serve the public weal.

These were questions that brutally, senselessly, he was denied the opportunity to explore. Nothing speaks better to that tragedy than a passage from an article on a "horrible event" that appeared nine years before his murder: "Its most important meaning, it seems to me, is that, although it is full of consequences, it has no saving meaning. Thinking about it is hard because there is something irreducibly unthinkable about it. It was an event that didn't have to be; it was gratuitous and, in historical terms, madly accidental. . . . This was an event that had the idiotic irrelevance of a natural disaster, and yet was a human deed, an intended premeditated act." These were words written on the occasion of the murder of Robert Kennedy, and their author was Charles Frankel. The essay ends: "We lay plans, we hope in some systematic way to deal with our collective problems, we try to make the public world orderly, and then wildness breaks out, sheer, private, dreaming malice, which cuts across everyone's hopes and cuts them down."[66]

NOTES

1. Charles Frankel, "Out of Touch in Washington," *Saturday Review* 52 (1 November 1969): 21.
2. The word "humanist" is used throughout this essay to denote a scholar in the humanities and never in its other meaning of a secular attitude toward religion.
3. James Gutmann, Columbia Oral History Collection, p. 54.
4. Abram Kardiner, Columbia Oral History Collection, p. 413.
5. To the disappointment of his publisher, who regarded Frankel as a "wonderful man" and "a great teacher," *The Case for Modern Man* did not sell well. Evan Thomas explained, "The college department did not get acceptance on the campuses, and they told me they weren't going to, and I was surprised, because he's such an attractive guy and such a good thinker, but I gather there's a whole new wave of philosophical thinking" (Evan Thomas, Columbia Oral History Collection, pp. 107, 113).
6. Remarks at Memorial Service for Professor and Mrs. Charles Frankel, St. Paul's Chapel, Columbia University, 15 May 1979, typescript in Oral History Research Office, Columbia University.
7. Quoted by C. Vann Woodward at Memorial Service for Professor and Mrs. Charles Frankel, St. Paul's Chapel, Columbia University, 15 May 1979, typescript in Oral History Research Office, Columbia University.
8. Charles Frankel, "The Political Responsibility of the Intellectual," in Paul Kurtz, ed., *Moral Problems in Contemporary Society: Essays in Humanistic Ethics* (Buffalo: Prometheus, 1973), pp. 174–75. The essay originally appeared as "Politics and the Intellectual," *The Humanist* 28 (1968): 14–20.
9. "Is Democracy Dying?: Verdict of 8 Leading World Scholars," *U.S. News & World Report*, 8 March 1976, p. 60.
10. Charles Frankel, *High on Foggy Bottom: An Outsider's Inside View of the Government* (New York: Harper and Row, 1969), p. 16.
11. Ibid., p. 11.

12. Memo to the president from Senator J. W. Fulbright, 23 July 1965, WHCF Name File, Lyndon B. Johnson MSS, LBJ Library, Austin, Texas.

13. Frankel, *High on Foggy Bottom*, pp. 16–17.

14. *New York Times*, 24 May 1969.

15. Frankel, *High on Foggy Bottom*, pp. 19–20.

16. Ibid., pp. 20–21.

17. *New York Times*, 6 November 1967.

18. *Choice* 6 (April 1969): 258.

19. Program Notes, "In Pursuit of Liberty," in National Endowment for the Humanities, "A Tribute in Memory of Charles Frankel, 1917–1979," mimeographed. Frankel's interest in television was longstanding. At the UNESCO conference in 1966, he promoted fellowships to permit observers from foreign countries, especially underdeveloped ones, to come to the United States to study educational television (Charles Frankel to Douglass Cater, Jr., 10 October 1966, WHCF Name File, Lyndon B. Johnson MSS, LBJ Library, Austin, Texas).

20. Among many examples of his preoccupation with ambiguity, note Charles Frankel, "Intellectual Foundations of Liberalism," in Columbia University, Program of Liberal Education in the Humanities, *Seminar Reports* 5 (Fall 1976): 9; and Charles Frankel, "Thoughts on Fame: Infamous and Otherwise," *New York Times Magazine*, 23 October 1960, p. 110.

21. Charles Frankel in *Saturday Review* 35 (11 October 1952): 15.

22. Charles Frankel, *The Democratic Prospect* (New York: Harper and Row, 1962), pp. 62–64.

23. *Washington Post*, 15 May 1979.

24. Charles Frankel, "Definition of the True Egghead," *New York Times Magazine*, 21 October 1956, p. 62.

25. *New York Times*, 22 February 1952.

26. Frankel, "The Political Responsibility of the Intellectual," in Kurtz, ed., *Moral Problems in Contemporary Society*, p. 173.

27. Charles Frankel, *The Case for Modern Man* (Boston: Beacon, 1959), p. 205.

28. Charles Frankel, "The Relation of Theory to Practice," in Herman D. Stein, ed., *Social Theory and Social Invention* (Cleveland: The Press of Case Western Reserve University, 1968), p. 42.

29. Charles Frankel, "Student Power: The Rhetoric and the Possibilities," *Saturday Review* 51 (2 November 1968): 23.

30. *New York Times*, 6 November 1967.

31. Ibid., 12 January 1970.

32. Charles Frankel, "Memorandum: Planning Meeting on the Rules of Scholarly Self-Government," mimeographed, in Frankel to the author, 29 July 1970.

33. Charles Frankel, "'We Must Not Let Moscow Set Our Pace,'" *New York Times Magazine*, 2 October 1960, p. 98.

34. Charles Frankel, *The Neglected Aspect of Foreign Affairs: American Educational and Cultural Policy Abroad* (Washington: Brookings Institution, 1965), p. 89.

35. Charles Frankel, "The Era of Educational and Cultural Relations," *Department of State Bulletin* 54 (6 June 1966): 896.

36. Frankel, *High on Foggy Bottom*, p. 48.

37. Ibid., pp. 49–50.

38. In December 1965, a high-ranking member of the White House staff wrote him: "You have had a notable launching as a statesman. Your first baby, the task force report, shows high promise of a long life" (Douglass Cater to Charles Frankel, 22 December 1965, WHCF Name File, Lyndon B. Johnson MSS, LBJ Library, Austin, Texas).

39. Charles Frankel, "International Education Act of 1966," *Department of State Bulletin* 54 (9 May 1966): 754–57.

40. Frankel, *High on Foggy Bottom*, pp. 127–28.

41. *New York Times*, 30 October 1966.

42. Frankel, *High on Foggy Bottom*, p. 136.

43. D. S. G., "International Programs: Frankel Resigns from State," *Science* 158 (15 December 1967): 1436.

44. *St. Louis Post-Dispatch*, 10 January 1968.

45. *New York Times*, 3 December 1967.

46. *St. Louis Post-Dispatch*, 10 January 1968. On his resignation, see,

too, Lyndon B. Johnson to Charles Frankel, 29 November 1967, Johnson MSS, LBJ Library, Austin, Texas; Charles Frankel, "The Silenced Majority," *Saturday Review* 52 (13 December 1969): 22, 51; "Frankel Speaks Out," *Nation* 206 (5 February 1968): 165. The Johnson administration, however, did not display the same magnanimity. In the fall of 1967, a White House aide sent a pointed memorandum to President Johnson: "This may interest you in light of the fact that you put [Robert A.] Scalapino on the United States Advisory Commission on International Educational and Cultural Affairs to replace Charles Frankel's nominee, Walter Johnson, who was bombing us right and left on Vietnam" (John P. Roche, Memorandum for the President, 9 November 1967, Lyndon B. Johnson MSS, WHCF Name File, LBJ Library, Austin, Texas).

47. Frankel, "Out of Touch in Washington," p. 23.

48. Charles Frankel, *The Faith of Reason: The Idea of Progress in the French Enlightenment* (New York: Octagon, 1969), p. 157.

49. Frankel, *High on Foggy Bottom*, p. 240.

50. Charles Frankel, *Education and the Barricades* (New York: Norton, 1968), p. 82; Frankel to the author, 25 February 1977; "The Report on German Universities: Comment by Charles Frankel," International Council on the Future of the University, *Newsletter* 6 (May 1979): 1, 3–6.

51. Charles Frankel, *A Stubborn Case* (New York: Norton, 1972), p. 124.

52. Charles Frankel, "The Academy Enshrouded," *Change* 9 (December 1977): 64.

53. William J. Bennett, "Charles and Helen Frankel: A Personal Remembrance," *The National Humanities Center Newsletter* 1 (Fall 1979): 23.

54. *New York Times*, 2 July 1978.

55. The first year's class of fellows included scholars examining such areas as citizenship, but also humanists engaged in studying matters that had no palpable utilitarian function, such as the plays of the Elizabethan dramatist John Webster. Though

Frankel organized a seminar to bring the perspective of humanists to bear on the work of the American Bar Association's committee revising its code of ethics, he also took pains to encourage applications for the second year's class of fellows from scholars working on the poetry of Fernando Pessoa and the human experience of time (Peter Riesenberg, "Habitat for Humanists," *Washington University Magazine* 49 [Summer 1979]: 14–15).

56. Quoted by C. Vann Woodward at Memorial Service for Professor and Mrs. Charles Frankel, St. Paul's Chapel, Columbia University, 15 May 1979, typescript in Oral History Research Office, Columbia University.

57. International Council on the Future of the University, *Newsletter* 6 (November 1979): 7.

58. Transcript of Proceedings of symposium on Government and the Humanities, 4–5 December 1978, Lyndon B. Johnson Library, Austin, Texas.

59. *New York Times*, 27 June 1969.

60. Frankel, *High on Foggy Bottom*, p. 67. On his prospectus for a public television series, he noted: "John Stuart Mill, Alexis de Tocqueville, George Santayana, not to mention Plato, feared that democracies, in which the voice of the majority was sovereign, would be less congenial, often, as settings for intellectual liberty than societies in which creative people could receive the protection of powerful patrons. Are democracy and equality threats to the liberties of the mind?" ("The Program Series," mimeographed, in Charles Frankel to the author, 25 July 1974).

61. Transcript of Proceedings of symposium on Government and the Humanities, 4–5 December 1978, Lyndon B. Johnson Library, Austin, Texas.

62. Charles Frankel, "Toward Deeper Cultural Relations in the Hemisphere," *Department of State Bulletin* 54 (7 February 1966): 205.

63. Frankel, *High on Foggy Bottom*, p. 25.

64. *New York Times*, 24 May 1969. See, too, Charles Frankel, "The United States Commitment to UNESCO," *Department of State Bulletin* 55 (12 December 1966): 888.

65. Frankel, "The Political Responsibility of the Intellectual," in Kurtz, ed., *Moral Problems in Contemporary Society*, p. 178.

66. Charles Frankel, "The Meaning of Political Murder," *Saturday Review* 51 (22 June 1968): 18.

BIBLIOGRAPHY

❦ BIBLIOGRAPHY OF

CHARLES FRANKEL

BOOKS

The Bear and the Beaver. New York: Sloane, 1951.

The Case for Modern Man. New York: Harper and Brothers, 1956.

The Case for Modern Man. With a New Preface by the Author. Boston: Beacon Press, 1959. Reprinted, Beacon Press, 1967. Reprinted, Books for Libraries Press, 1972.

The Democratic Prospect. New York: Harper and Row, 1962.

Education and the Barricades. New York: W. W. Norton, 1968.

The Faith of Reason: The Idea of Progress in the French Enlightenment. New York: King's Crown Press, 1948. Reprinted, New York: Octagon Books, 1969.

High on Foggy Bottom: An Outsider's Inside View of the Government. New York: Harper and Row, 1969.

Human Rights and Foreign Policy. New York: Foreign Policy Association, 1978.

The Love of Anxiety and Other Essays. New York: Harper and Row, 1965. Reprinted, New York: Dell Publishing Co., 1967.

Morality and U.S. Foreign Policy. New York: Foreign Policy Association, 1975.

The Neglected Aspect of Foreign Affairs: American Educational and Cultural Policy Abroad. Washington: Brookings Institution, 1965.

A Stubborn Case: A Novel. New York: W. W. Norton, 1972.

EDITED BOOKS

Controversies and Decisions: The Social Sciences and Public Policy. New York: Russell Sage Foundation, 1976.

The Golden Age of American Philosophy. New York: G. Braziller, 1960.
Introduction to Contemporary Civilization in the West. New York: Columbia University Press, 1941.
Issues in University Education: Essays by Ten American Scholars. New York: Harper and Brothers, 1959.
The Pleasures of Philosophy. New York: W. W. Norton, 1972.
The Social Contract, by Jean Jacques Rousseau. New York: Hafner Publishing Co., 1947.
The Uses of Philosophy, by Irwin Edman. New York: Simon and Schuster, 1955.

CONTRIBUTIONS TO BOOKS

"The Autonomy of the Social Sciences." In *Controversies and Decisions: The Social Sciences and Public Policy*, edited by Charles Frankel, pp. 9–30. New York: Russell Sage Foundation, 1976.
"Bureaucracy and Democracy in the New Europe." In *A New Europe*, edited by Stephen R. Graubard, pp. 538–59. Boston: Houghton-Mifflin Co., 1964.
"The Cultural Contest." In *Soviet-American Rivalry in the Middle East*, edited by J. C. Hurewitz, pp. 139–55. New York: Praeger, 1969.
"Cultural Understanding of the Caribbean." In *Carribbean: Current United States Relations*, edited by Alva Curtis Wilgus, pp. 160–66. Gainesville: University of Florida Press, 1966.
"Education in Fever." In *In Defense of Academic Freedom*, edited by Sidney Hook, pp. 34–45. New York: Pegasus, 1971.
"The Educational Impact of American Foreign Policy." In *Stress and Campus Response*, edited by G. Kerry Smith, pp. 52–63. San Francisco: Jossey-Bass, 1968.
"Efficient Power and Inefficient Virtue." In *Great Moral Dilemmas in Literature*, edited by R. M. MacIver, pp. 15–23. Institute for Religious and Social Studies. New York: Cooper Square, 1964.
"The Elite and the Electorate." In *Challenges to Democracy*, edited by Edward Reed, pp. 89–93. New York: Praeger Paperbacks, 1963.
"The Enlightenment," with Donald O'Connell. In *Chapters in Western Civilization*, 1:336–87. New York: Columbia University Press, 1948.
"Epilogue: Reflections on a Worn-out Model." In *Universities in the*

Western World, edited by Paul Seabury, pp. 279–89. New York: Free Press, 1975.

"Facts, Values, and Responsible Choice." In *The Ethics of Teaching and Scientific Research*, edited by Sidney Hook, Paul Kurtz, and Miro Todorovich, pp. 23–28. Buffalo, N.Y.: Prometheus Books, 1977.

"Freedom, Authority, and Orthodoxy." In *Freedom and Authority in Our Time*, pp. 419–30. New York: Conference on Science, Philosophy, and Religion in their Relation to the Democratic Way of Life, 1953.

"Information and Communication in the Not-So-New Society." In *Prologue to the Future: The United States and Japan in the Postindustrial Age*, edited by James William Morley, pp. 195–218. Lexington, Mass.: D. C. Heath and Co., 1974.

"John Dewey's Legacy." In *American Scholar Reader*, edited by Hiram Haydn and Betsy Saunders, pp. 506–22. New York: Athenaeum, 1960.

"John Dewey's Social Philosophy." In *New Studies in the Philosophy of John Dewey*, edited by Steven M. Cahn, pp. 3–44. Hanover, N.H.: The University Press of New England, 1977.

"Liberalism and Political Symbols." In *Symbols and Values: An Initial Study*, pp. 361–70. New York: Conference on Science, Philosophy, and Religion in their Relation to the Democratic Way of Life, 1954.

"Naturalism." In *Basic Beliefs: The Religious Philosophies of Mankind*, edited by Johnson E. Fairchild, pp. 148–55. New York: Sheridan House, 1959.

"Obstacles to Action for Human Welfare." In *Social Welfare Forum, 1961*, pp. 272–83. National Conference on Social Welfare. New York: Columbia University Press, 1961.

"Philosophy and the Social Sciences." In *Both Human and Humane: the Humanities and Social Sciences in Graduate Education*, edited by Charles E. Boewe and Roy F. Nichols, pp. 94–117. Philadelphia: University of Pennsylvania Press, 1960.

"Philosophy of Practice." In *Ethics and Social Justice*, edited by Howard E. Kiefer and Milton K. Munitz, pp. 1–15. Albany, N.Y.: State University of New York Press, 1968.

"The Philosophy of the Enlightenment." In *A History of Philosophical Systems*, edited by Vergilius Ferm, pp. 266–79. New York: Philosophical Library, 1950.

"The Political Responsibility of the Intellectual." in *Moral Problems*

in Contemporary Society: Essays in Humanistic Ethics, edited by
Paul W. Kurtz, pp. 173–88. Englewood Cliffs, N.J.: Prentice-
Hall, 1969. Reprinted, Buffalo, N.Y.: Prometheus Books, 1973.
"Positivism." In *A History of Philosophical Systems*, edited by Ver-
gilius Ferm, pp. 329–39. New York: Philosophical Library,
1950.
"The Power of the Democratic Idea." In *Prospect for America: The
Rockefeller Panel Report*, pp. 393–94. New York: Doubleday and
Co., 1960.
"Pressures Away from Intellectuality." In *Dilemmas of Youth: In
America Today*, edited by R. M. MacIver, pp. 65–75. New York:
Institute for Religious and Social Studies, 1961.
"Private Rights and the Public Good." In *Small Comforts for Hard
Times: Humanists on Public Policy*, edited by Michael Mooney
and Florian Stuber, pp. 87–102. New York: Columbia Univer-
sity Press, 1977.
"The Relation of Theory to Practice: Some Standard Views." In
Social Theory and Social Invention, edited by Herman D. Stein,
pp. 1–21. Cleveland: Press of the Case Western Reserve Uni-
versity, 1968.
"The Rights of Nature." In *When Values Conflict: Essays on Environ-
mental Analysis, Discourse, and Decision*, edited by Laurence H.
Tribe, Corinne S. Schelling, and John Voss, pp. 93–113. Cambridge, Mass.: Ballinger Publishing Co., 1976.
"Social Viewpoints Since 1850." In *Chapters in Western Civilization*,
2:186–222. New York: Columbia University Press, 1948.
"The Third Great Revolution of Mankind." In *A Contemporary
Reader: Essays for Today and Tomorrow*, edited by Harry W. Rud-
man and Irving Rosenthal, pp. 275–81. New York: Ronald
Press, 1961.

ARTICLES IN JOURNALS

"The Academy Enshrouded." *Change* 9 (December 1977): 24–29,
64.
"America: A Failure of Nerve?" *Current* 175 (September 1975):
25–29.
"Are we Really Crazy?" *Harper's Magazine* 210 (June 1955): 66–70.
"Barges on the Seine." *Harper's Magazine* 230 (May 1965): 60–65.
"Bureaucracy and Democracy in the New Europe." *Daedalus* 93
(Winter 1964): 471–92.

"Definition of the True Egghead." *New York Times Magazine* (21 October 1956): 14, 56, 58, 60, 62.

"Dilemma of Progress." *American Scholar* 11 (April 1942): 181–89.

"Discussion: Philosophy of Education." *Harvard Educational Review* 33 (Spring 1963): 224–29.

"Education and Telecommunications." *Journal of Higher Education* 41 (January 1970): 1–15.

"Education and the Barricades." *Official Report of the American Association of School Administrators* (1969): 75–85.

"Education for World Responsibility." *Vital Speeches* 32 (August 1966): 621–25.

"Education for World Responsibility: An Old Phrase, a Transformed Problem." *Department of State Bulletin* 55 (18 July 1966): 84–90.

"Empiricism and Moral Imperatives." *Journal of Philosophy* 50 (April 1953): 257–68.

"Equality of Opportunity." *Ethics* 81 (April 1971): 191–211.

"Era of Educational and Cultural Relations." *Department of State Bulletin* 54 (6 June 1966): 889–97.

"The Etiquette of Scholarship." *Educational Forum* 20 (November 1955): 95–106.

"Explanation and Interpretation in History." *Philosophy of Science* 24 (April 1957): 137–55.

"Fevered Philosophes." *Saturday Review* 35 (11 October 1952): 14–15.

"Foreign Policy for the Future." *PTA Magazine* 62 (October 1967): 4, 10–12.

"Four Illusions that Beset Us." *New York Times Magazine* (22 September 1963): 31, 86, 88.

"Freedom, Authority, and Orthodoxy." *Antioch Review* 12 (June 1952): 182–94.

"The Government of Scholarship." *Bulletin of the American Association of University Professors* 41 (December 1955): 696–712.

"The Impact of Changing Values on the Family." *Social Casework* 57 (1976): 355–65.

"In One Way We're Worse Off." *New York Times Magazine* (10 June 1962): 36.

"Intellectual Foundations of Liberalism." Columbia University, Program of Liberal Education in the Humanities, *Seminar Reports* 5 (Fall 1976): 9.

"International Education Act of 1966; Statement, March 31, 1966." *Department of State Bulletin* 54 (9 May 1966): 754–57.

"Is it Ever Right to Break the Law?" *New York Times Magazine* (12 January 1964): 17, 36, 39, 41.

"Is It Just TV, or Most of Us?" *New York Times Magazine* (15 November 1959): 15, 105.

"Is Solzhenitsyn Right? (American Responses to Harvard Address)" *Time* 111 (26 June 1978): 18–20.

"John Dewey's Legacy." *American Scholar* 29 (Summer 1960): 313–31.

"Justice, Utilitarianism, and Rights." *Social Theory and Practice* 3 (Spring 1974): 27–46.

"A Liberal Is a Liberal Is a ——." *New York Times Magazine* (28 February 1960): 21, 82–83.

"Liberalism and Political Symbols." *Antioch Review* 13 (September 1953): 351–60.

"Man's Stance, Brains, and Troubles." *Saturday Review* 38 (31 December 1955): 13.

"The Meaning of Political Murder." *Saturday Review* 51 (22 June 1968): 17–18.

"The Nature and Sources of Irrationalism." *Science* 180 (1 June 1973): 927–31.

"The New Egalitarianism and the Old." *Commentary* 56 (September 1973): 54–61.

"On the Nature of Proof in Philosophy." *Revue Internationale de Philosophie* 8 (1954): 109–23.

"Our Colleges: Inside View by Outsiders." *New York Times Magazine* (24 February 1957): 23, 42, 44–45.

"Our Far-Flung Correspondents." *New Yorker* 39 (25 May 1963): 74–109, and 40 (6 June 1964): 136–52.

"Out of Touch in Washington." Excerpt from *High on Foggy Bottom: An Outsider's Inside View of the Government*. *Saturday Review* 52 (1 November 1969): 21–23, 54.

"The Philosopher as Teacher." *Proceedings of the Catholic Philosophical Association* 47 (1973): 1–11.

"Philosophy." *Saturday Review* 36 (14 April 1953): 23.

"Philosophy and History." *Political Science Quarterly* 72 (September 1957): 350–69.

"Plea for Moderation in Moderation." *New York Times Magazine* (21 October 1956): 9.

"The Plight of the Humanist Intellectual." *Encounter* 43 (August 1974): 11–17.

"Political Disobedience and the Denial of Political Authority." *Social Theory and Practice* 2 (Spring 1972): 85–98.

"Politics and the Intellectual." *Humanist* 28 (July–August 1968): 14–20.

"Problems, Yes—But Other Systems are Worse Off." *U.S. News and World Report* 80 (8 March 1976): 59–61.

"Professional Education as University Education." *Social Service Review* 32 (September 1958): 234–46.

"Proper and Improper Ways to Support Higher Education." *NUEA Spectator* 38 (September 1974): 6–11.

"Reflections on a Worn-out Model." *Daedalus* 103 (Fall 1974): 25–32.

"Report of the Committee on Professional Ethics." *Bulletin of the American Association of University Professors* 44 (Winter 1958): 781–84.

"Report on Current Research." *Saturday Review* 36 (4 April 1953): 23.

"Review for the Teacher: Philosophy." *NEA Journal* 51 (December 1962): 50–53.

"Roots of Treason." *Saturday Review* 39 (March 1956): 16.

"Scholar's Freedom." *Antioch Review* 15 (September 1955): 339–54.

"The Scribblers and International Relations." *Foreign Affairs* 44 (October 1965): 1–14.

"Seeing Things in Double Focus." *Saturday Review* 36 (5 September 1953): 7–8.

"Shifting Currents in French Education." *Columbia Forum* 13 (Summer 1970): 11–16.

"Silenced Majority." *Saturday Review* 52 (13 December 1969): 22, 51.

"Sketches in an Octogenarian's Notebook." *Saturday Review* 39 (17 November 1956): 23.

"Social Philosophy and the Professional Education of Social Workers." *Social Service Review* 33 (December 1959): 345–59.

"Sociobiology and Its Critics." *Commentary* 68 (July 1979): 39–47.

"Some Thoughts on Education for World Responsibility." *School and Society* 95 (1 April 1967): 219–23.

"Sorry Socialism." *Saturday Review* 38 (13 August 1955): 10.

"Specter of Eugenics." *Commentary* 57 (March 1974): 25–33.

"Student Power: The Rhetoric and the Possibilities." *Saturday Review* 51 (2 November 1968): 23–25, 73.

"Student Power: A Symposium." *Humanist* 29 (May–June 1969): 11–16.

"Teachers in an Atomic Society." *The Ethical Outlook* 46 (January–February 1960): 5–11.

"The Third Great Revolution of Mankind." *New York Times Magazine* (9 February 1958): 11, 70–71, 78.

"Thoughts on Fame." *New York Times Magazine* (23 October 1960): 110.

"Toward a Humanistic Revolution in Education." *Journal of Educational Measurement* 6 (Fall 1969): 4–11.

"Toward Deeper Cultural Relations in the Hemisphere." *Department of State Bulletin* 54 (7 February 1966): 202–7.

"Trouble with Togetherness." *New York Times Magazine* (27 April 1958): 26, 30, 32.

"United States Commitment to UNESCO: Statement, October 27, 1966." *Department of State Bulletin* 55 (12 December 1966): 883–89.

"U.S. Problems and Those of Others." *Current* 183 (May 1976): 33–38.

"The Unpredictable in History." *Current* 45 (January 1954): 38.

"We Must Not Let Moscow Set Our Pace." *New York Times Magazine* (2 October 1960): 9, 98–99.

"What Has Happened to Our Morality." *New York Times Magazine* (10 June 1962): 12.

"What Is a Philosophy of Education?" *Harvard Educational Review* 26 (Spring 1956): 131–33.

"What Is the Verdict on Marx? Excerpt from Address, May 1968." *Saturday Review* 51 (25 May 1968): 10–13, 41.

"Who is Santayana?" *Saturday Review* 39 (7 January 1956): 11.

"Why the Humanities?" *Ideas: A Publication of the National Humanities Center* 1 (Winter, 1979): 2–3, 13–14.

CONTRIBUTORS

JOHN AGRESTO, Project Director of the National Humanities Center, has written numerous articles on legal theory, political philosophy, and American political thought. He is also the author of a forthcoming book entitled *The Supreme Court and Constitutional Democracy*.

WILLIAM BENNETT, President and Director of the National Humanities Center, is coauthor of *Counting by Race: Equality in American Thought from the Founding Fathers to Bakke*. His articles have appeared in *Harvard Civil Rights*, *Stanford Law Review*, *Newsweek*, *The Wall Street Journal*, *Commentary*, and *Encounter*.

MURIEL BRADBROOK is Professor Emerita, Fellow, and former Mistress of Girton College, Cambridge University. She is the author of numerous essays and books on Shakespeare and Elizabethan Drama, including *John Webster, Citizen and Dramatist* and the six-volume *A History of Elizabethan Drama*.

NICHOLAS P. CHRISTY is Chief of Staff at the Brooklyn Veterans Administration Medical Center. His articles, both on medical language and on endocrinology, have appeared in medical journals such as the *New England Journal of Medicine* and the *American Journal of Medicine*.

B. J. T. DOBBS, Associate Professor of History at Northwestern University, has done extensive research on alchemy and early chemistry. She is the author of *The Foundations of Newton's Alchemy, or "The Hunting of the Greene Lyon."*

RICHARD M. DORSON, Distinguished Professor of History and Folklore and Director of the Folklore Institute at Indiana University, is the author of *American Folklore* and *America in Legend* and General Editor of the series *Folktales of the World*. He has served as President of the American Folklore Society and Editor of the *Journal of American Folklore*.

ABRAHAM EDEL, Research Professor of Philosophy at the University of Pennsylvania, is the author of numerous books, including the two-volume work *Science, Ideology, and Value* and *Aristotle and His Philosophy: A Contemporary Reading*.

GERALD F. ELSE, Professor Emeritus of Classics at the University of Michigan, has published widely in scholarly journals on ancient Greek and Latin literature. He is the author of *Aristotle's Poetics: The Argument* and *The Origins and Early Form of Greek Tragedy*.

ELIZABETH FLOWER, Professor of Philosophy at the University of Pennsylvania, is coauthor of the two-volume *A History of Philosophy in America* and has written numerous articles for various scholarly publications.

TORSTEN HUSÉN, International Chair of International Education at the University of Stockholm, is the author of *The School in Question: A Comparative Study of School and Its Future in Western Societies* and *Talent, Equality, and Meritocracy*. He has served as Editor-in-Chief of the Swedish *Encyclopedia of Psychology and Education*.

LEWIS LEARY is William Rand Kenan, Jr., Professor of English Emeritus at the University of North Carolina at Chapel Hill. He has written numerous books on American authors, including *That Rascal Freneau*, *Mark Twain*, and *Emerson: An Interpretive Essay*, and he is the compiler of the three-volume *Articles on American Literature, 1968–1975*.

WILLIAM E. LEUCHTENBURG, De Witt Clinton Professor of History at Columbia University, has done extensive research and writing on Franklin D. Roosevelt and the New Deal. He is the author of *A Troubled Feast: American Society since 1945* and coauthor of the Oxford University Press history *The Growth of the American Republic*.

CARL NORDENFALK, Director Emeritus of the Nationalmuseum of Stockholm, has written extensively on medieval book illuminations. He is the author of *Treasures of Swedish Art* and *Celtic and Anglo-Saxon Painting*, and he is coauthor of the Skira editions *Early Medieval Painting* and *Romanesque Painting*.

PETER RIESENBERG, Professor of History at Washington, has worked primarily on the history of the idea of citizenship in the Middle Ages. He is the author of *Inalienability of Sovereignty in Medieval Political Thought* and coauthor of *The Medieval Town*.

SAMUEL SCOLNICOV is Senior Lecturer in Philosophy and Education at The Hebrew University of Jerusalem. He has published widely in professional journals on classical Greek philosophy and on the philosophy of education, and he is the author of *A Short History of Greek Philosophy: I. The Pre-Socratic Philosophers*.

JOHN SITTER, Professor of English at Emory University, is a scholar of eighteenth-century English literature. His articles have appeared in numerous journals, and he is the author of *The Poetry of Pope's 'Dunciad'*.

JACOB L. TALMON was Professor of Modern General History at The Hebrew University of Jerusalem. His books include *The Unique and the Universal*, *Romanticism and Revolt*, *Israel Among Nations*, and a trilogy on the evolution of totalitarian democracy and the distortions of democracy, the last volume of which is entitled *The Myth of the Nation and the Vision of Revolution: The Origins of Ideological Polarization in the Twentieth Century*.

WALTER ALAN TUTTLE is the Librarian of the National Humanities Center.